COLLECTED POEMS

1943—2004

OTHER WORKS BY RICHARD WILBUR

Mayflies: New Poems and Translations

The Beautiful Changes and Other Poems

Ceremony and Other Poems

A Bestiary (editor, with Alexander Calder)

Molière's *The Misanthrope* (translator)

Things of This World

Poems 1943–1956

Candide (with Lillian Hellman)

Poe: Complete Poems (editor)

Advice to a Prophet and Other Poems

Molière's *Tartuffe* (translator)

The Poems of Richard Wilbur

Loudmouse (for children)

Shakespeare: Poems (co-editor, with Alfred Harbage)

Walking to Sleep: New Poems and Translations

Molière's *The School for Wives* (translator)

Opposites

The Mind-Reader: New Poems

Responses: Prose Pieces, 1948–1976

Molière's *The Learned Ladies* (translator)

Racine's *Andromache* (translator)

Racine's *Phaedra* (translator)

New and Collected Poems

More Opposites

The Catbird's Song: Prose Pieces 1963–1995

RICHARD WILBUR

COLLECTED POEMS

1943–2004

HARCOURT, INC.

Orlando Austin New York San Diego Toronto London

www.HarcourtBooks.com

Permissions acknowledgments appear on page 579 and constitute
a continuation of the copyright page.

Library of Congress Cataloging-in-Publication Data
Wilbur, Richard, 1921–
[Poems. Selections]
Collected poems, 1943–2004/Richard Wilbur.—1st ed.
p.   cm.
Includes index.
ISBN 0-15-101105-2
I. Title.
PS3545.I32165A6   2004
811'.54—dc22   2004009228

Text set in Minion
Designed by Cathy Riggs

Printed in the United States of America
First edition
A C E G I K J H F D B

CONTENTS

AN INTRODUCTORY NOTE   xv

NEW POEMS (2004)

    ONE

        The Reader   5
        Sir David Brewster's Toy   6
        Security Lights, Key West   7
        Man Running   8
        Asides   10
        Tanka   11
        In Trackless Woods   12
        The Sleepwalker   13
        Green   15
        Blackberries for Amelia   16

    TWO

        Twelve Riddles from Symphosius   19
        To a Comedian   21
        An Eightieth-Birthday Ballade for   22
        Anthony Hecht
        Notes   23

MAYFLIES: NEW POEMS AND TRANSLATIONS (2000)

        Changes
        A Barred Owl   29
        For C.   30
        Zea   31
        At Moorditch   32
        Bonds   33
        The Gambler   34

Three Tankas 35
    On Lyman Flat 35
    All Hallows' Eve 35
    Wild Asters 35
Mayflies 36
A Short History 37
Fabrications 38
Signatures 40
Icons 41
Crow's Nests 43
STÉPHANE MALLARMÉ: Sea Breeze 44
NINA CASSIAN: Ballad of the Jack 45
of Diamonds
Once 46
Bone Key 47
Personae 48
VALERI PETROV: A Cry from Childhood 49
VALERI PETROV: Photos from the Archives 50
A Digression 51
A Wall in the Woods: Cummington 52
    1. "What is it for . . ." 52
    2. "He will hear . . ." 52
Elsewhere 54
CHARLES BAUDELAIRE: The Albatross 55
CHARLES BAUDELAIRE: Correspondences 56
This Pleasing Anxious Being 57
    1. "In no time you are back . . ." 57
    2. "The shadow of whoever . . ." 57
    3. "Wild, lashing snow . . ." 58

Transformations
The Prologue to Molière's *Amphitryon* 61
DANTE ALIGHIERI: Canto xxv of the *Inferno* 66
Notes 72

NEW AND COLLECTED POEMS (1987)

ONE

The Ride 79
Gnomons 80

Alatus   81
Lying   83
On Having Mis-identified a Wild Flower   86
JOSEPH BRODSKY: Six Years Later   87
Leaving   89
The Catch   91
VINICIUS DE MORAES: Song   93
Icarium Mare   94
Some Riddles from Symphosius   96
Under a Tree   98
Wyeth's Milk Cans   99
For W. H. Auden   100
Orchard Trees, January   101
GUILLAUME APOLLINAIRE: Mirabeau Bridge   102
Trolling for Blues   103
Advice from the Muse   104
The Rule   106
A Fable   107
Transit   108
Shad-Time   109
Worlds   111
All That Is   112
A Finished Man   114
Hamlen Brook   115

TWO   For Music
On Freedom's Ground   119
       I. Back Then   119
       II. Our Risen States   119
       III. Like a Great Statue   120
       IV. Come Dance   121
       V. Immigrants Still   122

THE MIND-READER: NEW POEMS (1976)

ONE   The Eye
A Storm in April   127
The Writer   128
To the Etruscan Poets   130
The Eye   131

Sleepless at Crown Point	*133*
Piccola Commedia	*134*
A Wedding Toast	*136*
March	*137*
In Limbo	*138*
A Sketch	*140*
Peter	*142*
Cottage Street, 1953	*143*
The Fourth of July	*144*
A Shallot	*146*
A Black Birch in Winter	*147*
For the Student Strikers	*148*
C Minor	*149*
To His Skeleton	*151*
John Chapman	*152*
April 5, 1974	*153*
Teresa	*154*
Children of Darkness	*155*

TWO

FRANÇOIS VILLON: Ballade of Forgiveness	*159*
JEAN DE LA FONTAINE: The Grasshopper and the Ant	*160*
JOACHIM DU BELLAY: Happy the Man	*161*
VOLTAIRE: To Madame du Châtelet	*162*

THREE

Flippancies	*167*
Two Riddles from Aldhelm	*168*
Rillons, Rillettes	*169*
The Prisoner of Zenda	*170*

FOUR

JOSEPH BRODSKY: The Funeral of Bobò	*173*
ANDREI VOZNESENSKY: Phone Booth	*175*
ANDREI VOZNESENSKY: An Arrow in the Wall	*177*
NIKOLAI MORSHEN: Two Poems	*179*

FIVE   *The Mind-Reader*

The Mind-Reader	*183*
Notes	*188*

WALKING TO SLEEP: NEW POEMS AND TRANSLATIONS (1969)

ONE   *In the Field*

The Lilacs   195
On the Marginal Way   197
Complaint   200
Fern-Beds in Hampshire County   202
In a Churchyard   203
Seed Leaves   205
In the Field   207
A Wood   210
For Dudley   211
Running   213
     I. 1933   213
     II. Patriots' Day   213
     III. Dodwells Road   214
Under Cygnus   216

TWO   *Thyme*

Thyme Flowering among Rocks   219
A Miltonic Sonnet for Mr. Johnson on His Refusal of Peter Hurd's Official Portrait   221
A Riddle   222
Playboy   223
The Mechanist   224
The Agent   225
The Proof   228
A Late Aubade   229
Matthew VIII, 28 ff.   230
For K. R. on Her Sixtieth Birthday   231

THREE   *Walking to Sleep*

Walking to Sleep   235

FOUR   *Translations*

JORGE LUIS BORGES: Compass   241
JORGE LUIS BORGES: Everness   242
JORGE LUIS BORGES: Ewigkeit   243
ANNA AKHMATOVA: Lot's Wife   244
ANDREI VOZNESENSKY: Foggy Street   245
ANDREI VOZNESENSKY: Antiworlds   247
ANDREI VOZNESENSKY: Dead Still   249

CHARLES D'ORLÉANS: Rondeau 250

FRANÇOIS VILLON: Ballade of the Ladies 251
of Time Past

FRANÇOIS VILLON: Ballade in Old French 252

FRANÇOIS VILLON: A Ballade to End With 253

Notes 254

ADVICE TO A PROPHET AND OTHER POEMS (1961)

Two Voices in a Meadow 257

Advice to a Prophet 258

Stop 260

Junk 261

Loves of the Puppets 263

A Summer Morning 264

A Hole in the Floor 265

JORGE GUILLÉN: The Horses 267

JORGE GUILLÉN: Death, from a Distance 268

She 269

Gemini 271

The Undead 272

October Maples, Portland 274

Eight Riddles from Symphosius 275

Shame 277

A Grasshopper 278

SALVATORE QUASIMODO: 280
The Agrigentum Road

The Aspen and the Stream 281

A Fire-Truck 283

Someone Talking to Himself 284

In the Smoking-Car 286

Ballade for the Duke of Orléans 287

GÉRARD DE NERVAL: Antéros 288

To Ishtar 289

Pangloss's Song: A Comic-Opera Lyric 290

Two Quatrains for First Frost 292

Another Voice 293

MOLIÈRE: Tartuffe, Act I, Scene 4 294

Fall in Corrales 297

Next Door 298

A Christmas Hymn   300

Notes   302

THINGS OF THIS WORLD (1956)

Altitudes   305

Love Calls Us to the Things of This World   307

Sonnet   309

Piazza di Spagna, Early Morning   310

John Chrysostom   311

A Black November Turkey   312

Mind   314

After the Last Bulletins   315

Lamarck Elaborated   317

A Plain Song for Comadre   318

Merlin Enthralled   319

A Voice from under the Table   321

The Beacon   323

Statues   325

Looking into History   326

CHARLES BAUDELAIRE: L'Invitation au Voyage   328

Digging for China   330

FRANCIS JAMMES: A Prayer to Go to Paradise with the Donkeys   331

PHILIPPE DE THAUN: The Pelican   333

Apology   335

PAUL VALÉRY: Helen   336

Beasts   337

Exeunt   338

Marginalia   339

Boy at the Window   340

Speech for the Repeal of the McCarran Act   341

All These Birds   342

A Baroque Wall-Fountain in the Villa Sciarra   344

An Event   347

A Chronic Condition   348

The Mill   349

For the New Railway Station in Rome   350

CEREMONY AND OTHER POEMS (1950)

Then	355
Conjuration	356
"A World without Objects Is a Sensible Emptiness"	357
The Pardon	358
Part of a Letter	359
La Rose des Vents	360
Epistemology	361
Castles and Distances	362
Museum Piece	365
Ode to Pleasure	366
In the Elegy Season	368
Marché aux Oiseaux	369
Juggler	370
Parable	371
The Good Servant	372
Pity	373
The Sirens	374
Year's End	375
The Puritans	376
Grasse: The Olive Trees	377
The Avowal	378
The Gifts	379
Five Women Bathing in Moonlight	380
The Terrace	381
A Problem from Milton	383
A Glance from the Bridge	384
Clearness	385
Games One	386
Games Two	387
Beowulf	388
Still, Citizen Sparrow	390
Wellfleet: The House	391
The Death of a Toad	392
Driftwood	393
A Courtyard Thaw	395
Lament	396

Flumen Tenebrarum   397

From the Lookout Rock   399

To an American Poet Just Dead   401

Giacometti   402

He Was   404

A Simile for Her Smile   405

Ceremony   406

THE BEAUTIFUL CHANGES AND OTHER POEMS (1947)

Cicadas   409

Water Walker   410

Tywater   413

Mined Country   414

Potato   416

First Snow in Alsace   418

On the Eyes of an SS Officer   419

Place Pigalle   420

Violet and Jasper   421

The Peace of Cities   422

The Giaour and the Pacha   423

Up, Jack   424

In a Bird Sanctuary   425

June Light   427

A Song   428

The Walgh-Vogel   429

The Melongène   430

Objects   431

A Dutch Courtyard   433

My Father Paints the Summer   434

Folk Tune   435

Sun and Air   436

Two Songs in a Stanza of Beddoes'   437

The Waters   439

Superiorities   441

A Simplification   442

A Dubious Night   443

L'Etoile   444

Sunlight Is Imagination   445

    &   447

    O   448

    The Regatta   449

    Bell Speech   451

    Poplar, Sycamore   452

    Winter Spring   453

    Attention Makes Infinity   454

    Grace   455

    Lightness   457

    For Ellen   458

    Caserta Garden   459

    Praise in Summer   461

    The Beautiful Changes   462

    Notes   463

APPENDIX A: SHOW LYRICS

    Oh, Happy We!   465

    Glitter and Be Gay   468

    The Ragpicker's Song   470

APPENDIX B: POEMS FOR CHILDREN AND OTHERS

    Opposites   473

    More Opposites   515

    A Few Differences   559

    The Disappearing Alphabet   567

    The Pig in the Spigot   573

    Permissions Acknowledgments   579

    Title Index   581

AN INTRODUCTORY NOTE

I once asked Wallace Stevens whether he liked such-and-such a poem of his, and he heartily replied, "I like *all* my poems." Every poet has moments of feeling that way, moved by gratitude for all the times when he got something decently said, or hoped to have done so, and could in conscience add another poem to his manuscript. That, I think, is the mood in which a collected poems—as opposed to a sternly winnowed selected—should be assembled. This book begins with some new work from the last few years, and then offers all of my previous books of poems in reverse order of publication. Nothing has been thrown out, and any changes of wording are too few and too slight to mention.

Most of my poems have been written out of my own need to write them, and not for special uses and occasions. Yet writing of the latter kind, if it turns out well, deserves to be included in a poet's books, and can at the least provide variety. Back in 1959 or so, I wrote a hymn at the request of Richard Winslow, who set it for a Wesleyan Christmas concert, and that text will be found here. So will the text of a cantata, done in collaboration with William Schuman, which was performed at the Lincoln Center in 1986 to celebrate the hundredth anniversary of the Statue of Liberty. Most show lyrics are a bit watery when read without the music, but I think that "Pangloss's Song," which was done for the Broadway show *Candide,* can stand fairly well without the support of Leonard Bernstein's excellent setting. I have put one or two other samples of show-lyric in an appendix. Finally, with the encouragement of my editor and of several fellow poets, I have put into a second appendix five small books of verse for children, three of which are accompanied by my own drawings. I don't think that my work in this genre need seem too out of keeping with the rest of the collection. Some of the poems were first published in grown-up periodicals, adults have admitted to enjoying them, and when published abroad in translation the books have not always been earmarked for juveniles. They are, as I have some-times said in subtitles, "for children and others."

I had better mention that, when I have translated a poem from an-other language, my usual practice has been to give the original author's name in capitals, followed by the poem's title. An example might be "JORGE LUIS BORGES: Compass." What I like about that form of ascription is that it is economical, declares at once that what follows is a transla-tion, and gives immediate credit to the author of the original. No one, I hope, will find it confusing.

R. W.
Cummington, Massachusetts
2004

NEW POEMS

2004

———•———

For Charlee
in this and the other kingdom

ONE

THE READER

She is going back, these days, to the great stories
That charmed her younger mind. A shaded light
Shines on the nape half-shadowed by her curls,
And a page turns now with a scuffing sound.
Onward they come again, the orphans reaching
For a first handhold in a stony world,
The young provincials who at last look down
On the city's maze, and will descend into it,
The serious girl, once more, who would live nobly,
The sly one who aspires to marry so,
The young man bent on glory, and that other
Who seeks a burden. Knowing as she does
What will become of them in bloody field
Or Tuscan garden, it may be that at times
She sees their first and final selves at once,
As a god might to whom all time is now.
Or, having lived so much herself, perhaps
She meets them this time with a wiser eye,
Noting that Julien's calculating head
Is from the first too severed from his heart.
But the true wonder of it is that she,
For all that she may know of consequences,
Still turns enchanted to the next bright page
Like some Natasha in the ballroom door—
Caught in the flow of things wherever bound,
The blind delight of being, ready still
To enter life on life and see them through.

Sir David Brewster's Toy

In this tube you see
At the far end a batch of
Colored-glass debris—

Which, however, grows
Upon reflection to an
Intricate pied rose,

Flushed with sun, that might,
Set in some cathedral's wall,
Paraphrase the light.

Now, at the least shake,
The many colors jumble
And abruptly make

The rose rearrange,
Adding to form and splendor
The release of change.

Rattle it afresh
And see its coruscating
Flinders quickly mesh,

Fashioning once more
A fine sixfold gaudiness
Never seen before.

Many prophets claim
That Heaven's joys, though endless,
Are not twice the same;

This kaleidoscope
Can, in that connection, give
Exercise in hope.

SECURITY LIGHTS, KEY WEST

Mere minutes from Duval Street's goings-on,
The midnight houses of this quiet block,
With their long-lidded shutters, are withdrawn
In sleep past bush and picket, bolt and lock,

Yet each façade is raked by the strange glare
Of halogen, in which fantastic day
Veranda, turret, balustraded stair
Glow like the settings of some noble play.

As if the isle were Prospero's, you seem
To glimpse great summoned spirits as you pass.
Cordelia tells her truth, and Joan her dream,
Becket prepares the sacrifice of Mass,

A dog-tired watchman in that mirador
Waits for the flare that tells of Troy's defeat,
And other lofty ghosts are heard, before
You turn into a narrow, darker street.

There, where no glow or glare outshines the sky,
The pitch-black houses loom on either hand
Like hulks adrift in fog, as you go by.
It comes to mind that they are built on sand,

And that there may be drama here as well,
Where so much murk looks up at star on star:
Though, to be sure, you cannot always tell
Whether those lights are high or merely far.

MAN RUNNING

Whatever he has done
Against our law and peace of mind,
Our mind's eye looks with pity of a kind
At the scared, stumbling fellow on the run

Who hears a siren scream
As through the thickets we conceive
He ploughs with fending arms, and to deceive
The snuffling dogs now flounders up a stream

Until he doubles back,
Climbing at length a rocky rise
To where he crumples and, exhausted, lies
In the scorched brush beside a railroad track.

*

If then he hops a freight
And clatteringly rides as far
As the next county in a cattle-car,
We feel our sense of him disintegrate

In rumors, warnings, claims
That here or there he has appeared—
Tall, short, fierce, furtive, with or without a beard.
Still, in fidelity to childhood games

And outlaws of romance,
We darkly cheer him, whether or not
He robbed that store, or bank, or fired that shot,
And wish him, guiltily, a sporting chance.

*

Ditching the stolen truck,
He disappears into a vast
Deep-wooded wilderness, and is at last
Beyond the reach of law, and out of luck,

And we are one with him,
Sharing with him that eldest dread
Which, when it gathers in a sleeping head,
Is a place mottled, ominous, and dim

Remembered from the day
When we descended from the trees
Into the shadow of our enemies,
Not lords of nature yet, but naked prey.

ASIDES

Though the season's begun to speak
Its long sentence of darkness,
The upswept boughs of the larch
Bristle with gold for a week,

And then there is only the willow
To make bright interjection,
Its drooping branches decked
With thin leaves, curved and yellow,

Till winter, loosening these
With a first flurry and bluster,
Shall scatter across the snow-crust
Their dropped parentheses.

TANKA

Black-and-white Holsteins
Crowd downfield at feeding-time,
Mingling their blotches.
It is like ice breaking up
In a dark, swollen river.

In Trackless Woods

In trackless woods, it puzzled me to find
Four great rock maples seemingly aligned,
As if they had been set out in a row
Before some house a century ago,
To edge the property and lend some shade.
I looked to see if ancient wheels had made
Old ruts to which the trees ran parallel,
But there were none, so far as I could tell—
There'd been no roadway. Nor could I find the square
Depression of a cellar anywhere,
And so I tramped on further, to survey
Amazing patterns in a hornbeam spray
Or spirals in a pine cone, under trees
Not subject to our stiff geometries.

THE SLEEPWALKER

Like an axe-head sunk in a stump,
His face is wedged into the pillow's dark,
The nose and mouth scarcely breathing,
The mind without a picture.

But now a window shade
Floats inward, to admit the ashen moonlight,
Hovers, and then in haste falls back
To crash against the screen.

In a room like this, a harrowing
Dream takes shape, although he can't yet tell
Whether abductors keep him here
Or foes without besiege him.

Afoot now in that dream,
He moves through half-familiar shapes, through shapes
Made vague as if by attic-dust
Or oxides undersea,

Until a doorknob's glint
Alerts him, and the opening door reveals
Obsidian gloom from which emerge
Eight shoe-tips in a row.

Shutting the door against
That bodiless surveillance, he begins
To waken, and his eyes to clear,
Conforming room to room

And shaking off the dream
For good, except that later on, in daylight,
Walking down street or corridor
Upon a clear-cut errand,

His mood will briefly yield
To an odd notion like an undertow,
A sense that he is mortally
Beset, and in need of ransom.

GREEN

Tree-leaves which, till the growing season's done,
Change into wood the powers of the sun,

Take from that radiance only reds and blues.
Green is a color that they cannot use,

And so their rustling myriads are seen
To wear all summer an extraneous green,

A green with no apparent role, unless
To be the symbol of a great largesse

Which has no end, though autumns may revoke
That shade from yellowed ash and rusted oak.

BLACKBERRIES FOR AMELIA

Fringing the woods, the stone walls, and the lanes,
Old thickets everywhere have come alive,
Their new leaves reaching out in fans of five
From tangles overarched by this year's canes.

They have their flowers too, it being June,
And here or there in brambled dark-and-light
Are small, five-petaled blooms of chalky white,
As random-clustered and as loosely strewn

As the far stars, of which we now are told
That ever faster do they bolt away,
And that a night may come in which, some say,
We shall have only blackness to behold.

I have no time for any change so great,
But I shall see the August weather spur
Berries to ripen where the flowers were—
Dark berries, savage-sweet and worth the wait—

And there will come the moment to be quick
And save some from the birds, and I shall need
Two pails, old clothes in which to stain and bleed,
And a grandchild to talk with while we pick.

TWO

Twelve Riddles from Symphosius

MALUM

My Latin name sounds evil. Goddesses three
I set at odds, three sisters guard my tree,
And Troy was drowned in blood because of me.

CAPILLUS

Though many cut me, I am never split.
My hue can change, and I like it not a whit
That Fate will make me whiten, bit by bit.

SPECULUM

I've no fixed image; all forms in me convene.
Within me is a region bright and keen
In which you see what I, just now, have seen.

CENTAURUS

Because I've four feet and two hands beside,
My self's in doubt; I blend and yet divide.
Borne by my bodies, I both walk and ride.

MULA

I favor neither parent, as you see.
I'm a mixed breed unfit for progeny.
Though others bred me, none is bred by me.

TAURUS

I served a wooden beast whose head was crowned.
In wild Cilicia are my mountains found.
I ride in heaven, and walk upon the ground.

FUMUS

To make men weep, though griefless, is my lot.
I seek to climb, but in damp air can not.
Without me, my begetter's not begot.

FARINA

I have been pressed and ground 'twixt stone and stone,
Escaping by diminishment alone.
My size is smaller now, my numbers grown.

LAPIS

Like old Deucalion, I was not drowned.
Though hard, I'm cousin to the spongy ground.
Without my *S*, I am a kind of sound.

FOLLIS

When breath departs from me, I do not die,
For back it comes, then leaves me with a sigh—
Now blown away, and now in fresh supply.

TRIDENS

With me, who have three sharp teeth in a row,
A long neck, and a single tooth below,
A god makes winds obey and waters flow.

VITIS

I'll marry, but I want no marriage-bed,
No mate; by me my issue shall be bred.
Dig me no grave; I'll dig my own instead.

To a Comedian

You stand up for the interests of folk
Who need a bedroom or a bathroom joke,
Told with a drumfire of such words as *shit*,
To jog their jaded spirits for a bit.
It pays, you find, to give them what they're after.
You are the clown who put the *ugh* in laughter.

An Eightieth-Birthday Ballade for Anthony Hecht

Who is the man whose poems dare
Describe man's inhumanities,
And count our deadly sins, and bare
Such truths as cause the blood to freeze,
Yet in whose darkest verse one sees
How style and agile intellect
Can both instruct and greatly please?
I speak, of course, of Tony Hecht.

Who is the man who has a flair
For double-dactyl drolleries
And other forms, as light as air,
That call for wit and expertise,
Whose "Dover Bitch," moreover, frees
His comic gifts to play unchecked?
Who is his own antipodes?
The many-sided Tony Hecht.

Who has translated Baudelaire,
Avoiding all translationese?
Who rendered Brodsky and Voltaire
And Horace's urbanities,
And would be named by all of these
As one of their august elect?
Can there be any question? He's
That true Parnassian, Tony Hecht.

By now, Prince, you must be aware
Of what bard most deserves respect.
There is but one beyond compare,
The incomparable Tony Hecht.

Sir David Brewster's Toy Brewster (1781–1868) was a Scottish natural philosopher who made a number of discoveries in the refraction of light, and is generally held to have been the inventor of the kaleidoscope.

Twelve Riddles from Symphosius The answers to these ancient riddles, translated here from the Latin, are as follows: Apple, Hair, Mirror, Centaur, Mule, Bull, Smoke, Flour, Stone, Bellows, Trident, Vine.

Mayflies

NEW POEMS AND TRANSLATIONS

2000

———•———

For my daughter Ellen

Changes

A BARRED OWL

The warping night air having brought the boom
Of an owl's voice into her darkened room,
We tell the wakened child that all she heard
Was an odd question from a forest bird,
Asking of us, if rightly listened to,
"Who cooks for you?" and then "Who cooks for you?"

Words, which can make our terrors bravely clear,
Can also thus domesticate a fear,
And send a small child back to sleep at night
Not listening for the sound of stealthy flight
Or dreaming of some small thing in a claw
Borne up to some dark branch and eaten raw.

For C.

After the clash of elevator gates
And the long sinking, she emerges where,
A slight thing in the morning's crosstown glare,
She looks up toward the window where he waits,
Then in a fleeting taxi joins the rest
Of the huge traffic bound forever west.

On such grand scale do lovers say good-bye—
Even this other pair whose high romance
Had only the duration of a dance,
And who, now taking leave with stricken eye,
See each in each a whole new life forgone.
For them, above the darkling clubhouse lawn,

Bright Perseids flash and crumble; while for these
Who part now on the dock, weighed down by grief
And baggage, yet with something like relief,
It takes three thousand miles of knitting seas
To cancel out their crossing, and unmake
The amorous rough and tumble of their wake.

We are denied, my love, their fine tristesse
And bittersweet regrets, and cannot share
The frequent vistas of their large despair,
Where love and all are swept to nothingness;
Still, there's a certain scope in that long love
Which constant spirits are the keepers of,

And which, though taken to be tame and staid,
Is a wild sostenuto of the heart,
A passion joined to courtesy and art
Which has the quality of something made,
Like a good fiddle, like the rose's scent,
Like a rose window or the firmament.

ZEA

Once their fruit is picked,
The cornstalks lighten, and though
Keeping to their strict

Rows, begin to be
The tall grasses that they are—
Lissom, now, and free

As canes that clatter
In island wind, or plumed reeds
Rocked by lake water.

Soon, if not cut down,
Their ranks grow whistling-dry, and
Blanch to lightest brown,

So that, one day, all
Their ribbon-like, down-arcing
Leaves rise up and fall

In tossed companies,
Like goose-wings beating southward
Over the changed trees.

Later, there are days
Full of bare expectancy,
Downcast hues, and haze,

Days of an utter
Calm, in which one white corn-leaf,
Oddly aflutter,

Its fabric sheathing
A gaunt stem, can seem to be
The sole thing breathing.

At Moorditch

"Now," said the voice of lock and window-bar,
"You must confront things as they truly are.
          Open your eyes at last, and see
The desolateness of reality."

"Things have," I said, "a pallid, empty look,
Like pictures in an unused coloring book."

"Now that the scales have fallen from your eyes,"
Said the sad hallways, "you must recognize
          How childishly your former sight
Salted the world with glory and delight."

"This cannot be the world," I said. "Nor will it,
Till the heart's crayon spangle and fulfill it."

BONDS

1
The bully focuses the coward's fears;
The grateful coward weeps the bully's tears.

2
The reader's tyrannous desires compel
The weary, bored pornographer to tell
Again, and then once more, and then anew,
The shameful things that lustful monsters do
To a blameless victim—chained, or drugged, or tied—
With whom the reader feels identified.

The Gambler

Full of a cold excitement, he betrays
      His creditors and all he loves
With long-shot wagers, till at length he shoves
A last few chips across the glowing baize.

It thrills him to be almost free of hope.
      The tossed white ball begins to strike
The spinning wheel-compartments, sounding like
The stutter of a stretching gallows-rope.

Still, not until the ball has come to rest
      Will he be able to achieve
A pure despair. Meanwhile he must believe
As best he can in luck, which at its best

Affects him as a love both great and grim—
      A love whose boyish pet he is,
A love of prodigal indulgences,
Doting, divine, and cold to all but him.

THREE TANKAS

ON LYMAN FLAT

Scattered raindrops fall
On the roadside trees, jolting
A leaf here or there:
So troops stand at attention,
Motionless but for eye-blinks.

ALL HALLOWS' EVE

They are not the dead,
These sheeted tykes at the door,
Asking for candy:
But they are our successors,
And we their ghostly elders.

WILD ASTERS

In the frost-quelled field,
Asters yet fly the yearning
Colors of desire.
All honor to Aaron Burr,
Whose last whisper was *"Madame..."*

MAYFLIES

In somber forest, when the sun was low,
I saw from unseen pools a mist of flies
    In their quadrillions rise
And animate a ragged patch of glow
With sudden glittering—as when a crowd
    Of stars appear
Through a brief gap in black and driven cloud,
One arc of their great round-dance showing clear.

It was no muddled swarm I witnessed, for
In *entrechats* each fluttering insect there
    Rose two steep yards in air,
Then slowly floated down to climb once more,
So that they all composed a manifold
    And figured scene,
And seemed the weavers of some cloth of gold,
Or the fine pistons of some bright machine.

Watching those lifelong dancers of a day
As night closed in, I felt myself alone
    In a life too much my own,
More mortal in my separateness than they—
Unless, I thought, I had been called to be
    Not fly or star
But one whose task is joyfully to see
How fair the fiats of the caller are.

A Short History

Corn planted us; tamed cattle made us tame.
Thence hut and citadel and kingdom came.

FABRICATIONS

As if to prove again
The bright resilience of the frailest form,
A spider has repaired her broken web
Between the palm-trunk and the jasmine tree.

Etched on the clear new light
Above the still-imponderable ground,
It is a single and gigantic eye
Whose golden pupil, now, the spider is.

Through it you catch the flash
Of steeples brightened as a cloud slips over,
One loitering star, and off there to the south
Slow vultures kettling in the lofts of air.

Each day men frame and weave
In their own way whatever looms in sight,
Though they must see with human scale and bias,
And though there is much unseen. The Talmud tells

How dusty travelers once
Came to a river where a roc was wading,
And would have hastened then to strip and bathe,
Had not a booming voice from heaven said,

"Step not into that water:
Seven years since, a joiner dropped his axe
Therein, and it hath not yet reached the bottom."
Whether beneath our senses or beyond them,

The world is bottomless,
A drift of star-specks or the Red King's dream,
And fogs our thought, although it is not true
That we grasp nothing till we grasp it all.

Witness this ancient map
Where so much blank and namelessness surround
A little mushroom-clump of coastal towers
In which we may infer civility,

A harbor-full of spray,
And all those loves which hint of love itself,
Imagining too a pillar at whose top
A spider's web upholds the architrave.

SIGNATURES

False Solomon's Seal—
So called because it lacks a
Star-scar on the heel,

And ends its arched stem
In a spray of white florets,
Later changing them

To a red, not blue,
Spatter of berries—is no
Falser than the true.

Solomon, who raised
The temple and wrote the song,
Wouldn't have dispraised

This bowed, graceful plant
So like an aspergillum,
Nor its variant

With root duly scarred,
Whose bloom-hung stem is like the
Bell-branch of a bard.

Liking best to live
In the deep woods whose light is
Most contemplative,

Both are often found
Where mandrake, wintergreen, and
Dry leaves strew the ground,

Their heads inclining
Toward the dark earth, one blessing
And one divining.

ICONS

They are one answer to the human need
For a second life, and they exist for us
In the secular heaven of photography,
    Safe in emulsion's cloud

Through which we glimpse them, knowing them as we know
The angels, by report and parched surmise.
Like Milton's seraphim who veil their gaze
    Against the beams of God,

Often we see them handsomely asquint
When captured by a bursting photoflash,
Or dazzling and bedazzled on that beach
    Where currently they sun;

And yet perhaps they seem most brilliant when,
Putting away all glamour, they appear
In their old clothes at home, with dog and child,
    Projecting toward the lens

From a couch not unlike our own, a smile
Sublimely confident of mattering.
They smile, too, when we spot their avatars
    Upon the actual street,

Sharing with us the little joke that we
Have known them in a different dimension;
But since they strike us then as subtly changed—
    Pale, short, a trifle older—

It is not hard to yield them back to dream,
From which their images immutably
Bestow a flourish on our muted lives,
    Even though death betray them.

Still, there are fewer sightings year by year
Of the trenchcoat carried niftily over the shoulder,
The innocent sultry look, the heaved guitar,
   The charming pillbox hat,

And fewer of their dreamers left to grieve
As all those glossy selves, transcendent still,
Slip unaccountably into the morgues
   And archives of this world.

CROW'S NESTS

That lofty stand of trees beyond the field,
Which in the storms of summer stood revealed

As a great fleet of galleons bound our way
Across a moiled expanse of tossing hay,

Full-rigged and swift, and to the topmost sail
Taking their fill and pleasure of the gale,

Now, in this leafless time, are ships no more,
Though it would not be hard to take them for

A roadstead full of naked mast and spar
In which we see now where the crow's nests are.

STÉPHANE MALLARMÉ

Sea Breeze

The flesh grows weary. And books, I've read them all.
Off, then, to where I glimpse through spray and squall
Strange birds delighting in their unknown skies!
No antique gardens mirrored in my eyes
Can stay my sea-changed spirit, nor the light
Of my abstracted lamp which shines (O Night!)
On the guardian whiteness of the empty sheet,
Nor the young wife who gives the babe her teat.
Come, ship whose masts now gently rock and sway,
Raise anchor for a stranger world! Away!

How strange that Boredom, all its hopes run dry,
Still dreams of handkerchiefs that wave good-bye!
Those gale-inviting masts might creak and bend
In seas where many a craft has met its end,
Dismasted, lost, with no green island near it...
But hear the sailors singing, O my spirit!

from the French

NINA CASSIAN

BALLAD OF THE JACK OF DIAMONDS

Here is the Jack of Diamonds, clad
In the rusty coat he's always had.
His two dark brothers wish him dead,
As does the third, whose hue is red.

Here is the Jack of Diamonds, whom
The fates have marked for certain doom.
He is a mediocre fellow,
A scrawny jack whose chest is hollow
And spattered with a dismal yellow—
No model for a Donatello.

The two dark brothers of this jack,
Abetted by the third, alack,
(Who, draped in hearts from head to foot,
Is the most knavish of the lot),
Have vowed by all means to be free
Of him who gives them symmetry,
Making a balanced set of four
Whose equilibrium they abhor.

One brother, on his breast and sleeves,
Is decked with tragic, spadelike leaves.
The next has crosses for décor.
The motif of the third is gore.

The Jack of Diamonds is dead,
Leaving a vacuum in his stead.

This ballad seems at least twice-told.
Well, all Romanian plots are old.

from the Romanian

45

ONCE

The old rock-climber cries out in his sleep,
Dreaming without enthusiasm
Of a great cliff immeasurably steep,
Or of the sort of yawning chasm,
Now far too deep,
That once, made safe by rashness, he could leap.

BONE KEY

He used to call his body Brother Ass...
—St. Bonaventure, *Life of St. Francis*

You would think that here, at least,
In dens by night, on tawny sands by day,
Poor Brother Ass would be a kingly beast.
So does the casuarina seem to say,

Whose kindred haziness
Of head is flattering to a bloodshot eye;
So too the palm's blown shadows, which caress
Anointed brows and bodies where they lie,

And angel's-trumpets, which
Proclaim a musky scent in fleshly tones.
Yet in this island soil, that's only rich
In rock and coral and Calusa bones,

It's hardihood that thrives,
As when a screw pine that the gale has downed,
Shooting new prop-roots from its trunk, survives
In bristling disarray by change of ground,

Or the white mangrove, nursed
In sea-soaked earth and air, contrives to expel
From leafstalk glands the salt with which it's cursed,
Or crotons, scorched as by the flames of Hell,

Protectively attire
Their leaves in leather, and so move to and fro
In the hot drafts that stir the sun's harsh fire,
Like Shadrach, Meshach, and Abednego.

PERSONAE

1

The poet, mindful of the daring lives
Of bards who dwelt in garrets, drank in dives,
And bought in little shops within the means
Of working folk their soup-bone, salt, and beans,
Becoming, in the cause of literature,
Adjunctive members of the laboring poor,

Ascends the platform now to read his verse
Dressed like a sandhog, stevedore, or worse,
And wears a collar of memorial blue
To give the brave Bohemian past its due.

2

Musicians, who remember when their sort
Were hirelings at some duke's or prince's court,
Obliged to share the noble patron's feast
Belowstairs, or below the salt at least,
Now sweep onto the concert stage disguised
As those by whom they once were patronized.

How princely are their tailcoats! How refined
Their airs, their gracious gestures! And behind
The great conductor who urbanely bows
Rise rank on rank on rank of noble brows.

A Cry from Childhood

Why must it come just now to trouble me,
This sudden, shrill, and dreamlike cry
Of children calling "Valeri! Valeri!"
Out in the street nearby?

It is not for me, that distant childhood call;
Alas, it is for me no more.
They are calling now to someone else, my small
Namesake who lives next door.

Though such disturbances, I must admit,
Are troubling to my train of thought,
I keep my feelings to myself, for it
Would be comical, would it not,

If, from his high and studious retreat,
A gaunt old man leaned out to say
"I can't come out" to the children in the street,
"I'm not allowed to play."

from the Bulgarian

VALERI PETROV

Photos from the Archives

Those manly brows, those eyes so steady,
Those mouths unwilling to betray,
And under them those thin necks, ready
To wear a gallows-rope next day:

Old Nazi archives saved for us
These pictures of our friends who died.
Mug shots, we know, look always thus,
Full face and profile, side by side,

Yet sometimes guilty thoughts arise
Which make us fancy that these men
Have looked once deep into our eyes,
And turned their faces from us then.

from the Bulgarian

A DIGRESSION

Having confided to the heavy-lipped
Mailbox his great synoptic manuscript,
He stands light-headed in the lingering clang.
How lightly, too, he feels his briefcase hang!

And now it swings beside his knees, as they
From habit start him on his evening way,
With the tranced rhythm of a metronome,
Past hall and grove and stadium toward his home.

Yet as the sun-bathed campus slips behind,
A giddy lack of purpose fills his mind,
Making him swerve into a street which for
Two decades he has managed to ignore.

What stops him in his tracks is that his soul,
Proposing nothing, innocent of goal,
Sees no perspective narrowing between
Gold-numbered doors and frontages of green,

But for the moment an obstructive storm
Of specks and flashes that will take no form,
A roiled mosaic or a teeming scrim
That seems to have no pertinence to him.

It is his purpose now as, turning 'round,
He takes his bearings and is homeward bound,
To ponder what the world's confusion meant
When he regarded it without intent.

A WALL IN THE WOODS: CUMMINGTON

1

What is it for, now that dividing neither
Farm from farm nor field from field, it runs
Through deep impartial woods, and is transgressed
By boughs of pine or beech from either side?
Under that woven tester, buried here
Or there in laurel-patch or shrouding vine,
It is for grief at what has come to nothing,
What even in this hush is scarcely heard—
Whipcrack, the ox's lunge, the stoneboat's grating,
Work-shouts of young men stooped before their time
Who in their stubborn heads foresaw forever
The rose of apples and the blue of rye.
It is for pride, as well, in pride that built
With levers, tackle, and abraded hands
What two whole centuries have not brought down.
Look how with shims they made the stones weigh inward,
Binding the water-rounded with the flat;
How to a small ravine they somehow lugged
A long, smooth girder of a rock, on which
To launch their wall in air, and overpass
The narrow stream that still slips under it.
Rosettes of lichen decorate their toils,
Who labored here like Pharaoh's Israelites;
Whose grandsons left for Canaans in the west.
Except to prompt a fit of elegy
It is for us no more, or if it is,
It is a sort of music for the eye,
A rugged ground bass like the bagpipe's drone
On which the leaf-light like a chanter plays.

2

He will hear no guff
About Jamshýd's court, this small,
Striped, duff-colored resident
On top of the wall,

Who, having given
An apotropaic shriek
Echoed by crows in heaven,
Is off like a streak.

There is no tracing
The leaps and scurries with which
He braids his long castle, ra-
Cing, by gap, ledge, niche

And Cyclopean
Passages, to reappear
Sentry-like on a rampart
Thirty feet from here.

What is he saying
Now, in a steady chipping
Succinctly plucked and cadenced
As water dripping?

It is not drum-taps
For a lost race of giants,
But perhaps says something, here
In Mr. Bryant's

Homiletic woods,
Of the brave art of forage
And the good of a few nuts
In burrow-storage;

Of agility
That is not sorrow's captive,
Lost as it is in being
Briskly adaptive;

Of the plenum, charged
With one life through all changes,
And of how we are enlarged
By what estranges.

ELSEWHERE

The delectable names of harsh places:
Cilicia Aspera, Estremadura.
In that smooth wave of cello-sound, Mojave,
We hear no ill of brittle parch and glare.

So late October's pasture-fringe,
With aster-blur and ferns of toasted gold,
Invites to barrens where the crop to come
Is stone prized upward by the deepening freeze.

Speechless and cold the stars arise
On the small garden where we have dominion.
Yet in three tongues we speak of Taurus' name
And of Aldebaran and the Hyades,

Recalling what at best we know,
That there is beauty bleak and far from ours,
Great reaches where the Lord's delighting mind,
Though not inhuman, ponders other things.

CHARLES BAUDELAIRE

The Albatross

Often, for pastime, mariners will ensnare
The albatross, that vast sea-bird who sweeps
On high companionable pinion where
Their vessel glides upon the bitter deeps.

Torn from his native space, this captive king
Flounders upon the deck in stricken pride,
And pitiably lets his great white wing
Drag like a heavy paddle at his side.

This rider of winds, how awkward he is, and weak!
How droll he seems, who was all grace of late!
A sailor pokes a pipestem into his beak;
Another, hobbling, mocks his trammeled gait.

The Poet is like this monarch of the clouds,
Familiar of storms, of stars, and of all high things;
Exiled on earth amidst its hooting crowds,
He cannot walk, borne down by giant wings.

from the French

CHARLES BAUDELAIRE

CORRESPONDENCES

Nature's a temple whose living colonnades
Breathe forth a mystic speech in fitful sighs;
Man wanders among symbols in those glades,
Where all things watch him with familiar eyes.

Like dwindling echoes gathered far away
Into a deep and thronging unison
Huge as the night or as the light of day,
All scents and sounds and colors meet as one.

Perfumes there are as sweet as the oboe's sound,
Green as the prairies, fresh as a child's caress,
—And there are others, rich, corrupt, profound

And of an infinite pervasiveness,
Like myrrh, or musk, or amber, that excite
The ecstasies of sense, the soul's delight.

from the French

THIS PLEASING ANXIOUS BEING

1

In no time you are back where safety was,
Spying upon the lambent table where
Good family faces drink the candlelight
As in a manger scene by de La Tour.
Father has finished carving at the sideboard
And Mother's hand has touched a little bell,
So that, beside her chair, Roberta looms
With serving bowls of yams and succotash.
When will they speak, or stir? They wait for you
To recollect that, while it lived, the past
Was a rushed present, fretful and unsure.
The muffled clash of silverware begins,
With ghosts of gesture, with a laugh retrieved,
And the warm, edgy voices you would hear:
Rest for a moment in that resonance.
But see your small feet kicking under the table,
Fiercely impatient to be off and play.

2

The shadow of whoever took the picture
Reaches like Azrael's across the sand
Toward grown-ups blithe in black and white, encamped
Where surf behind them floods a rocky cove.
They turn with wincing smiles, shielding their eyes
Against the sunlight and the future's glare,
Which notes their bathing caps, their quaint maillots,
The wicker picnic hamper then in style,
And will convict them of mortality.
Two boys, however, do not plead with time,
Distracted as they are by what?—perhaps
A whacking flash of gull-wings overhead—
While off to one side, with his back to us,
A painter, perched before his easel, seeing
The marbled surges come to various ruin,

Seeks out of all those waves to build a wave
That shall in blue summation break forever.

3
Wild, lashing snow, which thumps against the windshield
Like earth tossed down upon a coffin-lid,
Half clogs the wipers, and our Buick yaws
On the black roads of 1928.
Father is driving; Mother, leaning out,
Tracks with her flashlight beam the pavement's edge,
And we must weather hours more of storm
To be in Baltimore for Christmastime.
Of the two children in the back seat, safe
Beneath a lap-robe, soothed by jingling chains
And by their parents' pluck and gaiety,
One is asleep. The other's half-closed eyes
Make out at times the dark hood of the car
Ploughing the eddied flakes, and might foresee
The steady chugging of a landing craft
Through morning mist to the bombarded shore,
Or a deft prow that dances through the rocks
In the white water of the Allagash,
Or, in good time, the bedstead at whose foot
The world will swim and flicker and be gone.

Transformations

The Prologue to Molière's *Amphitryon*

Mercury, on a cloud: Night, in a chariot drawn through the air by two horses

MERCURY   Whoa, charming Night! I beg you, stop and tarry.
                  There is a favor I would ask of you.
                      I bring you a word or two
                      As Jupiter's emissary.

NIGHT   So it's you, Lord Mercury! Heaven knows,
                  I scarcely knew you in that languid pose!

MERCURY   Ah me! I was so weary and so lame
                  From running errands at great Jove's behest,
                  I sat down on a little cloud to rest
                      And wait until you came.

NIGHT   Oh, come now, Mercury. Is it proper for
                  A god to say that he is tired and sore?

MERCURY   Are we made of iron?

NIGHT   No; but we must maintain
                  A tone befitting our divinity.
                  Some words, if uttered by the gods, profane
                      Our lofty rank and high degree,
                      And such base language ought to be
                      Restricted to the human plane.

MERCURY   That's easy enough for you to say;
                You have, my sweet, a chariot and a pair
                  Of splendid steeds to whisk you everywhere
                  In a most nonchalant and queenly way.
                    But my life's not like that at all;
                  And, given my unjust and dismal fate,
                      I owe the poets endless hate
                      For their unutterable gall
                      In having heartlessly decreed,

Ever since Homer sang of Troy,
That each god, for his use and need,
Should have a chariot to enjoy,
While I must go on foot, indeed,
Like some mere village errand-boy—
I, who in heaven and on earth am known
As the famed messenger of Jove's high throne,
And who, without exaggeration,
Considering all the chores I'm given,
Need, more than anyone in Heaven,
To have some decent transportation.

NIGHT   Too bad, but there's no help for it;
The poets treat us as they please.
There's no end to the idiocies
That those fine gentlemen commit.
Still, you are wrong to chide them so severely;
They gave you wingèd heels; that's quite a gift.

MERCURY   Oh, yes: they've made my feet more swift,
But does that make my legs less weary?

NIGHT   Lord Mercury, your point is made.
Now, what's this message that you bear?

MERCURY   It comes from Jove, as you're aware.
He wishes you to cloak him with your shade
While, in a gallant escapade,
He consummates a new affair.
To you, Jove's habits can be nothing new;
You know how often he forsakes the skies;
How much he likes to put on human guise
When there are mortal beauties to pursue,
And how he's full of tricks and lies
That purest maids have yielded to.
Alcmena's bright eyes lately turned his head;
And while, upon the far Boeotian plain,
Amphitryon, her lord, has led

His Thebans in a fierce campaign,
Jove's taken his form and, acting in his stead,
Is eased now of his amorous pain
By the soft pleasures of the lady's bed.
It serves his purpose that the couple were
But lately married; and the youthful heat
Of their amours, their ardor keen and sweet,
Were what inclined the crafty Jupiter
To this particular deceit.
His tactic has succeeded, in this case:
Though, doubtless, such impersonations
Would, with most wives, be vain and out of place;
It isn't always that her husband's face
Will give a woman palpitations.

NIGHT Jove baffles me, and I have trouble seeing
Why these impostures give him such delight.

MERCURY He likes to sample every state of being,
And in so doing he's divinely right.
However high the role that men assign him,
I'd not think much of him if he
Forever played the awesome deity
And let the jeweled bounds of Heaven confine him.
It is, I think, the height of silly pride
Always to be imprisoned in one's splendor;
Above all, if one would enjoy the tender
Passions, one must set one's rank aside.
Jove is a connoisseur of pleasures, who
Is practiced in descending from on high;
When he would enter into any new
Delight, he lays his selfhood by,
And Jupiter the god is lost to view.

NIGHT One might excuse his leaving our high station
To mix with mankind in a lower place,
And sample human passions, however base,
And share men's foolish agitation,

If only, in his taste for transformation,
He'd join no species save the human race.
    But for great Jupiter to change
    Into a bull, or swan, or snake,
    Is most unsuitable and strange,
And causes tongues to cluck and heads to shake.

MERCURY   Let critics carp, in their conceit:
    Such metamorphoses are sweet
    In ways they cannot comprehend.
Jove knows what he's about, in all his dealings;
And in their passions and their tender feelings,
Brutes are less brutish than some folk contend.

NIGHT   Let us revert to the current lady-friend.
    If Jove's sly trick has proved auspicious,
    What does he ask of me? What more can he need?

MERCURY That you rein in your horses, check their speed,
    And thereby satisfy his amorous wishes,
    Stretching a night that's most delicious
    Into a night that's long indeed;
    That you allow his fires more time to burn,
    And stave the daylight off, lest it awaken
    The man whose place he's taken,
    And hasten his return.

NIGHT   It's not the prettiest of tasks
    That Jupiter would have me do!
    There's a sweet name for creatures who
    Perform the service that he asks!

MERCURY For a young goddess, you embrace
    Old-fashioned notions, it seems to me;
    To do such service isn't base
    Except in those of low degree.
When one is blessed with high estate and standing,
    All that one does is good as gold,

And things have different names, depending
On what position one may hold.

NIGHT   In matters of this dubious kind
You've more experience than I;
I'll trust your counsel, then, and try
To do this thing that Jove's assigned.

MERCURY   Ho! Dearest Madam Night, take care;
Don't overdo it, pray; go easy.
Your reputation everywhere
Is not for being prim and queasy.
In every clime, you've played a shady part
In many a tryst and rendezvous;
As far as morals are concerned, dear heart,
There's little to choose between us two.

NIGHT   Enough. Let's cease to bicker thus;
Let us maintain our dignities,
And let's not prompt mankind to laugh at us
By too much frankness, if you please.

MERCURY   Farewell. I must descend now, right away,
And, putting off the form of Mercury,
So change that I may seem to be
Amphitryon's valet.

NIGHT   I shall ride on but, as you ask of me,
I'll often dawdle and delay.

MERCURY   Good day, dear Night.

NIGHT   Good Mercury, good day.

DANTE ALIGHIERI

CANTO XXV OF THE *INFERNO*

The thief, when he had done with prophecy,
    made figs of both his lifted hands, and cried,
    "Take these, O God, for they are aimed at Thee!"

Then was my heart upon the serpents' side,
    for 'round his neck one coiled like a garrote
    as if to say, "Enough of ranting pride,"

And another pinned his arms, and tied a knot
    of head and tail in front of him again,
    so tightly that they could not stir one jot.

Alas, Pistoia, why dost thou not ordain
    that thou be burnt to ashes, since thou hast
    out-sinned the base begetters of thy strain?

In the dark rounds of Hell through which I passed,
    I saw no spirit so blaspheme his Lord,
    not him who from the Theban wall was cast.

He fled then, speaking not another word,
    and into sight a raging centaur came:
    "Where has that half-cooked sinner gone?" he roared.

So many snakes Maremma cannot claim
    as covered all his back in dense array,
    to where his form took on a human frame.

Behind his nape, upon his shoulders, lay
    a seething dragon with its wings outspread,
    which sets afire whatever comes its way.

"Him you behold is Cacus," my master said,
    "who underneath the rock of the Aventine
    so often made a lake of bloody red.

He is not with his brothers, since condign
    justice has set him here, who to his den
    so craftily made off with Geryon's kine:

For that, his crooked ways were ended then
    by the club of Hercules, which dealt him nigh
    a hundred blows, of which he felt not ten."

While thus he spoke, the centaur hastened by,
    and from below three spirits came in view,
    whose coming neither my great guide nor I

Perceived until they shouted, "Who are you?"
    At that, we two broke off our talk together
    and turned our whole attention to that crew.

Who they might be I did not promptly gather;
    but, as may chance in meetings of the kind,
    one had occasion then to name another,

Saying, "Where's Cianfa? Why did he fall behind?"
    I put my finger to my lips, to show
    my guide that he should wait and pay them mind.

'Twill be no wonder, Reader, if you are slow
    to trust the thing that I shall now impart,
    for I, who saw it, scarce believe it so.

I watched a vile, six-footed serpent dart
    toward one of them, and then, with never a pause,
    fasten itself to him with every part.

It clasped his belly with its middle claws,
 its forefeet clutched his arms as in a vise,
 and into either cheek it sank its jaws.

The hindmost feet it dug into his thighs,
 and twixt them thrust its tail so limberly
 that up his spine its clambering tip could rise.

Never did ivy cling so to a tree
 as did that hideous creature bind and braid
 its limbs and his in pure ferocity;

And then they stuck together, as if made
 of melting wax, and mixed their colors; nor
 did either now retain his former shade;

Just so, when paper burns, there runs before
 the creeping flame a stain of darkish hue
 that, though not black as yet, is white no more.

The other two cried out to him they knew,
 saying, "Agnello, how you change! Ah me,
 already you are neither one nor two."

The two heads now were one, and we could see
 two faces fuse in one blear visage, where
 no vestiges of either seemed to be.

Four forelimbs now combined to make a pair
 of arms, and strange new members grew in place
 of the bellies, legs, and chests that had been there.

Their erstwhile shapes were gone without a trace,
 and the monstrous form that was and was not they
 now moved away with slow and stumbling pace.

As lizards, in the cruelest heat of day,
    skitter from hedge to hedge along a lane,
    and flash like lightning if they cross the way,

So, toward the bellies of the other twain,
    there sped a little reptile, fiery-hot
    and blackly glinting as a pepper-grain:

It now transfixed, in one of them, the spot
    through which our earliest nourishment must come;
    then fell, and sprawled before him like a sot.

The victim gazed at it, and yet was dumb;
    he stood stock-still, and did but yawn a bit,
    as if some drowsy fever made him numb.

The serpent looked on him, and he on it;
    from the one's mouth and the other's wound, a spate
    of smoke poured out, and the fumes converged and knit.

Of poor Sabellus' and Nasidius' fate
    let Lucan tell no more, but listen now
    to what I saw. Let Ovid not relate

Of Cadmus and of Arethusa, how
    they turned to snake or fountain by his grace;
    no envy of those feats need I avow,

For he never made two creatures, face to face,
    so change that each one let the other seize
    its very substance, as in the present case.

Incited by their mutual sympathies,
    the serpent caused its tail now to divide,
    and the wretch pressed together his feet and knees.

His legs and thighs adhered then, side to side,
    soon blending, so that nowhere, low or high,
    could any seam or juncture be descried.

The cloven tail took on the form that by
    degrees the other lost, and now its skin
    turned soft, while the other's hardened in reply.

I saw the armpits of the man begin
    to engulf the arms, while the beast's short forelegs grew
    by just that length to which the arms sank in.

Its two hind feet entwined, and turned into
    that member which by mankind is concealed,
    and the thief's one member branched then into two.

Now, while the smoke by which they both were veiled
    transposed their hues, and planted on one crown
    the hair that from the other it plucked and peeled,

The one arose, the other toppled down,
    and each, still grimly staring, set about
    to make the other's lineaments his own.

The upright one drew back his upper snout,
    and from his brow the excess matter ran
    downward, till from the cheeks two ears grew out;

Then the nether remnant of the snout began,
    out of its superfluity, to make
    a human nose, and the full lips of a man.

The prone one thrust his jaws out like a snake,
    and at the same time drew his ears inside,
    as a snail retracts its horns for safety's sake,

And cleft his tongue, that once was unified
    and shaped for speech. Then, in the other's head,
    the forked tongue healed, and the smoke could now subside.

The soul that had become a beast now fled
    hissing away; the other, who had begun
    to speak in sputters, followed where it led,

Yet turned his new-made shoulders toward the one
    who lingered, saying, "Buoso shall crawl through this
    stony terrain awhile, as I have done."

Thus did the cargo of the seventh abyss
    change and re-change; let the strangeness of it, pray,
    excuse me if my pen has gone amiss.

Although my thoughts were fuddled by dismay
    and my eyes a bit uncertain, all the same
    those darkling spirits did not steal away

Ere I knew one for Puccio, called the Lame;
    and he had been the only one to keep
    his form, of the three thieves who earlier came.

The other was he, Gaville, who made thee weep.

Zea   The title is one half of the botanical name (*Zea mays*) for Indian corn or maize.

At Moorditch   In act 1, scene 2, of *Henry the Fourth, Part I*, Prince Hal says to Falstaff, "What sayest thou to a hare, or the melancholy of Moor Ditch?" Moorditch seemed to me a good name for the sort of hospital where people are treated for depression.

Signatures   Gerard's *Herball* (1597) says of Solomon's Seal that "The root is white and thicke, full of knobs or joints, in some places resembling the mark of a seale, whereof I thinke it tooke the name *Sigillum Solomonis.*" Evidently some herbalists saw in the "raised orbicular scars of the stems of former years" (Homer D. House, *Wild Flowers*) a pattern resembling the magical five-pointed or six-pointed star called Solomon's Seal. The rootstock of False Solomon's Seal also bears the scars of former stems, but no such pattern has been discerned in them. Yeats's poems mention more than once the bell-branch which was the insignia of the ancient Celtic bard or ollave. And Robert Graves, in his *White Goddess,* tells of "the branch of golden bells which were the ollave's emblem of office."

Bone Key   The name "Key West" comes from Spanish "Cayo Hueso" (Bone Island), which may or may not derive from intertribal Indian warfare, the final massacre of the Calusas, and the littering of the island with their bones. The casuarina, a feathery tree that takes its name from the cassowary bird, has an aptitude for growing in seacoast sand and is also known as Australian pine. Angel's-trumpet is a poisonous, narcotic tree of the genus *Datura.* Screw pine is a common name for the large Asiatic shrub pandanus. White mangroves and crotons are well-known, and so, surely, are Shadrach, Meshach, and Abednego.

A Wall in the Woods: Cummington   Jamshýd, a legendary king of ancient Persia, is mentioned in an *ubi sunt* manner by FitzGerald's Omar Khayyám: "They say the Lion and the Lizard keep / The courts where Jamshýd gloried and drank deep." William Cullen Bryant (1794–1878), whose poems often found lessons in nature, was born and raised in Cummington, Massachusetts, and returned there in his latter years.

This Pleasing Anxious Being   The title is taken from the twenty-second stanza of Thomas Gray's "Elegy Written in a Country Churchyard."

The Prologue to Molière's *Amphitryon*   Molière's three-act comedy *Amphitryon* (1668) was based on a Latin tragicomedy of the second century B.C., the

Amphitruo of Plautus, and was influenced as well by Jean de Rotrou's prior French adaptation, *Les Sosies* (1636). It is generally agreed that Molière greatly improved upon his sources. In any case, the prologue is wholly Molière's idea and owes nothing to any earlier play. The form of the prologue, and that of the play as a whole, is the system of *vers libres* which Molière's friend La Fontaine was then employing for his *Fables*: in writing *vers libres,* one is free at any moment to alter line length or rhyme pattern for expressive reasons.

Dante Alighieri: Canto xxv of the *Inferno* This translation was done for Daniel Halpern's *Dante's Inferno: Translations by Twenty Contemporary Poets* (Ecco, 1993). Of my notes, included in the Ecco volume and much indebted to such scholars as Charles Singleton, I give here the summarizing first paragraph.

Dante and Virgil are still in the Seventh Chasm, to which the souls of thieves are assigned. As Canto xxiv has shown, it is a dark place, and full of reptiles that variously punish the sinners—twining around them so as to bind their thievish hands, or (as happened to Vanni Fucci in xxiv) causing them to burn to ashes and then reform. What first occurs in Canto xxv is that Vanni Fucci, at the conclusion of a prophecy grievous to Dante, makes a gesture of obscene defiance toward God, is therefore throttled and bound by serpents, and flees, pursued by the centaur Cacus. The remainder of the canto is concerned with the transformations undergone by five thieves of Florence, all of noble family, who have been identified as Agnello de' Brunelleschi, Buoso (degli Abati?), Puccio "Sciancato" de' Galigai, Cianfa de' Donati, and Francesco de' Cavalcanti. Cianfa, who has been changed into a six-footed serpent, attacks Agnello and merges with him to create a monster that is neither reptile nor man. Then Francesco, who is temporarily a small reptile, assaults Buoso and exchanges shapes with him, the man becoming a serpentello *and the reptile becoming a man. Puccio remains unchanged, but for the moment only. The logic of these painful transformations is that the thieves, who in life appropriated what was not theirs, are here punished by the repeated loss even of their own persons.*

New and Collected Poems

1987

———•———

For my grandchildren,
Amelia and Gabriel

ONE

THE RIDE

The horse beneath me seemed
To know what course to steer
Through the horror of snow I dreamed,
And so I had no fear,

Nor was I chilled to death
By the wind's white shudders, thanks
To the veils of his patient breath
And the mist of sweat from his flanks.

It seemed that all night through,
Within my hand no rein
And nothing in my view
But the pillar of his mane,

I rode with magic ease
At a quick, unstumbling trot
Through shattering vacancies
On into what was not,

Till the weave of the storm grew thin,
With a threading of cedar-smoke,
And the ice-blind pane of an inn
Shimmered, and I awoke.

How shall I now get back
To the inn-yard where he stands,
Burdened with every lack,
And waken the stable-hands

To give him, before I think
That there was no horse at all,
Some hay, some water to drink,
A blanket and a stall?

GNOMONS

In April, thirteen centuries ago,
Bede cast his cassocked shadow on the ground
Of Jarrow and, proceeding heel-to-toe,
Measured to where a head that could contain
The lore of Christendom had darkly lain,
And thereby, for that place and season, found
That a man's shade, at the third hour from dawn,
Stretches eleven feet upon the lawn.

This morning, with his tables in my hand,
Adapting them as near as I can gauge,
Foot after foot, on Massachusetts land,
I pace through April sunlight toward a wall
On which he knew my shadow's end would fall
Whatever other dark might plague the age,
And, warmed by the fidelity of time,
Make with his sun-ringed head a dusky rhyme.

ALATUS

for R. P. W.

Their supply-lines cut,
The leaves go down to defeat,
Turning, flying, but

Bravely so, the ash
Shaking from blade and pennon
May light's citron flash;

And rock maple, though
Its globed array be shivered,
Strews its fallen so

As to mock the cold,
Blanketing earth with earnest
Of a summer's gold.

Still, what sumac-gore
Began, and rattling oak shall
End, is not a war;

Nor are leaves the same
(Though May come back in triumph),
Crumpled once by flame.

This time's true valor
Is a rash consent to change,
To crumbling pallor,

Dust, and dark re-merge.
See how the fire-bush, circled
By a crimson verge

Of its own sifting,
Bristles aloft its every
Naked stem, lifting

Beyond the faint sun,
Toward the hid pulse of things, its
Wingèd skeleton.

LYING

To claim, at a dead party, to have spotted a grackle,
When in fact you haven't of late, can do no harm.
Your reputation for saying things of interest
Will not be marred, if you hasten to other topics,
Nor will the delicate web of human trust
Be ruptured by that airy fabrication.
Later, however, talking with toxic zest
Of golf, or taxes, or the rest of it
Where the beaked ladle plies the chuckling ice,
You may enjoy a chill of severance, hearing
Above your head the shrug of unreal wings.
Not that the world is tiresome in itself:
We know what boredom is: it is a dull
Impatience or a fierce velleity,
A champing wish, stalled by our lassitude,
To make or do. In the strict sense, of course,
We invent nothing, merely bearing witness
To what each morning brings again to light:
Gold crosses, cornices, astonishment
Of panes, the turbine-vent which natural law
Spins on the grill-end of the diner's roof,
Then grass and grackles or, at the end of town
In sheen-swept pastureland, the horse's neck
Clothed with its usual thunder, and the stones
Beginning now to tug their shadows in
And track the air with glitter. All these things
Are there before us; there before we look
Or fail to look; there to be seen or not
By us, as by the bee's twelve thousand eyes,
According to our means and purposes.
So too with strangeness not to be ignored,
Total eclipse or snow upon the rose,
And so with that most rare conception, nothing.
What is it, after all, but something missed?
It is the water of a dried-up well
Gone to assail the cliffs of Labrador.

There is what galled the arch-negator, sprung
From Hell to probe with intellectual sight
The cells and heavens of a given world
Which he could take but as another prison:
Small wonder that, pretending not to be,
He drifted through the bar-like boles of Eden
In a *black mist low creeping,* dragging down
And darkening with moody self-absorption
What, when he left it, lifted and, if seen
From the sun's vantage, seethed with vaulting hues.
Closer to making than the deftest fraud
Is seeing how the catbird's tail was made
To counterpoise, on the mock-orange spray,
Its light, up-tilted spine; or, lighter still,
How the shucked tunic of an onion, brushed
To one side on a backlit chopping-board
And rocked by trifling currents, prints and prints
Its bright, ribbed shadow like a flapping sail.
Odd that a thing is most itself when likened:
The eye mists over, basil hints of clove,
The river glazes toward the dam and spills
To the drubbed rocks below its crashing cullet,
And in the barnyard near the sawdust-pile
Some great thing is tormented. Either it is
A tarp torn loose and in the groaning wind
Now puffed, now flattened, or a hip-shot beast
Which tries again, and once again, to rise.
What, though for pain there is no other word,
Finds pleasure in the cruellest simile?
It is something in us like the catbird's song
From neighbor bushes in the grey of morning
That, harsh or sweet, and of its own accord,
Proclaims its many kin. It is a chant
Of the first springs, and it is tributary
To the great lies told with the eyes half-shut
That have the truth in view: the tale of Chiron
Who, with sage head, wild heart, and planted hoof
Instructed brute Achilles in the lyre,

Or of the garden where we first mislaid
Simplicity of wish and will, forgetting
Out of what cognate splendor all things came
To take their scattering names; and nonetheless
That matter of a baggage-train surprised
By a few Gascons in the Pyrenees
Which, having worked three centuries and more
In the dark caves of France, poured out at last
The blood of Roland, who to Charles his king
And to the dove that hatched the dove-tailed world
Was faithful unto death, and shamed the Devil.

On Having Mis-identified a Wild Flower

A thrush, because I'd been wrong,
Burst rightly into song
In a world not vague, not lonely,
Not governed by me only.

JOSEPH BRODSKY

SIX YEARS LATER

So long had life together been that now
The second of January fell again
On Tuesday, making her astonished brow
Lift like a windshield-wiper in the rain,
    So that her misty sadness cleared, and showed
    A cloudless distance waiting up the road.

So long had life together been that once
The snow began to fall, it seemed unending;
That, lest the flakes should make her eyelids wince,
I'd shield them with my hand, and they, pretending
    Not to believe that cherishing of eyes,
    Would beat against my palm like butterflies.

So alien had all novelty become
That sleep's entanglements would put to shame
Whatever depths the analysts might plumb;
That when my lips blew out the candle-flame,
    Her lips, fluttering from my shoulder, sought
    To join my own, without another thought.

So long had life together been that all
That tattered brood of papered roses went,
And a whole birch-grove grew upon the wall,
And we had money, by some accident,
    And tonguelike on the sea, for thirty days,
    The sunset threatened Turkey with its blaze.

So long had life together been without
Books, chairs, utensils—only that ancient bed,
That the triangle, before it came about,
Had been a perpendicular, the head
    Of some acquaintance hovering above
    Two points which had been coalesced by love.

So long had life together been that she
And I, with our joint shadows, had composed
A double door, a door which even if we
Were lost in work or sleep, was always closed:
　　Somehow, it would appear, we drifted right
　　On through it into the future, into the night.

LEAVING

As we left the garden-party
By the far gate,
There were many loitering on
Who had come late

And a few arriving still,
Though the lawn lay
Like a fast-draining shoal
Of ochre day.

Curt shadows in the grass
Hatched every blade,
And now on pedestals
Of mounting shade

Stood all our friends—iconic,
Now, in mien,
Half-lost in dignities
Till now unseen.

There were the hostess' hands
Held out to greet
The scholar's limp, his wife's
Quick-pecking feet,

And there was wit's cocked head,
And there the sleek
And gaze-enameled look
Of beauty's cheek.

We saw now, loitering there
Knee-deep in night,
How even the wheeling children
Moved in a rite

Or masque, or long charade
Where we, like these,
Had blundered into grand
Identities,

Filling our selves as sculpture
Fills the stone.
We had not played so surely,
Had we known.

THE CATCH

From the dress-box's plashing tis-
Sue paper she pulls out her prize,
Dangling it to one side before my eyes
Like a weird sort of fish

That she has somehow hooked and gaffed
And on the dock-end holds in air—
Limp, corrugated, lank, a catch too rare
Not to be photographed.

I, in my chair, make shift to say
Some bright, discerning thing, and fail,
Proving once more the blindness of the male.
Annoyed, she stalks away

And then is back in half a minute,
Consulting, now, not me at all
But the long mirror, mirror on the wall.
The dress, now that she's in it,

Has changed appreciably, and gains
By lacy shoes, a light perfume
Whose subtle field electrifies the room,
And two slim golden chains.

With a fierce frown and hard-pursed lips
She twists a little on her stem
To test the even swirling of the hem,
Smooths down the waist and hips,

Plucks at the shoulder-straps a bit,
Then turns around and looks behind,
Her face transfigured now by peace of mind.
There is no question—it

Is wholly charming, it is she,
As I belatedly remark,
And may be hung now in the fragrant dark
Of her soft armory.

SONG

Never take her away,
The daughter whom you gave me,
The gentle, moist, untroubled
Small daughter whom you gave me;
O let her heavenly babbling
Beset me and enslave me.
Don't take her; let her stay,
Beset my heart, and win me,
That I may put away
The firstborn child within me,
That cold, petrific, dry
Daughter whom death once gave,
Whose life is a long cry
For milk she may not have,
And who, in the night-time, calls me
In the saddest voice that can be
Father, Father, and tells me
Of the love she feels for me.
Don't let her go away,
Her whom you gave—my daughter—
Lest I should come to favor
That wilder one, that other
Who does not leave me ever.

ICARIUM MARE

We have heard of the undimmed air
Of the True Earth above us, and how here,
    Shut in our sea-like atmosphere,
We grope like muddled fish. Perhaps from there,

    That fierce lucidity,
Came Icarus' body tumbling, flayed and trenched
    By waxen runnels, to be quenched
Near Samos riding in the actual sea,

    Where Aristarchus first
Rounded the sun in thought; near Patmos, too,
    Where John's bejeweled inward view
Descried an angel in the solar burst.

    The reckoner's instruments,
The saint's geodic skull bowed in his cave—
    Insight and calculation brave
Black distances exorbitant to sense,

    Which in its little shed
Of broken light knows wonders all the same.
    Where else do lifting wings proclaim
The advent of the fire-gapped thunderhead,

    Which swells the streams to grind
What oak and olive grip their roots into,
    Shading us as we name anew
Creatures without which vision would be blind?

    This is no outer dark
But a small province haunted by the good,
    Where something may be understood
And where, within the sun's coronal arc,

We keep our proper range,
Aspiring, with this lesser globe of sight,
To gather tokens of the light
Not in the bullion, but in the loose change.

SOME RIDDLES FROM SYMPHOSIUS

TEGULA

Earth gave me body; strong through fire am I;
Earth bore me, but my home is ever on high;
Though moisture drenches me, I soon am dry.

ROTAE

Four equal sisters equidistant run
As if they vied in skill and speed, but none
Gains on another, and their task is one.

PECUNIA

First I was earth, and deep in earth retired;
Another name I gained when I was fired;
I'm earth no more, but through me earth's acquired.

SPONGIA

Though light, I bear the water's clinging weight,
And all my guts in spreading caves dilate.
When pressed to go, the water leaves in spate.

SILEX

Fire dwells in me, but rarely meets the eye;
A knock will bring it forth, but else it's shy;
No wood it needs to live, no water to die.

TINEA

Though not well-read, on letters have I dined;
I've lived in books, but not improved my mind;
Devoured the Muses, and still am unrefined.

PHOENIX

My death is life; when born, I am unmade.
Ere life can kindle in me, I must fade;
Thus I alone am fathered by a shade.

SOMNUS

I come when good and ready, and I glut
Men's eyes with myriad forms and phantoms. But
None goes to me unless his eyes are shut.

Under a Tree

We know those tales of gods in hot pursuit
Who frightened wood-nymphs into taking root

And changing then into a branchy shape
Fair, but perplexing to the thought of rape:

But this, we say, is more how love is made—
Ply and reply of limbs in fireshot shade,

Where overhead we hear tossed leaves consent
To take the wind in free dishevelment

And, answering with supple blade and stem,
Caress the gusts that are caressing them.

WYETH'S MILK CANS

Beyond them, hill and field
Harden, and summer's easy
Wheel-ruts lie congealed.

What if these two bells tolled?
They'd make the bark-splintering
Music of pure cold.

For W. H. Auden

Now I am surer where they were going,
The brakie loping the tops of the moving freight,
The beautiful girls in their outboard, waving to someone
As the stern dug in and the wake pleated the water,

The uniformed children led by a nun
Through the terminal's uproar, the clew-drawn scholar descending
The cast-iron stair of the stacks, shuffling his papers,
The Indians, two to a blanket, passing in darkness,

Also the German prisoner switching
His dusty neck as the truck backfired and started—
Of all these noted in stride and detained in memory
I now know better that they were going to die,

Since you, who sustained the civil tongue
In a scattering time, and were poet of all our cities,
Have for all your clever difference quietly left us,
As we might have known that you would, by that common door.

Orchard Trees, January

It's not the case, though some might wish it so
Who from a window watch the blizzard blow

White riot through their branches vague and stark,
That they keep snug beneath their pelted bark.

They take affliction in until it jells
To crystal ice between their frozen cells,

And each of them is inwardly a vault
Of jewels rigorous and free of fault,

Unglimpsed by us until in May it bears
A sudden crop of green-pronged solitaires.

MIRABEAU BRIDGE

Under the Mirabeau Bridge there flows the Seine
　　Must I recall
　　Our loves recall how then
After each sorrow joy came back again

　　　Let night come on bells end the day
　　　The days go by me still I stay

Hands joined and face to face let's stay just so
　　While underneath
　　The bridge of our arms shall go
Weary of endless looks the river's flow

　　　Let night come on bells end the day
　　　The days go by me still I stay

All love goes by as water to the sea
　　All love goes by
　　How slow life seems to me
How violent the hope of love can be

　　　Let night come on bells end the day
　　　The days go by me still I stay

The days the weeks pass by beyond our ken
　　Neither time past
　　Nor love comes back again
Under the Mirabeau Bridge there flows the Seine

　　　Let night come on bells end the day
　　　The days go by me still I stay

TROLLING FOR BLUES

for John and Barbara

As with the dapper terns, or that sole cloud
Which like a slow-evolving embryo
Moils in the sky, we make of this keen fish
Whom fight and beauty have endeared to us
A mirror of our kind. Setting aside

His unreflectiveness, his flings in air,
The aberration of his flocking swerve
To spawning-grounds a hundred miles at sea,
How clearly, musing to the engine's thrum,
Do we conceive him as he waits below:

Blue in the water's blue, which is the shade
Of thought, and in that scintillating flux
Poised weightless, all attention, yet on edge
To lunge and seize with sure incisiveness,
He is a type of coolest intellect,

Or is so to the mind's blue eye until
He strikes and runs unseen beneath the rip,
Yanking imagination back and down
Past recognition to the unlit deep
Of the glass sponges, of chiasmodon,

Of the old darkness of Devonian dream,
Phase of a meditation not our own,
That long mêlée where selves were not, that life
Merciless, painless, sleepless, unaware,
From which, in time, unthinkably we rose.

ADVICE FROM THE MUSE

for T. W. W.

How credible, the room which you evoke:
At the far end, a lamplit writing-desk.
Nearer, the late sun swamps an arabesque
Carpet askew upon a floor of oak,
And makes a cherry table-surface glow,
Upon which lies an open magazine.
Beyond are shelves and pictures, as we know,
Which cannot in the present light be seen.

Bid now a woman enter in a mood
That we, because she brings a bowl of roses
Which, touch by delicate touch, she redisposes,
May think to catch with some exactitude.
And let her, in complacent silence, hear
A squirrel chittering like an unoiled joint
To tell us that a grove of beech lies near.
Have all be plain, but only to a point.

Not that the bearded man who in a rage
Arises ranting from a shadowy chair,
And of whose presence she was unaware,
Should not be fathomed by the final page,
And all his tale, and hers, be measured out
With facts enough, good ground for inference,
No gross unlikelihood or major doubt,
And, at the end, an end to all suspense.

Still, something should escape us, something like
A question one had meant to ask the dead,
The day's heat come and gone in infra-red,
The deep-down jolting nibble of a pike,
Remembered strangers who in picnic dress

Traverse a field and under mottling trees
Enter a midnight of forgetfulness
Rich as our ignorance of the Celebes.

Of motives for some act, propose a few,
Confessing that you can't yourself decide;
Or interpose a witness to provide,
Despite his inclination to be true,
Some fadings of the signal, as it were,
A breath which, drawing closer, may obscure
Mirror or window with a token blur—
That slight uncertainty which makes us sure.

THE RULE

The oil for extreme unction must be blessed
On Maundy Thursday, so the rule has ruled,
And by the bishop of the diocese.
Does that revolt you? If so, you are free
To squat beneath the deadly manchineel,
That tree of caustic drops and fierce aspersion,
And fancy that you have escaped from mercy.
Things must be done in one way or another.

A FABLE

Securely sunning in a forest glade,
 A mild, well-meaning snake
Approved the adaptations he had made
  For safety's sake.

 He liked the skin he had—
Its mottled camouflage, its look of mail,
And was content that he had thought to add
  A rattling tail.

The tail was not for drumming up a fight;
 No, nothing of the sort.
And he would only use his poisoned bite
  As last resort.

 A peasant now drew near,
Collecting wood; the snake, observing this,
Expressed concern by uttering a clear
  But civil hiss.

The simple churl, his nerves at once unstrung,
 Mistook the other's tone
And dashed his brains out with a deftly flung
  Pre-emptive stone.

MORAL

Security, alas, can give
 A threatening impression;
Too much defense-initiative
  Can prompt aggression.

TRANSIT

A woman I have never seen before
Steps from the darkness of her town-house door
At just that crux of time when she is made
So beautiful that she or time must fade.

What use to claim that as she tugs her gloves
A phantom heraldry of all the loves
Blares from the lintel? That the staggered sun
Forgets, in his confusion, how to run?

Still, nothing changes as her perfect feet
Click down the walk that issues in the street,
Leaving the stations of her body there
As a whip maps the countries of the air.

SHAD-TIME

Though between sullen hills,
Flat intervals, harsh-bristled bank and bank,
    The widening river-surface fills
        With sky-depth cold and blank,

The shadblow's white racemes
Burst here or there at random, scaled with red,
    As when the spitting fuse of dreams
        Lights in a vacant head,

Or as the Thracian strings,
Descending past the bedrock's muted staves,
    Picked out the signatures of things
        Even in death's own caves.

Shadblow; in farthest air
Toss three unsettled birds; where naked ledge
    Buckles the surge is a green glare
        Of moss at the water's edge;

And in this eddy here
A russet disc of maple-pollen spins.
    With such brave poverties the year
        Unstoppably begins.

It is a day to guess
What wide-deploying motives of delight
    Concert great fields of emptiness
        Beneath the mesh of sight,

So that this boulder, this
Scored obstacle atilt in whittling spray,
    This swarm of shadows, this abyss
        In which pure numbers play,

Though cloudily astrew
As rivers soon shall be with scattered roe,
Instant by instant chooses to
Affirm itself and flow.

WORLDS

For Alexander there was no Far East,
Because he thought the Asian continent
Ended with India. Free Cathay at least
Did not contribute to his discontent.

But Newton, who had grasped all space, was more
Serene. To him it seemed that he'd but played
With a few shells and pebbles on the shore
Of that profundity he had not made.

ALL THAT IS

Twilight approaches, with its last brief spot-lit
Galaxies of midges, its first star,
And having put in doubt its bats or swallows,
Enters the eastern suburbs. There the hedged
Air darkens like a fast-reducing broth,
Simmering the shapes of things. And counter to
Those topiary whims, those *carceri,*
That cypress dye which taints the arbor vitae,
Bright squares flash on in staggered patterns, block
By block, some few blacked out by lowered shades.
Meanwhile, through evening traffic and beneath
Checkered façades, a many-lighted bus,
Pausing or turning at the intersections,
Goes intricately home. One passenger
Already folds his paper to the left-
Hand lower corner of the puzzles page,
As elsewhere other hands are doing, whether
At kitchen tables under frazzled light,
In plumped-up sickbed, or the easy chair
Near which a faceted decanter glows.
Above this séance, in the common dark
Between the street-lamps and the jotted sky,
What now takes shape? It is a ghostly grille
Through which, as often, we begin to see
The confluence of the Oka and the Aare.

Is it a vision? Does the eye make out
A flight of ernes, rising from aits or aeries,
Whose shadows track across a harsh terrain
Of esker and arête? At waterside,
Does the shocked eeler lay his congers by,
Sighting a Reo driven by an edile?
And does the edile, from his running-board,
Step down to meet a ranee? Does she end
By reading to him from the works of Elia?
No, there are no such chance encounters here

As you imagined once, O Lautréamont,
No all-reflecting prism-grain of sand
Nor eyeful such as Markandeya got
When, stumbled into vacancy, he saw
A lambent god reposing on the sea,
Full of the knitted light of all that is.
It is a puzzle which, as puzzles do,
Dreams that there is no puzzle. It is a rite
Of finitude, a picture in whose frame
Roc, oast, and Inca decompose at once
Into the ABCs of every day.
A door is rattled shut, a deadbolt thrown.
Under some clipped euonymus, a mushroom,
Bred of an old and deep mycelium
As hidden as the webwork of the world,
Strews on the shifty night-wind, rising now,
A cast of spores as many as the stars.

A Finished Man

Of the four louts who threw him off the dock
Three are now dead, and so more faintly mock
The way he choked and splashed and was afraid.
His memory of the fourth begins to fade.

It was himself whom he could not forgive;
Yet it has been a comfort to outlive
That woman, stunned by his appalling gaffe,
Who with a napkin half-suppressed her laugh,

Or that grey colleague, surely gone by now,
Who, turning toward the window, raised his brow,
Embarrassed to have caught him in a lie.
All witness darkens, eye by dimming eye.

Thus he can walk today with heart at ease
Through the old quad, escorted by trustees,
To dedicate the monumental gym
A grateful college means to name for him.

Seated, he feels the warm sun sculpt his cheek
As the young president gets up to speak.
If the dead die, if he can but forget,
If money talks, he may be perfect yet.

HAMLEN BROOK

At the alder-darkened brink
Where the stream slows to a lucid jet
I lean to the water, dinting its top with sweat,
    And see, before I can drink,

A startled inchling trout
Of spotted near-transparency,
Trawling a shadow solider than he.
    He swerves now, darting out

To where, in a flicked slew
Of sparks and glittering silt, he weaves
Through stream-bed rocks, disturbing foundered leaves,
    And butts then out of view

Beneath a sliding glass
Crazed by the skimming of a brace
Of burnished dragon-flies across its face,
    In which deep cloudlets pass

And a white precipice
Of mirrored birch-trees plunges down
Toward where the azures of the zenith drown.
    How shall I drink all this?

Joy's trick is to supply
Dry lips with what can cool and slake,
Leaving them dumbstruck also with an ache
    Nothing can satisfy.

TWO

For Music

ON FREEDOM'S GROUND

A CANTATA

for William Schuman

I. Back Then
Back then, before we came
To this calm bay and savage oceanside,
When Bedloe's Island had no English name,
The waves were but the subjects of the tide
And vassals of the harnessed wind, which blew
Not as it chose, but as it had to do.

The river had no choice
But to create this basin to the south,
Where every springtime tuned the peeper's voice
And drove the shad-run through its narrow mouth,
And the high-hovering sea-birds, even they,
Were slaves to hunger, diving on their prey.

Where was the thought of freedom then?
It came ashore within the minds of men.

II. Our Risen States
It was an English thought
That there is no just government
Unless by free consent,
And in that English cause we fought.

Our George defied their George;
Our Continentals would not yield
On Saratoga's field,
Or to the snows of Valley Forge.

But Yorktown's fall we owe
Not to ourselves alone, and let
This nation not forget
Great Lafayette and Rochambeau.

It was our risen states
Which heartened France at last to rise
And beat with angry cries
On prison doors and palace gates,

Till Frenchmen all might say
With us, and by the world be heard,
The sweet and rousing word
Of liberty, of *liberté*.

III. *Like a Great Statue*

Mourn for the dead who died for this country,
Whose minds went dark at the edge of a field,
In the muck of a trench, on the beachhead sand,
In a blast amidships, a burst in the air.
What did they think of before they forgot us?
In the blink of time before they forgot us?
The glare and whiskey of Saturday evening?
The drone or lilt of their family voices?
The bend of a trout-stream? A fresh-made bed?
The sound of a lathe, or the scent of sawdust?
The mouth of a woman? A prayer? Who knows?
Let us not force them to speak in chorus,
These men diverse in their names and faces
Who lived in a land where a life could be chosen.
Say that they mattered, alive and after;
That they gave us time to become what we could.

*

Grieve for the ways in which we betrayed them,
How we robbed their graves of a reason to die:
The tribes pushed west, and the treaties broken,
The image of God on the auction block,
The immigrant scorned, and the striker beaten,
The vote denied to liberty's daughters.
From all that has shamed us, what can we salvage?
Be proud at least that we know we were wrong,
That we need not lie, that our books are open.

Praise to this land for our power to change it,
To confess our misdoings, to mend what we can,
To learn what we mean and to make it the law,
To become what we said we were going to be.
Praise to our peoples, who came as strangers,
Who more and more have been shaped into one
Like a great statue brought over in pieces,
Its hammered copper bolted together,
Anchored by rods in the continent's rock,
With a core of iron, and a torch atop it.
Praise to this land that its most oppressed
Have marched in peace from the dark of the past
To speak in our time, and in Washington's shadow,
Their invincible hope to be free at last—

    Lord God Almighty, free
    At last to cast their shackles down,
    And wear the common crown
    Of *liberté*, of liberty.

IV. Come Dance
Now in our lady's honor
Come dance on freedom's ground,
And do the waltz or polka,
Whatever spins around,

Or let it be the raspa,
The jig or Lindy hop,
Or else the tarantella,
Whatever doesn't stop,

The Highland fling, the hornpipe,
The schottische or the break,
Or, if you like, the cakewalk,
Whatever takes the cake,

But end it with the John Paul Jones,
Invented in this land,
That each of us may circle 'round
And take the other's hand.

V. Immigrants Still
Still, in the same great bay,
Now edged with towers and with piers,
Where for a hundred years
Our lady has been holding sway,

The risen tide comes flooding as before
To ramble north a hundred miles or more,
And the same sea-birds rise, though now they wheel
Above the crossing wakes of barge and keel.

These waters and these wings,
Whatever once they seemed, now wear
A bright, cavorting air,
And have the look of ransomed things:

To our free eyes the gulls go weaving now
Loose wreaths of flight about our lady's brow,
And toward her feet the motions of the sea
Leap up like hearts that hasten to be free.

*

Not that the graves of our dead are quiet,
Nor justice done, nor our journey over.
We are immigrants still, who travel in time,
Bound where the thought of America beckons;
But we hold our course, and the wind is with us.

The Mind-Reader

NEW POEMS

1976

———•———

For Charlee
Jusqu' à la fin du monde, lon-la

ONE

———•———

The Eye

A Storm in April

for Ben

Some winters, taking leave,
Deal us a last, hard blow,
Salting the ground like Carthage
Before they will go.

But the bright, milling snow
Which throngs the air today—
It is a way of leaving
So as to stay.

The light flakes do not weigh
The willows down, but sift
Through the white catkins, loose
As petal-drift,

Or in an up-draft lift
And glitter at a height,
Dazzling as summer's leaf-stir
Chinked with light.

This storm, if I am right,
Will not be wholly over
Till green fields, here and there,
Turn white with clover,

And through chill air the puffs of milkweed hover.

THE WRITER

In her room at the prow of the house
Where light breaks, and the windows are tossed with linden,
My daughter is writing a story.

I pause in the stairwell, hearing
From her shut door a commotion of typewriter-keys
Like a chain hauled over a gunwale.

Young as she is, the stuff
Of her life is a great cargo, and some of it heavy:
I wish her a lucky passage.

But now it is she who pauses,
As if to reject my thought and its easy figure.
A stillness greatens, in which

The whole house seems to be thinking,
And then she is at it again with a bunched clamor
Of strokes, and again is silent.

I remember the dazed starling
Which was trapped in that very room, two years ago;
How we stole in, lifted a sash

And retreated, not to affright it;
And how for a helpless hour, through the crack of the door,
We watched the sleek, wild, dark

And iridescent creature
Batter against the brilliance, drop like a glove
To the hard floor, or the desk-top,

And wait then, humped and bloody,
For the wits to try it again; and how our spirits
Rose when, suddenly sure,

It lifted off from a chair-back,
Beating a smooth course for the right window
And clearing the sill of the world.

It is always a matter, my darling,
Of life or death, as I had forgotten. I wish
What I wished you before, but harder.

To the Etruscan Poets

Dream fluently, still brothers, who when young
Took with your mothers' milk the mother tongue,

In which pure matrix, joining world and mind,
You strove to leave some line of verse behind

Like a fresh track across a field of snow,
Not reckoning that all could melt and go.

THE EYE

"...all this beastly seeing"

—D. H. Lawrence

for John and Bill

I.

One morning in St. Thomas, when I tried
Our host's binoculars, what was magnified?
In the green slopes about us, only green,
Brisked into fronds and paddles, could be seen,
Till by a lunging focus I was shown
Some portion of a terrace like our own.
Someone with ankles crossed, in tennis shoes,
Was turning sun-blank pages of the news,
To whom in time came espadrilles of pink
Bearing a tall and fruit-crowned tropic drink.
How long I witnessed, missing not a sip!—
Then, scanning down through photons to a ship
In the blue bay, spelt out along the bow
The queenly legend of her name; and now
Followed her shuttling lighter as it bore
Her jounced, gay charges landward to explore
Charlotte Amalie, with its duty-free
Leicas, binoculars, and jewelry.
What kept me goggling all that hour? The nice
Discernment of a lime or lemon slice?
A hope of lewd espials? An astounded
Sense of the import of a thing surrounded—
Of what a Z or almond-leaf became
Within the sudden premise of a frame?
All these, and that my eye should flutter there,
By shrewd promotion, in the outstretched air,
An unseen genius of the middle distance,
Giddy with godhead or with nonexistence.

II.

Preserve us, Lucy,
From the eye's nonsense, you by whom
Benighted Dante was beheld,
To whom he was beholden.

If the salesman's head
Rolls on the seat-back of the 'bus
In ugly sleep, his open mouth
Banjo-strung with spittle,

Forbid my vision
To take itself for a curious angel.
Remind me that I am here in body,
A passenger, and rumpled.

Charge me to see
In all bodies the beat of spirit,
Not merely in the *tout en l'air*
Or double pike with layout

But in the strong,
Shouldering gait of the legless man,
The calm walk of the blind young woman
Whose cane touches the curbstone.

Correct my view
That the far mountain is much diminished,
That the fovea is prime composer,
That the lid's closure frees me.

Let me be touched
By the alien hands of love forever,
That this eye not be folly's loophole
But giver of due regard.

Sleepless at Crown Point

All night, this headland
Lunges into the rumpling
Capework of the wind.

Piccola Commedia

He is no one I really know,
The sun-charred, gaunt young man
By the highway's edge in Kansas
Thirty-odd years ago.

On a tourist-cabin veranda
Two middle-aged women sat;
One, in a white dress, fat,
With a rattling glass in her hand,

Called "Son, don't you feel the heat?
Get up here into the shade."
Like a good boy, I obeyed,
And was given a crate for a seat

And an Orange Crush and gin.
"This state," she said, "is hell."
Her thin friend cackled, "Well, dear,
You've gotta fight sin with sin."

"No harm in a drink; my stars!"
Said the fat one, jerking her head.
"And I'll take no lip from Ed,
Him with his damn cigars."

Laughter. A combine whined
On past, and dry grass bent
In the backwash; liquor went
Like an ice-pick into my mind.

Beneath her skirt I spied
Two sea-cows on a floe.
"Go talk to Mary Jo, son,
She's reading a book inside."

As I gangled in at the door
A pink girl, curled in a chair,
Looked up with an ingénue stare.
Screenland lay on the floor.

Amazed by her starlet's pout
And the way her eyebrows arched,
I felt both drowned and parched.
Desire leapt up like a trout.

"Hello," she said, and her gum
Gave a calculating crack.
At once, from the lightless back
Of the room there came the grumble

Of someone heaving from bed,
A Zippo's click and flare,
Then, more and more apparent,
The shuffling form of Ed,

Who neither looked nor spoke
But moved in profile by,
Blinking one gelid eye
In his elected smoke.

This is something I've never told,
And some of it I forget.
But the heat! I can feel it yet,
And that conniving cold.

A Wedding Toast

M. C. H.
C. H. W.
14 July 1971

St. John tells how, at Cana's wedding-feast,
The water-pots poured wine in such amount
That by his sober count
There were a hundred gallons at the least.

It made no earthly sense, unless to show
How whatsoever love elects to bless
Brims to a sweet excess
That can without depletion overflow.

Which is to say that what love sees is true;
That the world's fullness is not made but found.
Life hungers to abound
And pour its plenty out for such as you.

Now, if your loves will lend an ear to mine,
I toast you both, good son and dear new daughter.
May you not lack for water,
And may that water smack of Cana's wine.

MARCH

Beech leaves which might have clung
Parching for six weeks more
Were stripped by last night's gale
Which made so black a roar

And drove the snow-streaks level.
So we see in the glare
Of a sun whose white combustion
Cannot warm the air.

From the edge of the woods, in gusts,
The leaves are scuttled forth
Onto a pasture drifted
Like tundras of the north,

To migrate there in dry
Skitter or fluttered brawl,
Then flock into some hollow
Like this, below the wall,

With veins swept back like feathers
To our prophetic sight,
And bodies of gold shadow
Pecking at sparks of light.

In Limbo

What rattles in the dark? The blinds at Brewster?
I am a boy then, sleeping by the sea,
Unless that clank and chittering proceed
From a bent fan-blade somewhere in the room,
The air-conditioner of some hotel
To which I came too dead-beat to remember.
Let me, in any case, forget and sleep.
But listen: under my billet window, grinding
Through the shocked night of France, I surely hear
A convoy moving up, whose treads and wheels
Trouble the planking of a wooden bridge.

For a half-kindled mind that flares and sinks,
Damped by a slumber which may be a child's,
How to know when one is, or where? Just now
The hinged roof of the Cinema Vascello
Smokily opens, beaming to the stars
Crashed majors of a final panorama,
Or else that spume of music, wafted back
Like a girl's scarf or laughter, reaches me
In adolescence and the Jersey night,
Where a late car, tuned in to wild casinos,
Guns past the quiet house towards my desire.

Now I could dream that all my selves and ages,
Pretenders to the shadowed face I wear,
Might, in this clearing of the wits, forgetting
Deaths and successions, parley and atone.
It is my voice which prays it; mine replies
With stammered passion or the speaker's pause,
Rough banter, slogans, timid questionings—
Oh, all my broken dialects together;
And that slow tongue which mumbles to invent
The language of the mended soul is breathless,
Hearing an infant howl demand the world.

Someone is breathing. Is it I? Or is it
Darkness conspiring in the nursery corner?
Is there another lying here beside me?
Have I a cherished wife of thirty years?
Far overhead, a long susurrus, twisting
Clockwise or counterclockwise, plunges east,
Twin floods of air in which our flagellate cries,
Rising from love-bed, childbed, bed of death,
Swim toward recurrent day. And farther still,
Couched in the void, I hear what I have heard of,
The god who dreams us, breathing out and in.

Out of all that I fumble for the lamp-chain.
A room condenses and at once is true—
Curtains, a clock, a mirror which will frame
This blinking mask the light has clapped upon me.
How quickly, when we choose to live again,
As Er once told, the cloudier knowledge passes!
I am a truant portion of the all
Misshaped by time, incorrigible desire
And dear attachment to a sleeping hand,
Who lie here on a certain day and listen
To the first birdsong, homelessly at home.

A SKETCH

Into the lower right
Square of the window frame
There came
   with scalloped flight

A goldfinch, lit upon
The dead branch of a pine,
Shining,
   and then was gone,

Tossed in a double arc
Upward into the thatched
And cross-hatched
    pine-needle dark.

Briefly, as fresh drafts stirred
The tree, he dulled and gleamed
And seemed
   more coal than bird,

Then, dodging down, returned
In a new light, his perch
A birch-
   twig, where he burned

In the sun's broadside ray,
Some seed pinched in his bill.
Yet still
   he did not stay,

But into a leaf-choked pane,
Changeful as even in heaven,
Even
   in Saturn's reign,

Tunneled away and hid.
And then? But I cannot well
Tell you
      all that he did.

It was like glancing at rough
Sketches tacked on a wall,
And all
      so less than enough

Of gold on beaten wing,
I could not choose that one
Be done
      as the finished thing.

PETER

There at the story's close
We could not stay awake.
The new wine made us doze,
And not for Jesus' sake

I struck the high-priest's slave
Who came at start of day,
But as a hand might wave
Some bugling fly away.

That hand warm by the flame,
I murmured no, no, no
To mutters of his name
And felt the rooster's crow

Flail me, yet did not waken
Out of that rocky sleep.
Dungeoned I stood there, shaken
Only enough to weep,

Only enough to fill,
At those predicted jeers,
Through the dropped lashes' grille
The socket's moat of tears.

COTTAGE STREET, 1953

Framed in her phoenix fire-screen, Edna Ward
Bends to the tray of Canton, pouring tea
For frightened Mrs. Plath; then, turning toward
The pale, slumped daughter, and my wife, and me,

Asks if we would prefer it weak or strong.
Will we have milk or lemon, she enquires?
The visit seems already strained and long.
Each in his turn, we tell her our desires.

It is my office to exemplify
The published poet in his happiness,
Thus cheering Sylvia, who has wished to die;
But half-ashamed, and impotent to bless,

I am a stupid life-guard who has found,
Swept to his shallows by the tide, a girl
Who, far from shore, has been immensely drowned,
And stares through water now with eyes of pearl.

How large is her refusal; and how slight
The genteel chat whereby we recommend
Life, of a summer afternoon, despite
The brewing dusk which hints that it may end.

And Edna Ward shall die in fifteen years,
After her eight-and-eighty summers of
Such grace and courage as permit no tears,
The thin hand reaching out, the last word *love*,

Outliving Sylvia who, condemned to live,
Shall study for a decade, as she must,
To state at last her brilliant negative
In poems free and helpless and unjust.

The Fourth of July

for I. A. R.

1.
Liddell, the Oxford lexicographer,
Allowed his three small daughters on this day
To row from Folly Bridge to Godstow, where
Their oarsman, Mr. Dodgson, gave them tea
Beneath a rick of hay,
Shading their minds with golden fantasy.
And it was all fool's gold,
Croquet or caucus madder than a hare,
That universe of which he sipped and told,
Mocking all grammars, codes, and theorems
Beside the spangled, blindly flowing Thames.

2.
Off to the west, in Memphis, where the sun's
Mid-morning fire beat on a wider stream,
His purpose headstrong as a river runs,
Grant closed a smoky door on aides and guards
And chewed through scheme on scheme
For toppling Vicksburg like a house of cards.
The haze at last would clear
On Hard Times Landing, Porter's wallowed guns,
The circling trenches that in just a year
Brought the starved rebels through the settling smoke
To ask for terms beside a stunted oak.

3.
The sun is not a concept but a star.
What if its rays were once conjointly blurred
By tea-fumes and a general's cigar?
Though, as for that, what grand arcanum saves
Appearances, what word
Holds all from foundering in points and waves?

No doubt the fairest game
Play only in those groves where creatures are
At one, distinct, and innocent of name,
As Alice found, who in the termless wood
Lacked words to thank the shade in which she stood.

4.

Nevertheless, no kindly swoon befell
Tree-named Linnaeus when the bald unknown
Encroached upon his memory, cell by cell,
And he, whose love of all things made had brought
Bird, beast, fish, plant, and stone
Into the reaches of his branchy thought,
Lost bitterly to mind
Their names' sweet Latin and his own as well.
Praise to all fire-fledged knowledge of the kind
That, stooped beneath a hospitable roof
Brings only hunch and gaiety for proof,

5.

But also to Copernicus, who when
His vision leapt into the solar disc
And set the earth to wheeling, waited then
To see what slate or quadrant might exact,
Not hesitant to risk
His dream-stuff in the fitting-rooms of fact;
And honor to these States,
Which come to see that black men too are men,
Beginning, after troubled sleep, debates,
Great bloodshed, and a century's delay,
To mean what once we said upon this day.

A Shallot

The full cloves
Of your buttocks, the convex
Curve of your belly, the curved
Cleft of your sex—

Out of this corm
That's planted in strong thighs
The slender stem and radiant
Flower rise.

A Black Birch in Winter

You might not know this old tree by its bark,
Which once was striate, smooth, and glossy-dark,
So deep now are the rifts which separate
Its roughened surface into flake and plate.

Fancy might less remind you of a birch
Than of mosaic columns in a church
Like Ara Coeli or the Lateran,
Or the trenched features of an agèd man.

Still, do not be too much persuaded by
These knotty furrows and these tesserae
To think of patterns made from outside-in
Or finished wisdom in a shriveled skin.

Old trees are doomed to annual rebirth,
New wood, new life, new compass, greater girth,
And this is all their wisdom and their art—
To grow, stretch, crack, and not yet come apart.

FOR THE STUDENT STRIKERS

Go talk with those who are rumored to be unlike you,
And whom, it is said, you are so unlike.
Stand on the stoops of their houses and tell them why
You are out on strike.

It is not yet time for the rock, the bullet, the blunt
Slogan that fuddles the mind toward force.
Let the new sound in our streets be the patient sound
Of your discourse.

Doors will be shut in your faces, I do not doubt.
Yet here or there, it may be, there will start,
Much as the lights blink on in a block at evening,
Changes of heart.

They are your houses; the people are not unlike you;
Talk with them, then, and let it be done
Even for the grey wife of your nightmare sheriff
And the guardsman's son.

written for the Wesleyan *Strike News*
Spring, 1970

C Minor

Beethoven during breakfast? The human soul,
Though stalked by hollow pluckings, winning out
(While bran-flakes crackle in the cereal-bowl)
    Over despair and doubt?

You are right to switch it off and let the day
Begin at hazard, perhaps with pecker-knocks
In the sugar bush, the rancor of a jay,
    Or in the letter box

Something that makes you pause and with fixed shadow
Stand on the driveway gravel, your bent head
Scanning the snatched pages until the sad
    Or fortunate news is read.

The day's work will be disappointing or not,
Giving at least some pleasure in taking pains.
One of us, hoeing in the garden plot
    (Unless, of course, it rains)

May rejoice at the knitting of light in fennel-plumes
And dew like mercury on cabbage-hide,
Or rise and pace through too-familiar rooms,
    Balked and dissatisfied.

Shall a plate be broken? A new thing understood?
Shall we be lonely, and by love consoled?
What shall I whistle, splitting the kindling-wood?
    Shall the night-wind be cold?

How should I know? And even if we were fated
Hugely to suffer, grandly to endure,
It would not help to hear it all fore-stated
    As in an overture.

There is nothing to do with a day except to live it.
Let us have music again when the light dies
(Sullenly, or in glory) and we can give it
    Something to organize.

To His Skeleton

Why will you vex me with
These bone-spurs in the ear,
With X-rayed phlebolith
And calculus? See here,

Noblest of armatures,
The grin which bares my teeth
Is mine as yet, not yours.
Did you not stand beneath

This flesh, I could not stand,
But would revert to slime
Informous and unmanned;
And I may come in time

To wish your peace my fate,
Your sculpture my renown.
Still, I have held you straight
And mean to lay you down

Without too much disgrace
When what can perish dies.
For now then, keep your place
And do not colonize.

JOHN CHAPMAN

Beside the Brokenstraw or Licking Creek,
Wherever on the virginal frontier
New men with rutting wagons came to seek
Fresh paradises for the axe to clear,

John Chapman fostered in a girdled glade
Or river-flat new apples for their need,
Till half the farmsteads of the west displayed
White blossom sprung of his authentic seed.

Trusting in God, mistrusting artifice,
He would not graft or bud the stock he sold.
And what, through nature's mercy, came of this?
No sanguine crops of vegetable gold

As in Phaeacia or Hesperides,
Nor those amended fruit of harsher climes
That bowed the McIntosh or Rambo trees,
Ben Davis, Chandler, Jonathan, or Grimes,

But the old *malus malus*, double-dyed,
Eurasia's wilding since the bitter fall,
Sparse upon branches as perplexed as pride,
An apple gnarled, acidulous, and small.

Out of your grave, John Chapman, in Fort Wayne,
May you arise, and flower, and come true.
We meanwhile, being of a spotted strain
And born into a wilder land than you,

Expecting less of natural tree or man
And dubious of working out the brute,
Affix such hopeful scions as we can
To the rude, forked, and ever savage root.

APRIL 5, 1974

The air was soft, the ground still cold.
In the dull pasture where I strolled
Was something I could not believe.
Dead grass appeared to slide and heave,
Though still too frozen-flat to stir,
And rocks to twitch, and all to blur.
What was this rippling of the land?
Was matter getting out of hand
And making free with natural law?
I stopped and blinked, and then I saw
A fact as eerie as a dream.
There was a subtle flood of steam
Moving upon the face of things.
It came from standing pools and springs
And what of snow was still around;
It came of winter's giving ground
So that the freeze was coming out,
As when a set mind, blessed by doubt,
Relaxes into mother-wit.
Flowers, I said, will come of it.

TERESA

After the sun's eclipse,
The brighter angel and the spear which drew
A bridal outcry from her open lips,
    She could not prove it true,
Nor think at first of any means to test
By what she had been wedded or possessed.

    Not all cries were the same;
There was an island in mythology
Called by the very vowels of her name
    Where vagrants of the sea,
Changed by a wand, were made to squeal and cry
As heavy captives in a witch's sty.

    The proof came soon and plain:
Visions were true which quickened her to run
God's barefoot errands in the rocks of Spain
    Beneath its beating sun,
And lock the O of ecstasy within
The tempered consonants of discipline.

CHILDREN OF DARKNESS

If groves are choirs and sanctuaried fanes,
What have we here?
An elm-bole cocks a bloody ear;
In the oak's shadow lies a strew of brains.
Wherever, after the deep rains,

The woodlands are morose and reek of punk,
These gobbets grow—
Tongue, lobe, hand, hoof or butchered toe
Amassing on the fallen branch half-sunk
In leaf-mold, or the riddled trunk.

Such violence done, it comes as no surprise
To notice next
How some, parodically sexed,
Puff, blush, or gape, while shameless phalloi rise,
To whose slimed heads come carrion flies.

Their gift is not for life, these creatures who
Disdain to root,
Will bear no stem or leaf, no fruit,
And, mimicking the forms which they eschew,
Make it their pleasure to undo

All that has heart and fiber. Yet of course
What these break down
Wells up refreshed in branch and crown.
May we not after all forget that Norse
Drivel of Wotan's panicked horse,

And every rumor bred of forest-fear?
Are these the brood
Of adders? Are they devil's food,
Minced witches, or the seed of rutting deer?
Nowhere does water stand so clear

As in stalked cups where pine has come to grief;
The chanterelle
And cèpe are not the fare of hell;
Where coral schools the beech and aspen leaf
To seethe like fishes of a reef,

Light strikes into a gloom in which are found
Red disc, grey mist,
Gold-auburn firfoot, amethyst,
Food for the eye whose pleasant stinks abound,
And dead men's fingers break the ground.

Gargoyles is what they are at worst, and should
They preen themselves
On being demons, ghouls, or elves,
The holy chiaroscuro of the wood
Still would embrace them. They are good.

TWO

BALLADE OF FORGIVENESS

Brothers and sisters, Celestine,
Carthusian, or Carmelite,
Street-loafers, fops whose buckles shine,
Lackeys, and courtesans whose tight
Apparel gratifies the sight,
And little ladies'-men who trot
In tawny boots of dreadful height:
I beg forgiveness of the lot.

Young whores who flash their teats in sign
Of what they hawk for men's delight,
Ape-handlers, thieves and, soused with wine,
Wild bullies looking for a fight,
And Jacks and Jills whose hearts are light,
Whistling and joking, talking rot,
Street-urchins dodging left and right:
I beg forgiveness of the lot.

Excepting for those bloody swine
Who gave me, many a morn and night,
The hardest crusts on which to dine;
Henceforth I'll fear them not a mite.
I'd belch and fart in their despite,
Were I not sitting on my cot.
Well, to be peaceful and polite,
I beg forgiveness of the lot.

May hammers, huge and heavy, smite
Their ribs, and likewise cannon-shot.
May cudgels pulverize them quite.
I beg forgiveness of the lot.

THE GRASSHOPPER AND THE ANT

Grasshopper, having sung her song
   All summer long,
Was sadly unprovided-for
When the cold winds began to roar:
Not one least bite of grub or fly
Had she remembered to put by.
Therefore she hastened to descant
On famine, to her neighbor Ant,
Begging the loan of a few grains
Of wheat to ease her hunger-pains
Until the winter should be gone.
"You shall be paid," said she, "upon
My honor as an animal,
Both interest and principal."
The Ant was not disposed to lend;
That liberal vice was not for her.
"What did you do all summer, friend?"
She asked the would-be borrower.
"So please your worship," answered she,
"I sang and sang both night and day."
"You sang? Indeed, that pleases me.
Then dance the winter-time away."

JOACHIM DU BELLAY

Happy the Man

Happy the man who, journeying far and wide
As Jason or Ulysses did, can then
Turn homeward, seasoned in the ways of men,
And claim his own, and there in peace abide!

When shall I see the chimney-smoke divide
The sky above my little town: ah, when
Stroll the small gardens of that house again
Which is my realm and crown, and more beside?

Better I love the plain, secluded home
My fathers built, than bold façades of Rome;
Slate pleases me as marble cannot do;

Better than Tiber's flood my quiet Loire,
Those little hills than these, and dearer far
Than great sea winds the zephyrs of Anjou.

VOLTAIRE

To Madame du Châtelet

If you would have my heart love on,
Grant me such years as suit the lover,
And teach my twilight to recover
(If but it could) the flush of dawn.

Time takes my elbow now, in sign
That I must bow and turn away
From gardens where the god of wine
Divides with Love his pleasant sway.

Let us from rigorous Time obtain
What timely blessings may assuage.
Whoever will not be his age
Knows nothing of his age but pain.

Leave then to sweet and giddy youth
Those ecstasies which youth can give:
Two moments only do we live;
Let there be one for sober truth.

What! Will you leave me thus forlorn,
O tenderness, illusion, folly—
Heavenly gifts whereby I've borne
Life's bitterness and melancholy?

Two deaths we suffer. To forgo
Loving, and being loved in turn,
Is deathly pain, as now I learn.
Ceasing to live is no such woe.

Thus did I mourn the loss of all
Those years when I was young and mad,
My slow heart sighing to recall
The furious beat which once it had.

Friendship, descending from above,
Came then in mercy to my aid;
She was as kind, perhaps, as Love,
But not so ardent, and more staid.

Touched by her charms, so fresh they were,
And by her radiance calm and clear,
I followed her; yet shed a tear
That I could follow none but her.

THREE

FLIPPANCIES

1.

The Star System

While you're a white-hot youth, emit the rays
Which, now unmarked, shall dazzle future days.
Burn for the joy of it, and waste no juice
On hopes of prompt discovery. Produce!

Then, white with years, live wisely and survive.
Thus you may be on hand when you arrive,
And, like Antares, rosily dilate,
And for a time be gaseous and great.

2.

What's Good for the Soul Is Good for Sales

If fictive music fails your lyre, confess—
Though not, of course, to any happiness.
So it be tristful, tell us what you choose:
Hangover, Nixon on the TV news,
God's death, the memory of your rocking-horse,
Entropy, housework, Buchenwald, divorce,
Those damned flamingoes in your neighbor's yard…
All hangs together if you take it hard.

Two Riddles from Aldhelm

I.

Once I was water, full of scaly fish,
But now am something else, by Fortune's wish.
Through fiery torment I was made to grow
As white as ashes, or as glinting snow.

II.

Ugly I am, capacious, brazen, round,
And hang between high heaven and the ground,
Seething with billows and aglow with flame.
Thus, as it were, I'm vexed upon two fronts
By both those raging elements at once.
    What's my name?

Rillons, Rillettes

RILLETTES: Hors d'oeuvre *made up of a mash of pigmeat, usually highly seasoned. Also used for making sandwiches. The* Rillettes *enjoying the greatest popularity are the* Rillettes *and* Rillons de Tours, *but there are* Rillettes *made in many other parts of France.*

RILLONS: *Another name for the* Rillettes, *a pigmeat* hors d'oeuvre. *The most popular* Rillons *are those of Blois.*

—A Concise Encyclopaedia of Gastronomy,
edited by André L. Simon

Rillons, Rillettes, they taste the same,
And would by any other name,
And are, if I may risk a joke,
Alike as two pigs in a poke.

The dishes are the same, and yet
While Tours provides the best *Rillettes*,
The best *Rillons* are made in Blois.
There must be some solution.
                              Ah!—

Does Blois supply, do you suppose,
The best *Rillettes de Tours*, while those
Now offered by the chefs of Tours
Are, by their ancient standards, poor?

Clever, but there remains a doubt.
It is a thing to brood about,
Like non-non-A, infinity,
Or the doctrine of the Trinity.

THE PRISONER OF ZENDA

At the end a
"The Prisoner of Zenda,"
The King being out of danger,
Stewart Granger
(As Rudolph Rassendyll)
Must swallow a bitter pill
By renouncing his co-star,
Deborah Kerr.

It would be poor behavia
In him and in Princess Flavia
Were they to put their own
Concerns before those of the Throne.
Deborah Kerr must wed
The King instead.

Rassendyll turns to go.
Must it be so?
Why can't they have their cake
And eat it, for heaven's sake?
Please let them have it both ways,
The audience prays.
And yet it is hard to quarrel
With a plot so moral.

One redeeming factor,
However, is that the actor
Who plays the once-dissolute King
(Who has learned through suffering
Not to drink or be mean
To his future Queen),
Far from being a stranger,
Is *also* Stewart Granger.

FOUR

The Funeral of Bobò

1.

Bobò is dead, but don't take off your hat.
No gesture we could make will help us bear it.
Why mount a butterfly upon the spit
Of the Admiralty tower? We'd only tear it.

On every side, no matter where you glance,
Are squares of windows. As for "What happened?"—well,
Open an empty can by way of answer
And say "Just that, as near as one can tell."

Bobò is dead. Wednesday is almost over.
On streets which offer you no place to go,
Such whiteness lies. Only the night river,
With its black water, does not wear the snow.

2.

Bobò is dead; there's sadness in this line.
O window-squares, O arches' semicircles,
And such fierce frost that if one's to be slain,
Let blazing firearms do the dirty-work.

Farewell, Bobò, my beautiful and sweet.
These tear-drops dot the page like holes in cheese.
We are too weak to follow you, and yet
To take a stand exceeds our energies.

Your image, as I here and now predict,
Whether in crackling cold or waves of heat,
Shall never dwindle—quite the reverse, in fact—
In Rossi's matchless, long, and tapering street.

Bobò is dead. Something I might convey
Slips from my grasp, as bath-soap sometimes does.
Today, within a dream, I seemed to lie
Upon my bed. And there, in fact, I was.

Tear off a page, but read the date aright:
It's with a zero that our woes commence.
Without her, dreams suggest the waking state,
And squares of air push through the window-vents.

Bobò is dead. One feels an impulse, with
Half-parted lips, to murmur "Why? What for?"
It's emptiness, no doubt, which follows death.
That's likelier than Hell—and worse, what's more.

You were all things, Bobò. But your decease
Has changed you. You are nothing; you are not;
Or, rather, you are a clot of emptiness—
Which also, come to think of it, is a lot.

Bobò is dead. To these round eyes, the view
Of the bare horizon-line is like a knife.
But neither Kiki nor Zazà, Bobò,
Will ever take your place. Not on your life.

Now Thursday. I believe in emptiness.
There, it's like Hell, but shittier, I've heard.
And the new Dante, pregnant with his message,
Bends to the empty page and writes a word.

PHONE BOOTH

Someone is loose in Moscow who won't stop
Ringing my 'phone.
Whoever-it-is listens, then hangs up.
Dial tone.

What do you want? A bushel of rhymes or so?
An autograph? A bone?
Hello?
Dial tone.

Someone's lucky number, for all I know,
Is the same, worse luck, as my own.
Hello!
Dial tone.

Or perhaps it's an angel calling collect
To invite me to God's throne.
Damn, I've been disconnected.
Dial tone.

Or is it my old conscience, my power of choice
To which I've grown
A stranger, and which no longer knows my voice?
Dial tone.

Are you standing there in some subway station, stiff
And hatless in the cold,
With your finger stuck in the dial as if
In a ring of gold?

And is there, outside the booth, a desperate throng
Tapping its coins on the glass, chafing its hands,
Like a line of people who have been waiting long
To be measured for wedding-bands?

I hear you breathe and blow into some remote
Mouthpiece, and as you exhale
The lapels of my coat
Flutter like pennants in a gale.

Speak up, friend! Are you deaf and dumb as a stone?
Dial tone.

The planet's communications are broken.
I'm tired of saying *hello*.
My questions might as well be unspoken.
Into the void my answers go.

Thrown together, together
With you, with you unknown.
Hello. Hello. Hello there.
Dial tone. Dial tone. Dial tone.

ANDREI VOZNESENSKY

AN ARROW IN THE WALL

You'd look right with a wolf from Tambov
For sidekick and friend,
As you tear my Punjabi bow
Down from the wall, and bend it.

Your hand pulls back from the shoulder
As if measuring cloth by the yard;
The arrow pants, and is eager,
Like a nipple extended and hard.

And now, with what feminine fury,
Into the wall it goes—
All the walls of the snug and secure.
There's a woman in that, God knows!

In towers of skeletal steel,—an arrow!
In pomposities one and all.
Who says it's the electronic era?
There's an arrow in the wall!

Burn, privilege and power!
There's an arrow in the wall.
Soon, in a drained and lonely hour,
Your tears will fall.

But dark now, doubly dark,
Over rich embrasures which crawl
With elaborate moldings, your stark
Arrow is in the wall!

All right, you cheeky blonde,
Checkmate me, and I'll say
"Oh, you Olympian!," thinking fondly
Of how your belly-dimples play.

"You Scythian," I shall add, "you shrew..."
And you'll say, "To hell with you..."

* * * * *

Release, O rawhide bowstring,
The stillest arrow, a dart
So incredibly hushed, one might suppose
An angel was departing.

In public, we're barely friends,
But for years it's been going on:
Beneath my high-rise window
Dark waters run.

A deep stream of love.
A bright rapids of sorrow.
A high wall of forgiveness.
And pain's clean, piercing arrow.

Two Poems

1.

A star in the sky. How many words and tears,
What promises, what wishes made upon it,
How many heart-cries! For what endless years!
What dashings-off of verse and rhyme and sonnet!

Yet to the clear mind, too, it signs from heaven:
The Magi followed it with reverence;
So did the navigators…Einstein, even,
Could not without some fixèd stars make sense.

Ah, to select a theme that once for all
Would captivate all men without exception—
Saint, atheist, hero, coward, freeman, thrall—
And then to realize one's high conception
On the night's canvas with a dot, just one.

What artist would not own himself outdone?

2.

Nights rolled upon the river's face,
Volcanoes flared and overflowed,
And ferns which towered into space
With paleozoic flashes glowed

When, with his Slavic eye, there crept
A saurian from paludal slime—
My reptile ancestor—and stepped
On the dry land for the first time.

He did not then, of course, predict
The spate of future generation,
Of linked phenomena in strict

And inextinguishable relation,
Or me, in that concatenation,
In whose world Planck and Blok connect!

But I...what breed am I, what kind?
What are my past, my destiny?
How should that far one be divined
Whose modest forebear I shall be,
Whose world's pure miracle to me,
Whose deeds, the manner of whose mind?

Hundreds of years will pass, perhaps
Millions, and then he will be there,
Remembering us across that lapse,
Our strange third partner, and our heir.

And then what magic time will do!
All distances will coalesce,
And all awareness flow into
The heaven of his consciousness.

From grey mist will materialize
His predecessors, one and all,
Whatever their degree or size,
No matter how obscure or small,

And to that joyous herd, that throng
Bound from creation and before,
You too shall certainly belong,
O my reptilian ancestor.

FIVE

———•—•———

The Mind-Reader

THE MIND-READER

Lui parla.
for Charles and Eula

Some things are truly lost. Think of a sun-hat
Laid for the moment on a parapet
While three young women—one, perhaps, in mourning—
Talk in the crenellate shade. A slight wind plucks
And budges it; it scuffs to the edge and cartwheels
Into a giant view of some description:
Haggard escarpments, if you like, plunge down
Through mica shimmer to a moss of pines
Amidst which, here or there, a half-seen river
Lobs up a blink of light. The sun-hat falls,
With what free flirts and stoops you can imagine,
Down through that reeling vista or another,
Unseen by any, even by you or me.
It is as when a pipe-wrench, catapulted
From the jounced back of a pick-up truck, dives headlong
Into a bushy culvert; or a book
Whose reader is asleep, garbling the story,
Glides from beneath a steamer chair and yields
Its flurried pages to the printless sea.

It is one thing to escape from consciousness
As such things do, another to be pent
In the dream-cache or stony oubliette
Of someone's head.
                    They found, when I was little,
That I could tell the place of missing objects.
I stood by the bed of a girl, or the frayed knee
Of an old man whose face was lost in shadow.
When did you miss it?, people would be saying,
Where did you see it last? And then those voices,
Querying or replying, came to sound
Like cries of birds when the leaves race and whiten
And a black overcast is shelving over.

The mind is not a landscape, but if it were
There would in such case be a tilted moon
Wheeling beyond the wood through which you groped,
Its fine spokes breaking in the tangled thickets.
There would be obfuscations, paths which turned
To dried-up stream-beds, hemlocks which invited
Through shiny clearings to a groundless shade;
And yet in a sure stupor you would come
At once upon dilapidated cairns,
Abraded moss, and half-healed blazes leading
To where, around the turning of a fear,
The lost thing shone.
                          Imagine a railway platform—
The long cars come to a cloudy halt beside it,
And the fogged windows offering a view
Neither to those within nor those without.
Now, in the crowd—forgive my predilection—
Is a young woman standing amidst her luggage,
Expecting to be met by you, a stranger.
See how she turns her head, the eyes engaging
And disengaging, pausing and shying away.
It is like that with things put out of mind,
As the queer saying goes: a lost key hangs
Trammeled by threads in what you come to see
As the webbed darkness of a sewing-basket,
Flashing a little; or a photograph,
Misplaced in an old ledger, turns its bled
Oblivious profile to rebuff your vision,
Yet glistens with the fixative of thought.
What can be wiped from memory? Not the least
Meanness, obscenity, humiliation,
Terror which made you clench your eyes, or pulse
Of happiness which quickened your despair.
Nothing can be forgotten, as I am not
Permitted to forget.
                          It was not far
From that to this—this corner café table
Where, with my lank grey hair and vatic gaze,

I sit and drink at the receipt of custom.
They come here, day and night, so many people:
Sad women of the quarter, dressed in black,
As to a black confession; blinking clerks
Who half-suppose that Taurus ruminates
Upon their destinies; men of affairs
Down from Milan to clear it with the magus
Before they buy or sell some stock or other;
My fellow-drunkards; fashionable folk,
Mocking and ravenously credulous,
And skeptics bent on proving me a fraud
For fear that some small wonder, unexplained,
Should leave a fissure in the world, and all
Saint Michael's host come flapping back.
                                    I give them
Paper and pencil, turn away and light
A cigarette, as you have seen me do;
They write their questions; fold them up; I lay
My hand on theirs and go into my frenzy,
Raising my eyes to heaven, snorting smoke,
Lolling my head as in the fumes of Delphi,
And then, with shaken, spirit-guided fingers,
Set down the oracle. All that, of course,
Is trumpery, since nine times out of ten
What words float up within another's thought
Surface as soon in mine, unfolding there
Like paper flowers in a water-glass.
In the tenth case, I sometimes cheat a little.
That shocks you? But consider: what I do
Cannot, so most conceive, be done at all,
And when I fail, I am a charlatan
Even to such as I have once astounded—
Whereas a tailor can mis-cut my coat
And be a tailor still. I tell you this
Because you know that I have the gift, the burden.
Whether or not I put my mind to it,
The world usurps me ceaselessly; my sixth
And never-resting sense is a cheap room

Black with the anger of insomnia,
Whose wall-boards vibrate with the mutters, plaints,
And flushings of the race.

                        What should I tell them?
I have no answers. *Set your fears at rest,*
I scribble when I must. *Your paramour*
Is faithful, and your spouse is unsuspecting.
You were not seen, that day, beneath the fig-tree.
Still, be more cautious. When the time is ripe,
Expect promotion. I foresee a message
From a far person who is rich and dying.
You are admired in secret. If, in your judgment,
Profit is in it, you should take the gamble.
As for these fits of weeping, they will pass.

It makes no difference that my lies are bald
And my evasions casual. It contents them
Not to have spoken, yet to have been heard.
What more do they deserve, if I could give it,
Mute breathers as they are of selfish hopes
And small anxieties? Faith, justice, valor,
All those reputed rarities of soul
Confirmed in marble by our public statues—
You may be sure that they are rare indeed
Where the soul mopes in private, and I listen.
Sometimes I wonder if the blame is mine,
If through a sullen fault of the mind's ear
I miss a resonance in all their fretting.
Is there some huge attention, do you think,
Which suffers us and is inviolate,
To which all hearts are open, which remarks
The sparrow's weighty fall, and overhears
In the worst rancor a deflected sweetness?
I should be glad to know it.

                           Meanwhile, saved
By the shrewd habit of concupiscence,
Which, like a visor, narrows my regard,
And drinking studiously until my thought

Is a blind lowered almost to the sill,
I hanker for that place beyond the sparrow
Where the wrench beds in mud, the sun-hat hangs
In densest branches, and the book is drowned.
Ah, you have read my mind. One more, perhaps…
A mezzo-litro. Grazie, professore.

The Eye St. Lucy (S. Lucia), patroness of eyesight, perceived Dante's plight in Canto II of the *Inferno*.

In Limbo Plato recounts the vision of Er at the close of his *Republic*.

Peter John's gospel says that it was Peter who "smote the high priest's servant." Mark, Luke, and John all tell how Peter "sat with the servants, and warmed himself at the fire."

Cottage Street Edna Ward was Mrs. Herbert D. Ward, my wife's mother. The poet Sylvia Plath (1932–1963) was the daughter of one of Mrs. Ward's Wellesley friends. The recollection is probably composite, but it is true in essentials.

The Fourth of July Lewis Carroll first told of Alice's adventures on July 4, 1862. Vicksburg capitulated to General Grant on July 4, 1863. Of the "stunted oak," the general wrote in his *Memoirs,*

> At three o'clock Pemberton appeared at the point suggested in my verbal message, accompanied by the same officers who had borne his letter of the morning. Generals Ord, McPherson, Logan, and A. J. Smith, and several officers of my staff, accompanied me. Our place of meeting was on a hillside within a few hundred feet of the rebel lines. Near by stood a stunted oak-tree, which was made historical by the event. It was but a short time before the last vestige of its body, root and limb had disappeared, the fragments taken as trophies. Since then the same tree has furnished as many cords of wood, in the shape of trophies, as "The True Cross."

The "termless wood" may be found in *Through the Looking Glass,* Chapter III. In *The Life of Sir Charles Linnaeus* (London, 1794), D. H. Stoever wrote:

> Several of his relatives, who had quitted the Plough for the Muses, in the last century, changed their family name with their profession, and borrowed the names of LINDELIUS, or TILIANDER (Linden-*tree-man*), of a lofty Linden-tree, which still stood in our time, in the vicinity of their native place, between *Tomsboda* and *Linnhult;* a custom not unfrequent in *Sweden,* to take fresh appellations from natural objects. The father of LINNAEUS, as the first learned man of his family, could not withstand following the example which his kindred had set before him.

Owing to a stroke, Linnaeus lost in his latter years "the knowledge even of his own name" (Loren Eiseley, *Darwin's Century*).

For the Student Strikers   This was written one afternoon at the request of Wesleyan students, during a "strike" against U.S. military actions in Southeast Asia. The poem supports a student-proposed "canvassing" program, under which the students were to go from door to door in the city of Middletown, discussing their views with the citizens. As the poem did not flatter the students in the manner to which they were accustomed, it was at first thrown into the wastebasket at the offices of *Strike News,* but later retrieved and published.

To His Skeleton   A phlebolith is a vein-stone.

John Chapman   was also known as "John Appleseed." With few exceptions, apple trees raised from the seed of cultivated varieties do not "come true," but revert to the wild Eurasian type.

Teresa   The name of Circe's island was Aeaea.

Children of Darkness   Fungi do not have true roots, stems, leaves, or fruit, and do not increase by means of chlorophyll and light. They were early associated with darkness, snake-pits, witches, devils, and evil in general. The Fly Agaric was said, in folklore, to grow from the bloody slaver of Wotan's horse, pursued by devils. Among the plants mentioned here are Ear, Coral, Disc, and Mist Fungi; Morels; Earth Tongues; Rusty Hooves; Stinkhorns *(Phallus impudicus);* Stalked Saucers, and Dead Man's Fingers *(Xylaria polymorpha).*

FRANÇOIS VILLON **Ballade of Forgiveness**   Villon spent the summer of 1461 in prison at Meung-sur-Loire. The third stanza refers to his jailers, and "the hardest crusts" may imply torture.

Two Riddles from Aldhelm   The answers are Salt and Cauldron. Aldhelm, Bishop of Sherborne, died in 709; he was the author of one hundred Latin riddles.

JOSEPH BRODSKY **The Funeral of Bobò**   The poem concerns a young woman who was drowned, under mysterious circumstances, in the Gulf of Finland.

For linguistic aid in translating from the Russian, I owe thanks to Professors Simon Karlinsky and Carl R. Proffer.

Walking to Sleep

NEW POEMS AND TRANSLATIONS

1969

For my Mother and my Father

ONE

In the Field

THE LILACS

Those laden lilacs
                at the lawn's end
Came stark, spindly,
                   and in staggered file,
Like walking wounded
                   from the dead of winter.
We watched them waken
                   in the brusque weather
To rot and rootbreak,
                to ripped branches,
And saw them shiver
                as the memory swept them
Of night and numbness
               and the taste of nothing.
Out of present pain
              and from past terror
Their bullet-shaped buds
                came quick and bursting,
As if they aimed
             to be open with us!
But the sun suddenly
               settled about them,
And green and grateful
             the lilacs grew,
Healed in that hush,
            that hospital quiet.
These lacquered leaves
             where the light paddles
And the big blooms
           buzzing among them
Have kept their counsel,
             conveying nothing
Of their mortal message,
              unless one should measure

The depth and dumbness
                                of death's kingdom
By the pure power
            of this perfume.

On the Marginal Way

for J. C. P.

Another cove of shale,
But the beach here is rubbled with strange rock
    That is sleek, fluent, and taffy-pale.
I stare, reminded with a little shock
How, by a shore in Spain, George Borrow saw
A hundred women basking in the raw.

    They must have looked like this,
That catch of bodies on the sand, that strew
    Of rondure, crease, and orifice,
Lap, flank, and knee—a too abundant view
Which, though he'd had the lenses of a fly,
Could not have waked desire in Borrow's eye.

    Has the light altered now?
The rocks flush rose and have the melting shape
    Of bodies fallen anyhow.
It is a Géricault of blood and rape,
Some desert town despoiled, some caravan
Pillaged, its people murdered to a man,

    And those who murdered them
Galloping off, a rumpling line of dust
    Like the wave's white, withdrawing hem.
But now the vision of a colder lust
Clears, as the wind goes chill and all is greyed
By a swift cloud that drags a carrion shade.

    If these are bodies still,
Theirs is a death too dead to look asleep,
    Like that of Auschwitz' final kill,
Poor slaty flesh abandoned in a heap

And then, like sea-rocks buried by a wave,
Bulldozed at last into a common grave.

      It is not tricks of sense
But the time's fright within me which distracts
      Least fancies into violence
And makes my thought take cover in the facts,
As now it does, remembering how the bed
Of layered rock two miles above my head

      Hove ages up and broke
Soundless asunder, when the shrinking skin
      Of Earth, blacked out by steam and smoke,
Gave passage to the muddled fire within,
Its crannies flooding with a sweat of quartz,
And lathered magmas out of deep retorts

      Welled up, as here, to fill
With tumbled rockmeal, stone-fume, lithic spray,
      The dike's brief chasm and the sill.
Weathered until the sixth and human day
By sanding winds and water, scuffed and brayed
By the slow glacier's heel, these forms were made

      That now recline and burn
Comely as Eve and Adam, near a sea
      Transfigured by the sun's return.
And now three girls lie golden in the lee
Of a great arm or thigh, and are as young
As the bright boulders that they lie among.

      Though, high above the shore
On someone's porch, spread wings of newsprint flap
      The tidings of some dirty war,
It is a perfect day: the waters clap
Their hands and kindle, and the gull in flight
Loses himself at moments, white in white,

And like a breaking thought
Joy for a moment floods into the mind,
    Blurting that all things shall be brought
To the full state and stature of their kind,
By what has found the manhood of this stone.
May that vast motive wash and wash our own.

COMPLAINT

In reality, each love is that of the divine image,
and each is pure.

—Ficino

Why is it that whenever I talk with the duchess
My belly growls and my nose waters? Why must it
Be my hand that tumbles her wine-glass over
Into the Cellini salt-dish?

Stiff as a gaffer, fidgety as a child,
After twenty years of struggling to be a courtier
I remain incapable of the least politeness,
Wit, song, or learning,

And I wonder sometimes, what is it in me that hates me?
Is it that rolling captain who should burst
Like surf into her presence, dumping down
His pillage of the seas,

And in a wink dissolve her castled pride?
She scorns no common magic, and could be pleased
To be manhandled like a kitchen-girl,
So it were sweet and reckless.

Or is it that idolatrous fool that's in me,
Who, lest she alter, should enchant the hour
With gentled sparrows and an aimless lute,
Enthralling her with tales

Of a king's daughter bound in mountain sleep,
Whose prince and wakener, detained by trials
In deserts, deeps, and grottoes of the world,
Approaches her forever?

Or am I spited by the priest I might be
There in the stone grove of her oratory?

No ship sails out so free as she at prayer,
With head bowed and shrouded.

Confessing her, and my delight in her,
To the great ways and haven of her beauty,
Would I not serve her better? Would not my hand
Be steady with the wine?

Jackass, again you turn and turn this prism,
Whose every light is of the purest water.
How should I fathom her whose white hands fold
The rainbow like a fan?

O maiden, muse, and maiden, O my love
Whose every moment is the quick of time,
I am your bumbling servant now and ever,
In this and the other kingdom.

FERN-BEDS IN HAMPSHIRE COUNTY

Although from them
Steep stands of beech and sugar-maple stem,
Varied with birch, or ash, or basswood trees
Which spring will throng with bees,
While intervening thickets grow complex
With flower, seed, and variance of sex,
And the whole wood conspires, by change of kind,
To break the purchase of the gathering mind,
The ferns are as they were.
Let but a trifling stir
Of air traverse their pools or touchy beds
And some will dip their heads,
Some switch a moment like a scribbling quill
And then be still,
Sporadic as in guarded bays
The rockweed slaps a bit, or sways.
Then let the wind grow bluff, and though
The sea lies far to eastward, far below,
These fluent spines, with whipped pale underside,
Will climb through timber as a smoking tide
Through pier-stakes, beat their sprays about the base
Of every boulder, scale its creviced face
And, wave on wave, like some green infantry,
Storm all the slope as high as eye can see.
Whatever at the heart
Of creatures makes them branch and burst apart,
Or at the core of star or tree may burn
At last to turn
And make an end of time,
These airy plants, tenacious of their prime,
Dwell in the swept recurrence of
An ancient conquest, shaken by first love
As when they answered to the boomed command
That the sea's green rise up and take the land.

In a Churchyard

That flower unseen, that gem of purest ray,
Bright thoughts uncut by men:
Strange that you need but speak them, Thomas Gray,
And the mind skips and dives beyond its ken,

Finding at once the wild supposèd bloom,
Or in the imagined cave
Some pulse of crystal staving off the gloom
As covertly as phosphorus in a grave.

Void notions proper to a buried head!
Beneath these tombstones here
Unseenness fills the sockets of the dead,
Whatever to their souls may now appear;

And who but those unfathomably deaf
Who quiet all this ground
Could catch, within the ear's diminished clef
A music innocent of time and sound?

What do the living hear, then, when the bell
Hangs plumb within the tower
Of the still church, and still their thoughts compel
Pure tollings that intend no mortal hour?

As when a ferry for the shore of death
Glides looming toward the dock,
Her engines cut, her spirits bating breath
As the ranked pilings narrow toward the shock,

So memory and expectation set
Some pulseless clangor free
Of circumstance, and charm us to forget
This twilight crumbling in the churchyard tree,

Those swifts or swallows which do not pertain,
Scuffed voices in the drive,
That light flicked on behind the vestry pane,
Till, unperplexed from all that is alive,

It shadows all our thought, balked imminence
Of uncommitted sound,
And still would tower at the sill of sense
Were not, as now, its honed abeyance crowned

With a mauled boom of summons far more strange
Than any stroke unheard,
Which breaks again with unimagined range
Through all reverberations of the word,

Pooling the mystery of things that are,
The buzz of prayer said,
The scent of grass, the earliest-blooming star,
These unseen gravestones, and the darker dead.

SEED LEAVES

Homage to R. F.

Here something stubborn comes,
Dislodging the earth crumbs
And making crusty rubble.
It comes up bending double,
And looks like a green staple.
It could be seedling maple,
Or artichoke, or bean.
That remains to be seen.

Forced to make choice of ends,
The stalk in time unbends,
Shakes off the seed-case, heaves
Aloft, and spreads two leaves
Which still display no sure
And special signature.
Toothless and fat, they keep
The oval form of sleep.

This plant would like to grow
And yet be embryo;
Increase, and yet escape
The doom of taking shape;
Be vaguely vast, and climb
To the tip end of time
With all of space to fill,
Like boundless Igdrasil
That has the stars for fruit.

But something at the root
More urgent than that urge
Bids two true leaves emerge,
And now the plant, resigned
To being self-defined

Before it can commerce
With the great universe,
Takes aim at all the sky
And starts to ramify.

In the Field

This field-grass brushed our legs
Last night, when out we stumbled looking up,
   Wading as through the cloudy dregs
     Of a wide, sparkling cup,

Our thrown-back heads aswim
In the grand, kept appointments of the air,
   Save where a pine at the sky's rim
     Took something from the Bear.

Black in her glinting chains,
Andromeda feared nothing from the seas,
   Preserved as by no hero's pains,
     Or hushed Euripides',

And there the dolphin glowed,
Still flailing through a diamond froth of stars,
   Flawless as when Arion rode
     One of its avatars.

But none of that was true.
What shapes that Greece or Babylon discerned
   Had time not slowly drawn askew
     Or like cat's cradles turned?

And did we not recall
That Egypt's north was in the Dragon's tail?
   As if a form of type should fall
     And dash itself like hail,

The heavens jumped away,
Bursting the cincture of the zodiac,
   Shot flares with nothing left to say
     To us, not coming back

Unless they should at last,
Like hard-flung dice that ramble out the throw,
Be gathered for another cast.
Whether that might be so

We could not say, but trued
Our talk awhile to words of the real sky,
Chatting of class or magnitude,
Star-clusters, nebulae,

And how Antares, huge
As Mars' big roundhouse swing, and more, was fled
As in some rimless centrifuge
Into a blink of red.

It was the nip of fear
That told us when imagination caught
The feel of what we said, came near
The schoolbook thoughts we thought,

And faked a scan of space
Blown black and hollow by our spent grenade,
All worlds dashed out without a trace,
The very light unmade.

Then, in the late-night chill,
We turned and picked our way through outcrop stone
By the faint starlight, up the hill
To where our bed-lamp shone.

Today, in the same field,
The sun takes all, and what could lie beyond?
Those holes in heaven have been sealed
Like rain-drills in a pond,

And we, beheld in gold,
See nothing starry but these galaxies

Of flowers, dense and manifold,
    Which lift about our knees—

    White daisy-drifts where you
Sink down to pick an armload as we pass,
    Sighting the heal-all's minor blue
      In chasms of the grass,

    And strews of hawkweed where,
Amongst the reds or yellows as they burn,
    A few dead polls commit to air
      The seeds of their return.

    We could no doubt mistake
These flowers for some answer to that fright
    We felt for all creation's sake
      In our dark talk last night,

    Taking to heart what came
Of the heart's wish for life, which, staking here
    In the least field an endless claim,
      Beats on from sphere to sphere

    And pounds beyond the sun,
Where nothing less peremptory can go,
    And is ourselves, and is the one
      Unbounded thing we know.

A WOOD

Some would distinguish nothing here but oaks,
Proud heads conversant with the power and glory
Of heaven's rays or heaven's thunderstrokes,
And adumbrators to the understory,
Where, in their shade, small trees of modest leanings
Contend for light and are content with gleanings.

And yet here's dogwood: overshadowed, small,
But not inclined to droop and count its losses,
It cranes its way to sunlight after all,
And signs the air of May with Maltese crosses.
And here's witch hazel, that from underneath
Great vacant boughs will bloom in winter's teeth.

Given a source of light so far away
That nothing, short or tall, comes very near it,
Would it not take a proper fool to say
That any tree has not the proper spirit?
Air, water, earth and fire are to be blended,
But no one style, I think, is recommended.

For Dudley

Even when death has taken
An exceptional man,
It is common things which touch us, gathered
In the house that proved a hostel.

Though on his desk there lie
The half of a sentence
Not to be finished by us, who lack
His gaiety, his Greek,

It is the straight back
Of a good woman
Which now we notice. For her guests' hunger
She sets the polished table.

And now the quick sun,
Rounding the gable,
Picks out a chair, a vase of flowers,
Which had stood till then in shadow.

It is the light of which
Achilles spoke,
Himself a shadow then, recalling
The splendor of mere being.

As if we were perceived
From a black ship—
A small knot of island folk,
The Light-Dwellers, pouring

A life to the dark sea—
All that we do
Is touched with ocean, yet we remain
On the shore of what we know.

We say that we are behaving
As he would have us—
He who was brave and loved this world,
Who did not hold with weeping,

Yet in the mind as in
The shut closet
Where his coats hang in black procession,
There is a covert muster.

One is moved to turn to him,
The exceptional man,
Telling him all these things, and waiting
For the deft, lucid answer.

At the sound of that voice's deep
Specific silence,
The sun winks and fails in the window.
Light perpetual keep him.

RUNNING

I. 1933
(North Caldwell, New Jersey)

What were we playing? Was it prisoner's base?
I ran with whacking keds
Down the cart-road past Rickard's place,
And where it dropped beside the tractor-sheds

Leapt out into the air above a blurred
Terrain, through jolted light,
Took two hard lopes, and at the third
Spanked off a hummock-side exactly right,

And made the turn, and with delighted strain
Sprinted across the flat
By the bull-pen, and up the lane.
Thinking of happiness, I think of that.

II. PATRIOTS' DAY
(Wellesley, Massachusetts)

Restless that noble day, appeased by soft
Drinks and tobacco, littering the grass
While the flag snapped and brightened far aloft,
We waited for the marathon to pass,

We fathers and our little sons, let out
Of school and office to be put to shame.
Now from the street-side someone raised a shout,
And into view the first small runners came.

Dark in the glare, they seemed to thresh in place
Like preening flies upon a window-sill,
Yet gained and grew, and at a cruel pace
Swept by us on their way to Heartbreak Hill—

Legs driving, fists at port, clenched faces, men,
And in amongst them, stamping on the sun,
Our champion Kelley, who would win again,
Rocked in his will, at rest within his run.

III. DODWELLS ROAD
(Cummington, Massachusetts)

I jog up out of the woods
To the crown of the road, and slow to a swagger there,
The wind harsh and cool to my throat,
A good ache in my rib-cage.

Loud burden of streams at run-off,
And the sun's rocket frazzled in blown tree-heads:
Still I am part of that great going,
Though I stroll now, and am watchful.

Where the road turns and debouches,
The land sinks westward into exhausted pasture.
From fields which yield to aspen now
And pine at last will shadow,

Boy-shouts reach me, and barking.
What is the thing which men will not surrender?
It is what they have never had, I think,
Or missed in its true season,

So that their thoughts turn in
At the same roadhouse nightly, the same cloister,
The wild mouth of the same brave river
Never now to be charted.

You, whoever you are,
If you want to walk with me you must step lively.
I run, too, when the mood offers,
Though the god of that has left me.

But why in the hell spoil it?
I make a clean gift of my young running
To the two boys who break into view,
Hurdling the rocks and racing,

Their dog dodging before them
This way and that, his yaps flushing a pheasant
Who lifts now from the blustery grass
Flying full tilt already.

UNDER CYGNUS

Who says I shall not straighten till I bend,
And must be broken if I hope to mend?
Did Samson gain by being chained and blind?
Dark heaven hints at something of the kind,
Seeing that as we beat toward Hercules
Our flank is compassed by the galaxy's,
And we drawn off from our intended course
By a grand reel of stars whose banded force,
Catching us up, makes light of all our loss,
And dances us into the Northern Cross.

Well, if I must surrender and be gay
In the wrong pasture of the Milky Way,
If in the Cross I must resign my Sword,
To hang among the trophies of the Lord,
Let my distinction not consist alone
In having let myself be overthrown.
It was my loves and labors, carried high,
Which drove the flight that heaven turns awry,
My dreams which told the stars what they should tell.
Let the Swan, dying, sing of that as well.

TWO

———•••———

Thyme

Thyme Flowering among Rocks

This, if Japanese,
Would represent grey boulders
Walloped by rough seas

So that, here or there,
The balked water tossed its froth
Straight into the air.

Here, where things are what
They are, it is thyme blooming,
Rocks, and nothing but—

Having, nonetheless,
Many small leaves implicit,
A green countlessness.

Crouching down, peering
Into perplexed recesses,
You find a clearing

Occupied by sun
Where, along prone, rachitic
Branches, one by one,

Pale stems arise, squared
In the manner of *Mentha,*
The oblong leaves paired.

One branch, in ending,
Lifts a little and begets
A straight-ascending

Spike, whorled with fine blue
Or purple trumpets, banked in
The leaf-axils. You

Are lost now in dense
Fact, fact which one might have thought
Hidden from the sense,

Blinking at detail
Peppery as this fragrance,
Lost to proper scale

As, in the motion
Of striped fins, a bathysphere
Forgets the ocean.

It makes the craned head
Spin. Unfathomed thyme! The world's
A dream, Basho said,

Not because that dream's
A falsehood, but because it's
Truer than it seems.

A Miltonic Sonnet for Mr. Johnson on His Refusal of Peter Hurd's Official Portrait

Heir to the office of a man not dead
Who drew our Declaration up, who planned
Range and Rotunda with his drawing-hand
And harbored Palestrina in his head,
Who would have wept to see small nations dread
The imposition of our cattle-brand,
With public truth at home mistold or banned,
And in whose term no army's blood was shed,

Rightly you say the picture is too large
Which Peter Hurd by your appointment drew,
And justly call that Capitol too bright
Which signifies our people in your charge;
Wait, Sir, and see how time will render you,
Who talk of vision but are weak of sight.

6 January 1967

A RIDDLE

For M. M.

Where far in forest I am laid,
In a place ringed around by stones,
Look for no melancholy shade,
And have no thoughts of buried bones;
For I am bodiless and bright,
And fill this glade with sudden glow;
The leaves are washed in under-light;
Shade lies upon the boughs like snow.

PLAYBOY

High on his stockroom ladder like a dunce
The stock-boy sits, and studies like a sage
The subject matter of one glossy page,
As lost in curves as Archimedes once.

Sometimes, without a glance, he feeds himself.
The left hand, like a mother-bird in flight,
Brings him a sandwich for a sidelong bite,
And then returns it to a dusty shelf.

What so engrosses him? The wild décor
Of this pink-papered alcove into which
A naked girl has stumbled, with its rich
Welter of pelts and pillows on the floor,

Amidst which, kneeling in a supple pose,
She lifts a goblet in her farther hand,
As if about to toast a flower-stand
Above which hovers an exploding rose

Fired from a long-necked crystal vase that rests
Upon a tasseled and vermillion cloth
One taste of which would shrivel up a moth?
Or is he pondering her perfect breasts?

Nothing escapes him of her body's grace
Or of her floodlit skin, so sleek and warm
And yet so strangely like a uniform,
But what now grips his fancy is her face,

And how the cunning picture holds her still
At just that smiling instant when her soul,
Grown sweetly faint, and swept beyond control,
Consents to his inexorable will.

The Mechanist

Advancing with a self-denying gaze, he
Looks closely at the love-divining daisy.

Since none but persons may of persons learn,
The frightened plant denies herself in turn,

And sways away as if to flee her fears,
Clashing her flower heads like clumsy gears.

THE AGENT

Behind his back, the first wave passes over
The city which at dawn he left for good,
His staff-car musing through the streets, its tires
Kissing the rainy cheeks of cobblestones,
Till at St. Basil's gate the tower clock
Roused with a groan, flung down the hour, and shook
The tears into his eyes. In those lapped roars
And souring resonance he heard as well
Hoarse trains that highball down the world's ravines,
Some boat-horn's whoop and shudder, all sick thrills
Of transit and forsaking. Now he is calm,
Here in this locust-copse, his rendezvous,
Laying his uniform away in leaves
For good, and lacing up a peasant jerkin.
The sky fills with a suave bombination
Of yet more planes in level swarm; the city
Rocks now with flash and thud; the guildhall windows
Blink him a leaden message, that the small
Park, with its fountains, where his custom was
To sip a *fine* and watch the *passeggiata,*
Is deep in rubble and its trees afire.
But still he looks away, less now from grief
Than from a fuddled lostness how unlike
The buoyant spirits of his coming, when,
Light as a milkweed-puff, his parachute
Fell swaying toward a flashlight in a field
Of moonlit grain, which softly hove to meet him.
Bedded that night amongst the bins and kegs
Of a damp cellar, he did not rehearse
His orders, or the fear that some small flaw
In his forged self or papers might betray him,
But lay rejoicing in the smell of roots
And age, as in a painted cart next morning,
Hid under hay, he listened to the ching
Of harness and the sound of rim-struck stones.
And then that train-ride!—all compartments filled

With folk returning from the holiday,
From bonfire-jumping, dancing in a round,
And tying amulets of mistletoe.
Like some collector steeped in catalogues
Who finds at last in some dim shop or attic
A Martinique *tête-bêche* imperforate
Or still unbroken egg by Fabergé,
He took possession, prizing the foreknown
Half-Tartar eyes, the slurring of the schwa,
The braids and lederhosen, and the near-
Telepathy of shrugs and eyebrow-cockings
In which the nuance of their speeches lay.
Rocked by the train, with festal smiles about him,
His belly warmed by proffered *akvavit,*
He felt his hands fill with authentic gestures:
He would not shift his fork from left to right,
Nor bless himself right-shoulder-foremost. Born
Not of a culture but a drafty state,
And having, therefore, little to unlearn,
He would put on with ease the tribal ways
And ritual demeanors of this land
Toward whose chief city he was chugging now
To savor and betray.
                    But now a torn
Blare, like the clearing of a monstrous throat,
Rolls from those fields which vanish toward the border;
Dark tanks and half-tracks come, breasting the wheat,
And after them, in combat scatterment,
Dark infantry. He can already spy
Their cold familiar eyes, their bodies heavy
With the bulk foods of home, and so remembers
A gravel playground full of lonely wind,
The warmth of a wet bed. How hard it is,
He thinks, to be cheated of a fated life
In a deep *patria,* and so to be
A foundling never lost, a pure impostor
Faithless to everything. An ill thought strikes him:
What if these soldiers, through some chance or blunder,

Have not been briefed about him and his mission?
What will they make of him—a nervous man
In farmer's costume, speaking a precious accent,
Who cannot name the streets of his own town?
Would they not, after all, be right to shoot him?
He shrinks against a trunk and waits to see.

THE PROOF

Shall I love God for causing me to be?
I was mere utterance; shall these words love me?

Yet when I caused his work to jar and stammer,
And one free subject loosened all his grammar,

I love him that he did not in a rage
Once and forever rule me off the page,

But, thinking I might come to please him yet,
Crossed out *delete* and wrote his patient *stet.*

A LATE AUBADE

You could be sitting now in a carrel
Turning some liver-spotted page,
Or rising in an elevator-cage
Toward Ladies' Apparel.

You could be planting a raucous bed
Of salvia, in rubber gloves,
Or lunching through a screed of someone's loves
With pitying head,

Or making some unhappy setter
Heel, or listening to a bleak
Lecture on Schoenberg's serial technique.
Isn't this better?

Think of all the time you are not
Wasting, and would not care to waste,
Such things, thank God, not being to your taste.
Think what a lot

Of time, by woman's reckoning,
You've saved, and so may spend on this,
You who had rather lie in bed and kiss
Than anything.

It's almost noon, you say? If so,
Time flies, and I need not rehearse
The rosebuds-theme of centuries of verse.
If you *must* go,

Wait for a while, then slip downstairs
And bring us up some chilled white wine,
And some blue cheese, and crackers, and some fine
Ruddy-skinned pears.

MATTHEW VIII, 28 FF.

Rabbi, we Gadarenes
Are not ascetics; we are fond of wealth and possessions.
Love, as you call it, we obviate by means
Of the planned release of aggressions.

We have deep faith in prosperity.
Soon, it is hoped, we will reach our full potential.
In the light of our gross product, the practice of charity
Is palpably inessential.

It is true that we go insane;
That for no good reason we are possessed by devils;
That we suffer, despite the amenities which obtain
At all but the lowest levels.

We shall not, however, resign
Our trust in the high-heaped table and the full trough.
If you cannot cure us without destroying our swine,
We had rather you shoved off.

For K. R. on Her Sixtieth Birthday

Blow out the candles of your cake.
They will not leave you in the dark,
Who round with grace this dusky arc
Of the grand tour which souls must take.

You who have sounded William Blake,
And the still pool, to Plato's mark,
Blow out the candles of your cake.
They will not leave you in the dark.

Yet, for your friends' benighted sake,
Detain your upward-flying spark;
Get us that wish, though like the lark
You whet your wings till dawn shall break:
Blow out the candles of your cake.

THREE

———•———

Walking to Sleep

WALKING TO SLEEP

As a queen sits down, knowing that a chair will be there,
Or a general raises his hand and is given the field-glasses,
Step off assuredly into the blank of your mind.
Something will come to you. Although at first
You nod through nothing like a fogbound prow,
Gravel will breed in the margins of your gaze,
Perhaps with tussocks or a dusty flower,
And, humped like dolphins playing in the bow-wave,
Hills will suggest themselves. All such suggestions
Are yours to take or leave, but hear this warning:
Let them not be too velvet green, the fields
Which the deft needle of your eye appoints,
Nor the old farm past which you make your way
Too shady-linteled, too instinct with home.
It is precisely from Potemkin barns
With their fresh-painted hex signs on the gables,
Their sparkling gloom within, their stanchion-rattle
And sweet breath of silage, that there comes
The trotting cat whose head is but a skull.
Try to remember this: what you project
Is what you will perceive; what you perceive
With any passion, be it love or terror,
May take on whims and powers of its own.
Therefore a numb and grudging circumspection
Will serve you best, unless you overdo it,
Watching your step too narrowly, refusing
To specify a world, shrinking your purview
To a tight vision of your inching shoes—
Which may, as soon you come to think, be crossing
An unseen gorge upon a rotten trestle.
What you must manage is to bring to mind
A landscape not worth looking at, some bleak
Champaign at dead November's end, its grass
As dry as lichen, and its lichens grey,
Such glumly simple country that a glance
Of flat indifference from time to time

Will stabilize it. Lifeless thus, and leafless,
The view should set at rest all thoughts of ambush.
Nevertheless, permit no roadside thickets
Which, as you pass, might shake with worse than wind;
Revoke all trees and other cover; blast
The upstart boulder which a flicking shape
Has stepped behind; above all, put a stop
To the known stranger up ahead, whose face
Half turns to mark you with a creased expression.
Here let me interject that steady trudging
Can make you drowsy, so that without transition,
As when an old film jumps in the projector,
You will be wading a dun hallway, rounding
A newel post, and starting up the stairs.
Should that occur, adjust to circumstances
And carry on, taking these few precautions:
Detach some portion of your thought to guard
The outside of the building; as you wind
From room to room, leave nothing at your back,
But slough all memories at every threshold;
Nor must you dream of opening any door
Until you have foreseen what lies beyond it.
Regardless of its seeming size, or what
May first impress you as its style or function,
The abrupt structure which involves you now
Will improvise like vapor. Groping down
The gritty cellar steps and past the fuse-box,
Brushing through sheeted lawn-chairs, you emerge
In some cathedral's pillared crypt, and thence,
Your brow alight with carbide, pick your way
To the main shaft through drifts and rubbly tunnels.
Promptly the hoist, ascending toward the pit-head,
Rolls downward past your gaze a dinted rock-face
Peppered with hacks and drill-holes, which acquire
Insensibly the look of hieroglyphics.
Whether to surface now within the vast
Stone tent where Cheops lay secure, or take
The proffered shed of corrugated iron

Which gives at once upon a vacant barracks,
Is up to you. Need I, at this point, tell you
What to avoid? Avoid the pleasant room
Where someone, smiling to herself, has placed
A bowl of yellow freesias. Do not let
The thought of her in yellow, lithe and sleek
As lemonwood, mislead you where the curtains,
Romping like spinnakers which taste the wind,
Bellying out and lifting till the sill
Has shipped a drench of sunlight, then subsiding,
Both warm and cool the love-bed. Your concern
Is not to be detained by dread, or by
Such dear acceptances as would entail it,
But to pursue an ever-dimming course
Of pure transition, treading as in water
Past crumbling tufa, down cloacal halls
Of boarded-up hotels, through attics full
Of glassy taxidermy, moping on
Like a drugged fire-inspector. What you hope for
Is that at some point of the pointless journey,
Indoors or out, and when you least expect it,
Right in the middle of your stride, like that,
So neatly that you never feel a thing,
The kind assassin Sleep will draw a bead
And blow your brains out.

                       What, are you still awake?
Then you must risk another tack and footing.
Forget what I have said. Open your eyes
To the good blackness not of your room alone
But of the sky you trust is over it,
Whose stars, though foundering in the time to come,
Bequeath us constantly a jetsam beauty.
Now with your knuckles rub your eyelids, seeing
The phosphenes caper like St. Elmo's fire,
And let your head heel over on the pillow
Like a flung skiff on wild Gennesaret.
Let all things storm your thought with the moiled flocking
Of startled rookeries, or flak in air,

Or blossom-fall, and out of that come striding
In the strong dream by which you have been chosen.
Are you upon the roads again? If so,
Be led past honeyed meadows which might tempt
A wolf to graze, and groves which are not you
But answer to your suppler self, that nature
Able to bear the thrush's quirky glee
In stands of chuted light, yet praise as well,
All leaves aside, the barren bark of winter.
When, as you may, you find yourself approaching
A crossroads and its laden gallows tree,
Do not with hooded eyes allow the shadow
Of a man moored in air to bruise your forehead,
But lift your gaze and stare your brother down,
Though the swart crows have pecked his sockets hollow.
As for what turn your travels then will take,
I cannot guess. Long errantry perhaps
Will arm you to be gentle, or the claws
Of nightmare flap you pathless God knows where,
As the crow flies, to meet your dearest horror.
Still, if you are in luck, you may be granted,
As, inland, one can sometimes smell the sea,
A moment's perfect carelessness, in which
To stumble a few steps and sink to sleep
In the same clearing where, in the old story,
A holy man discovered Vishnu sleeping,
Wrapped in his maya, dreaming by a pool
On whose calm face all images whatever
Lay clear, unfathomed, taken as they came.

FOUR

———

Translations

Compass

All things are words of some strange tongue, in thrall
To Someone, Something, who both day and night
Proceeds in endless gibberish to write
The history of the world. In that dark scrawl

Rome is set down, and Carthage, I, you, all,
And this my being which escapes me quite,
My anguished life that's cryptic, recondite,
And garbled as the tongues of Babel's fall.

Beyond the name there lies what has no name;
Today I have felt its shadow stir the aim
Of this blue needle, light and keen, whose sweep

Homes to the utmost of the sea its love,
Suggestive of a watch in dreams, or of
Some bird, perhaps, who shifts a bit in sleep.

EVERNESS

One thing does not exist: Oblivion.
God saves the metal and he saves the dross,
And his prophetic memory guards from loss
The moons to come, and those of evenings gone.
Everything *is*: the shadows in the glass
Which, in between the day's two twilights, you
Have scattered by the thousands, or shall strew
Henceforward in the mirrors that you pass.
And everything is part of that diverse
Crystalline memory, the universe;
Whoever through its endless mazes wanders
Hears door on door click shut behind his stride,
And only from the sunset's farther side
Shall view at last the Archetypes and the Splendors.

JORGE LUIS BORGES

EWIGKEIT

Turn on my tongue, O Spanish verse; confirm
Once more what Spanish verse has always said
Since Seneca's black Latin; speak your dread
Sentence that all is fodder for the worm.
Come, celebrate once more pale ash, pale dust,
The pomps of death and the triumphant crown
Of that bombastic queen who tramples down
The petty banners of our pride and lust.
Enough of that. What things have blessed my clay
Let me not cravenly deny. The one
Word of no meaning is Oblivion,
And havened in eternity, I know,
My many precious losses burn and stay:
That forge, that night, that risen moon aglow.

ANNA AKHMATOVA

Lot's Wife

The just man followed then his angel guide
Where he strode on the black highway, hulking and bright;
But a wild grief in his wife's bosom cried,
Look back, it is not too late for a last sight

Of the red towers of your native Sodom, the square
Where once you sang, the gardens you shall mourn,
And the tall house with empty windows where
You loved your husband and your babes were born.

She turned, and looking on the bitter view
Her eyes were welded shut by mortal pain;
Into transparent salt her body grew,
And her quick feet were rooted in the plain.

Who would waste tears upon her? Is she not
The least of our losses, this unhappy wife?
Yet in my heart she will not be forgot
Who, for a single glance, gave up her life.

FOGGY STREET

The air is grey-white as a pigeon-feather.
    Police bob up like corks on a fishing-net.
Foggy weather.
What century is it? What era? I forget.

As in a nightmare, everything is crumbling;
    people have come unsoldered; nothing's intact.
I plod on, stumbling,
Or flounder in cotton wool, to be more exact.

Noses. Parking-lights. Badges flash and blur.
    All's vague, as at a magic-lantern show.
Your hat-check, Sir?
Mustn't walk off with the wrong head, you know.

It's as if a woman who's scarcely left your lips
    Should blur in the mind, yet trouble it with recall—
Bereft now, widowed by your love's eclipse—
Still yours, yet suddenly not yours at all...

Can that be Venus? No—an ice-cream vendor!
    I bump into curbstones, bump into passersby.
Are they friends, I wonder?
Home-bred Iagos, how covert you are, how sly!

Why it's you, my darling, shivering there alone!
    Your overcoat's too big for you, my dear.
But why have you grown
That moustache? Why is there frost in your hairy ear?

I trip, I stagger, I persist.
    Murk, murk...there's nothing visible anywhere.

Whose is the cheek you brush now in the mist?
Ahoy there!
One's voice won't carry in this heavy air.

When the fog lifts, how brilliant it is, how rare!

ANTIWORLDS

The clerk Bukashkin is our neighbor:
His face is grey as blotting-paper.

But like balloons of blue or red,
Bright Antiworlds
                                float over his head!
On them reposes, prestidigitous,
Ruling the cosmos, a demon-magician,
Anti-Bukashkin the academician,
Lapped in the arms of Lollobrigidas.

But Anti-Bukashkin's dreams are the color
Of blotting-paper, and couldn't be duller.

Long live Antiworlds! They rebut
With dreams the rat-race and the rut.
For some to be clever, some must be boring.
No deserts? No oases, then.
There are no women—
                                just anti-men.
In the forests, anti-machines are roaring.
There's the dirt of the earth, as well as the salt.
If the earth broke down, the sun would halt.

Ah, my critics; how I love them.
Upon the neck of the keenest of them,
Fragrant and bald as fresh-baked bread,
There shines a perfect anti-head...

...I sleep with windows open wide;
Somewhere a falling star invites,
And skyscrapers,
                                like stalactites,

Hang from the planet's underside.
There, upside down
                    below me far,
Stuck like a fork into the earth,
Or perching like a carefree moth,
My little Antiworld,
                    there you are!

In the middle of the night, why is it
That Antiworlds are moved to visit?

Why do they sit together, gawking
At the television, and never talking?

Between them, not one word has passed.
Their first strange meeting is their last.

Neither can manage the least *bon ton.*
Oh, how they'll blush for it later on!

Their ears are burning like a pair
Of crimson butterflies, hovering there…

…A distinguished lecturer lately told me,
"Antiworlds are a total loss."

Still, my apartment-cell won't hold me;
I thrash in my sleep, I turn and toss.

And, radio-like, my cat lies curled
With his green eye tuned in to the world.

DEAD STILL

Now, with your palms on the blades of my shoulders,
Let us embrace:
Let there be only your lips' breath on my face,
Only, behind our backs, the plunge of rollers.

Our backs, which like two shells in moonlight shine,
Are shut behind us now;
We lie here huddled, listening brow to brow,
Like life's twin formula or double sign.

In folly's world-wide wind
Our shoulders shield from the weather
The calm we now beget together,
Like a flame held between hand and hand.

Does each cell have a soul within it?
If so, fling open all your little doors,
And all your souls shall flutter like the linnet
In the cages of my pores.

Nothing is hidden that shall not be known.
Yet by no storm of scorn shall we
Be pried from this embrace, and left alone
Like muted shells forgetful of the sea.

Meanwhile, O load of stress and bother,
Lie on the shells of our backs in a great heap!
It will but press us closer, one to the other.

We are asleep.

CHARLES D'ORLÉANS

RONDEAU

The year has cast its cloak away
That was of driving rains and snows,
And now in flowered arras goes,
And wears the clear sun's glossy ray.

No bird or beast but seems to say
In cries or chipper tremolos:
The year has cast its cloak away
That was of driving rains and snows.

Stream, brook and silver fountain play,
And each upon itself bestows
A spangled livery as it flows.
All creatures are in fresh array.
The year has cast its cloak away.

BALLADE OF THE LADIES OF TIME PAST

O tell me where, in lands or seas,
Flora, that Roman belle, has strayed,
Thais, or Archipiades,
Who put each other in the shade,
Or Echo who by bank and glade
Gave back the crying of the hound,
And whose sheer beauty could not fade.
But where shall last year's snow be found?

Where too is learned Héloïse,
For whom shorn Abélard was made
A tonsured monk upon his knees?
Such tribute his devotion paid.
And where's that queen who, having played
With Buridan, had him bagged and bound
To swim the Seine thus ill-arrayed?
But where shall last year's snow be found?

Queen Blanche the fair, whose voice could please
As does the siren's serenade,
Great Bertha, Beatrice, Alice—these,
And Arembourg whom Maine obeyed,
And Joan whom Burgundy betrayed
And England burned, and Heaven crowned:
Where are they, Mary, Sovereign Maid?
But where shall last year's snow be found?

Not next week, Prince, nor next decade,
Ask me these questions I propound.
I shall but say again, dismayed,
Ah, where shall last year's snow be found?

FRANÇOIS VILLON

BALLADE IN OLD FRENCH

(Car, ou soit ly sains apostolles)

Let it be Rome's great Pope, adored
Of all, in alb and amice dressed,
Who, girt with stole instead of sword,
Can knock the Devil galley-west,
By spite and sulphur unimpressed,
Yet he, like any poor valet,
Shall of this life be dispossessed.
Him too the wind shall blow away.

Be it Constantinople's lord,
The emperor of the golden fist,
Or that French king, whom Christ reward,
And whom of kings I count the best,
Since he to God (whose name be blest)
Built church and convent in his day.
Much fame he had, as books attest.
That too the wind shall blow away.

Grenoble's count, whom men accord
A wise head and a fearless breast,
What Dôle or Dijon can afford
Of nobles proud in shield and crest,
And such as jump at their behest,
Trumpeters, soldiers, footmen, they
Who stuff their guts with so much zest:
Them too the wind shall blow away.

Princes must die like all the rest,
Like all who are of mortal clay,
And should they grumble or protest,
That too the wind shall blow away.

A Ballade to End With

Here is poor Villon's final word;
The ink upon his will is dried.
Come see him properly interred
When by the bell you're notified,
And come in scarlet, since he died
Love's martyr, through his gentle heart:
This on one ball he testified
As he made ready to depart.

Nor do I think his claim absurd;
Love hounded him both far and wide,
By such contempt and malice spurred
That, clear to Roussillon, one spied
No thorn in all the countryside
But wore his tattered shirt in part.
So said he (and he never lied)
As he made ready to depart.

And thus and therefore it occurred
That one rag only clothed his hide
When he lay dead; what's more, we heard
How on his bed of death he cried
A pox on Love, who still applied,
Sharper than buckle-tongue, his dart
(A fact which left us saucer-eyed),
As he made ready to depart.

Prince, like a falcon in your pride,
Hear how his pilgrimage did start:
He swigged some dark-red wine, and sighed,
As he made ready to depart.

On the Marginal Way The reference is to George Borrow's *The Bible in Spain,* 1843, chapter 50.

In the Field Some think that Euripides' lost play *Andromeda* told of the transformation of Andromeda—with Perseus, Cepheus, Cassiopeia, and Cetus—into the constellations bearing their names. See the *Oxford Classical Dictionary,* "Andromeda."

"...beyond the limits we know, there is something boundless for our hearts." *A New Catechism,* p. 13.

A Wood The witch hazel's flowers come in fall, the petals often hanging on till spring.

Running April 19 is Patriots' Day in Massachusetts. On that day the Boston Marathon is run.

Under Cygnus Our solar system's movement toward Hercules is turned toward Cygnus by the rotation of the galaxy. The Swan, the Northern Cross, and the Sword are different names for the same constellation.

A Riddle Answer: a campfire.

Dead Still The seventeenth line ("Nothing is hidden that shall not be known") echoes Matthew 10:26, Mark 4:22, and Luke 8:17.

I am indebted, for linguistic and interpretive help, to Norman Thomas di Giovanni (*Everness, Ewigkeit*), Willis Barnstone (*Compass*), Olga Carlisle (the Akhmatova poem), and Max Hayward (the Voznesensky poems).

Advice to a Prophet
and Other Poems

1961

—•—

For Lillian Hellman

Two Voices in a Meadow

A MILKWEED

Anonymous as cherubs
Over the crib of God,
White seeds are floating
Out of my burst pod.
What power had I
Before I learned to yield?
Shatter me, great wind:
I shall possess the field.

A STONE

As casual as cow-dung
Under the crib of God,
I lie where chance would have me,
Up to the ears in sod.
Why should I move? To move
Befits a light desire.
The sill of Heaven would founder,
Did such as I aspire.

ADVICE TO A PROPHET

When you come, as you soon must, to the streets of our city,
Mad-eyed from stating the obvious,
Not proclaiming our fall but begging us
In God's name to have self-pity,

Spare us all word of the weapons, their force and range,
The long numbers that rocket the mind;
Our slow, unreckoning hearts will be left behind,
Unable to fear what is too strange.

Nor shall you scare us with talk of the death of the race.
How should we dream of this place without us?—
The sun mere fire, the leaves untroubled about us,
A stone look on the stone's face?

Speak of the world's own change. Though we cannot conceive
Of an undreamt thing, we know to our cost
How the dreamt cloud crumbles, the vines are blackened by frost,
How the view alters. We could believe,

If you told us so, that the white-tailed deer will slip
Into perfect shade, grown perfectly shy,
The lark avoid the reaches of our eye,
The jack-pine lose its knuckled grip

On the cold ledge, and every torrent burn
As Xanthus once, its gliding trout
Stunned in a twinkling. What should we be without
The dolphin's arc, the dove's return,

These things in which we have seen ourselves and spoken?
Ask us, prophet, how we shall call
Our natures forth when that live tongue is all
Dispelled, that glass obscured or broken

In which we have said the rose of our love and the clean
Horse of our courage, in which beheld
The singing locust of the soul unshelled,
And all we mean or wish to mean.

Ask us, ask us whether with the worldless rose
Our hearts shall fail us; come demanding
Whether there shall be lofty or long standing
When the bronze annals of the oak-tree close.

STOP

In grimy winter dusk
We slowed for a concrete platform;
The pillars passed more slowly;
A paper bag leapt up.

The train banged to a standstill.
Brake-steam rose and parted.
Three chipped-at blocks of ice
Sprawled on a baggage-truck.

Out in that glum, cold air
The broken ice lay glintless,
But the truck was painted blue
On side, wheels, and tongue,

A purple, glowering blue
Like the phosphorus of Lethe
Or Queen Persephone's gaze
In the numb fields of the dark.

JUNK

Huru Welandes
         worc ne geswiceð
monna ænigum
         ðara ðe Mimming can
heardne gehealdan.
                    —Waldere

An axe angles
                    from my neighbor's ashcan;
It is hell's handiwork,
                    the wood not hickory,
The flow of the grain
                    not faithfully followed.
The shivered shaft
                    rises from a shellheap
Of plastic playthings,
                    paper plates,
And the sheer shards
                    of shattered tumblers
That were not annealed
                    for the time needful.
At the same curbside,
                    a cast-off cabinet
Of wavily warped
                    unseasoned wood
Waits to be trundled
                    in the trash-man's truck.
Haul them off! Hide them!
                    The heart winces
For junk and gimcrack,
                    for jerrybuilt things
And the men who make them
                    for a little money,
Bartering pride
                    like the bought boxer

Who pulls his punches,

           or the paid-off jockey

Who in the home stretch

            holds in his horse.

Yet the things themselves

           in thoughtless honor

Have kept composure,

           like captives who would not

Talk under torture.

                Tossed from a tailgate

Where the dump displays

            its random dolmens,

Its black barrows

         and blazing valleys,

They shall waste in the weather

              toward what they were.

The sun shall glory

          in the glitter of glass-chips,

Foreseeing the salvage

           of the prisoned sand,

And the blistering paint

           peel off in patches,

That the good grain

          be discovered again.

Then burnt, bulldozed,

           they shall all be buried

To the depth of diamonds,

            in the making dark

Where halt Hephaestus

          keeps his hammer

And Wayland's work

        is worn away.

LOVES OF THE PUPPETS

Meeting when all the world was in the bud,
Drawn each to each by instinct's wooden face,
These lovers, heedful of the mystic blood,
Fell glassy-eyed into a hot embrace.

April, unready to be so intense,
Marked time while these outstripped the gentle weather,
Yielded their natures to insensate sense,
And flew apart the more they came together.

Where did they fly? Why, each through such a storm
As may be conjured in a globe of glass
Drove on the colder as the flesh grew warm,
In breathless haste to be at lust's impasse,

To cross the little bridge and sink to rest
In visions of the snow-occluded house
Where languishes, unfound by any quest,
The perfect, small, asphyxiated spouse.

That blizzard ended, and their eyes grew clear,
And there they lay exhausted yet unsated;
Why did their features run with tear on tear,
Until their looks were individuated?

One peace implies another, and they cried
For want of love as if their souls would crack,
Till, in despair of being satisfied,
They vowed at least to share each other's lack.

Then maladroitly they embraced once more,
And hollow rang to hollow with a sound
That tuned the brooks more sweetly than before,
And made the birds explode for miles around.

A SUMMER MORNING

Her young employers, having got in late
From seeing friends in town
And scraped the right front fender on the gate,
Will not, the cook expects, be coming down.

She makes a quiet breakfast for herself.
The coffee-pot is bright,
The jelly where it should be on the shelf.
She breaks an egg into the morning light,

Then, with the bread-knife lifted, stands and hears
The sweet efficient sounds
Of thrush and catbird, and the snip of shears
Where, in the terraced backward of the grounds,

A gardener works before the heat of day.
He straightens for a view
Of the big house ascending stony-gray
Out of his beds mosaic with the dew.

His young employers having got in late,
He and the cook alone
Receive the morning on their old estate,
Possessing what the owners can but own.

A Hole in the Floor

for René Magritte

The carpenter's made a hole
In the parlor floor, and I'm standing
Staring down into it now
At four o'clock in the evening,
As Schliemann stood when his shovel
Knocked on the crowns of Troy.

A clean-cut sawdust sparkles
On the grey, shaggy laths,
And here is a cluster of shavings
From the time when the floor was laid.
They are silvery-gold, the color
Of Hesperian apple-parings.

Kneeling, I look in under
Where the joists go into hiding.
A pure street, faintly littered
With bits and strokes of light,
Enters the long darkness
Where its parallels will meet.

The radiator-pipe
Rises in middle distance
Like a shuttered kiosk, standing
Where the only news is night.
Here it's not painted green,
As it is in the visible world.

For God's sake, what am I after?
Some treasure, or tiny garden?
Or that untrodden place,
The house's very soul,
Where time has stored our footbeats
And the long skein of our voices?

Not these, but the buried strangeness
Which nourishes the known:
That spring from which the floor-lamp
Drinks now a wilder bloom,
Inflaming the damask love-seat
And the whole dangerous room.

JORGE GUILLÉN

THE HORSES

Shaggy and heavily natural, they stand
Immobile under their thick and cumbrous manes,
Pent in a barbed enclosure which contains,
By way of compensation, grazing-land.

Nothing disturbs them now. In slow increase
They fatten like the grass. Doomed to be idle,
To haul no cart or wagon, wear no bridle,
They grow into a vegetable peace.

Soul is the issue of so strict a fate.
They harbor visions in their waking eyes,
And with their quiet ears participate
In heaven's pure serenity, which lies
So near all things—yet from the beasts concealed.
Serene now, superhuman, they crop their field.

JORGE GUILLÉN

DEATH, FROM A DISTANCE

Je soutenais l'éclat de la mort toute pure
                                        —Valéry

When that dead-certainty appals my thought,
My future trembles on the road ahead.
There where the light of country fields is caught
In the blind, final precinct of the dead,
A wall takes aim.
                        But what is sad, stripped bare
By the sun's gaze? It does not matter now,—
Not yet. What matters is the ripened pear
That even now my hand strips from the bough.

The time will come: my hand will reach, some day,
Without desire. That saddest day of all,
I shall not weep, but with a proper awe
For the great force impending, I shall say,
Lay on, just destiny. Let the white wall
Impose on me its uncapricious law.

SHE

What was her beauty in our first estate
When Adam's will was whole, and the least thing
Appeared the gift and creature of his king,
How should we guess? Resemblance had to wait

For separation, and in such a place
She so partook of water, light, and trees
As not to look like any one of these.
He woke and gazed into her naked face.

But then she changed, and coming down amid
The flocks of Abel and the fields of Cain,
Clothed in their wish, her Eden graces hid,
A shape of plenty with a mop of grain,

She broke upon the world, in time took on
The look of every labor and its fruits.
Columnar in a robe of pleated lawn
She cupped her patient hand for attributes,

Was radiant captive of the farthest tower
And shed her honor on the fields of war,
Walked in her garden at the evening hour,
Her shadow like a dark ogival door,

Breasted the seas for all the westward ships
And, come to virgin country, changed again—
A moonlike being truest in eclipse,
And subject goddess of the dreams of men.

Tree, temple, valley, prow, gazelle, machine,
More named and nameless than the morning star,
Lovely in every shape, in all unseen,
We dare not wish to find you as you are,

Whose apparition, biding time until
Desire decay and bring the latter age,
Shall flourish in the ruins of our will
And deck the broken stones like saxifrage.

Gemini

I

Because poor PUER's both unsure and vain,
Those who befriend him suffer his disdain,
While those who snub him gain his deference.
He loves his enemies, in a certain sense.

II

It is the power of Heaven to withdraw
Which fills PUELLA with religious awe.
She worships the remoteness of a wraith.
If God should die for her, she'd lose her faith.

THE UNDEAD

Even as children they were late sleepers,
Preferring their dreams, even when quick with monsters,
  To the world with all its breakable toys,
    Its compacts with the dying;

From the stretched arms of withered trees
They turned, fearing contagion of the mortal,
  And even under the plums of summer
    Drifted like winter moons.

Secret, unfriendly, pale, possessed
Of the one wish, the thirst for mere survival,
  They came, as all extremists do
    In time, to a sort of grandeur:

Now, to their Balkan battlements
Above the vulgar town of their first lives,
  They rise at the moon's rising. Strange
    That their utter self-concern

Should, in the end, have left them selfless:
Mirrors fail to perceive them as they float
  Through the great hall and up the staircase;
    Nor are the cobwebs broken.

Into the pallid night emerging,
Wrapped in their flapping capes, routinely maddened
  By a wolf's cry, they stand for a moment
    Stoking the mind's eye

With lewd thoughts of the pressed flowers
And bric-a-brac of rooms with something to lose,—
  Of love-dismembered dolls, and children
    Buried in quilted sleep.

Then they are off in a negative frenzy,
Their black shapes cropped into sudden bats
That swarm, burst, and are gone. Thinking
Of a thrush cold in the leaves

Who has sung his few summers truly,
Or an old scholar resting his eyes at last,
We cannot be much impressed with vampires,
Colorful though they are;

Nevertheless, their pain is real,
And requires our pity. Think how sad it must be
To thirst always for a scorned elixir,
The salt quotidian blood

Which, if mistrusted, has no savor;
To prey on life forever and not possess it,
As rock-hollows, tide after tide,
Glassily strand the sea.

OCTOBER MAPLES, PORTLAND

The leaves, though little time they have to live,
Were never so unfallen as today,
And seem to yield us through a rustled sieve
The very light from which time fell away.

A showered fire we thought forever lost
Redeems the air. Where friends in passing meet,
They parley in the tongues of Pentecost.
Gold ranks of temples flank the dazzled street.

It is a light of maples, and will go;
But not before it washes eye and brain
With such a tincture, such a sanguine glow
As cannot fail to leave a lasting stain.

So Mary's laundered mantle (in the tale
Which, like all pretty tales, may still be true),
Spread on the rosemary-bush, so drenched the pale
Slight blooms in its irradiated hue,

They could not choose but to return in blue.

Eight Riddles from Symphosius

I

Hung from a foot, I walk upon my head,
And leave a trail of headprints where I tread!
Yet many of my kind are thus bestead.

II

I have borne more than a body ought to bear.
Three souls I harbored; when I lost a pair,
The third one all but perished then and there.

III

I bite, when bitten; but because I lack
For teeth, no biter scruples to attack,
And many bite me to be bitten back.

IV

Unequal in degree, alike in size,
We make our flight, ascending toward the skies
And rise with those who by our help can rise.

V

Mine was the strangest birth under the sun;
I left the womb, yet life had not begun;
Entered the world, and yet was seen by none.

VI

Sweet purlings in an earth-walled inn resound.
Within that inn a silent guest is found.
Together, guest and inn are onward bound.

VII

All teeth from head to foot (yet friend to men),
I rip and tear my green-haired prey; but then,
All that I chew I spew right out again.

VIII

To me, and through me, Fortune is unkind.
Though iron-bound, yet many must I bind—
And many free, though I remain confined.

SHAME

It is a cramped little state with no foreign policy,
Save to be thought inoffensive. The grammar of the language
Has never been fathomed, owing to the national habit
Of allowing each sentence to trail off in confusion.
Those who have visited Scusi, the capital city,
Report that the railway-route from Schuldig passes
Through country best described as unrelieved.
Sheep are the national product. The faint inscription
Over the city gates may perhaps be rendered,
"I'm afraid you won't find much of interest here."
Census-reports which give the population
As zero are, of course, not to be trusted,
Save as reflecting the natives' flustered insistence
That they do not count, as well as their modest horror
Of letting one's sex be known in so many words.
The uniform grey of the nondescript buildings, the absence
Of churches or comfort-stations, have given observers
An odd impression of ostentatious meanness,
And it must be said of the citizens (muttering by
In their ratty sheepskins, shying at cracks in the sidewalk)
That they lack the peace of mind of the truly humble.
The tenor of life is careful, even in the stiff
Unsmiling carelessness of the border-guards
And *douaniers*, who admit, whenever they can,
Not merely the usual carloads of deodorant
But gypsies, g-strings, hasheesh, and contraband pigments.
Their complete negligence is reserved, however,
For the hoped-for invasion, at which time the happy people
(Sniggering, ruddily naked, and shamelessly drunk)
Will stun the foe by their overwhelming submission,
Corrupt the generals, infiltrate the staff,
Usurp the throne, proclaim themselves to be sun-gods,
And bring about the collapse of the whole empire.

A Grasshopper

But for a brief
Moment, a poised minute,
He paused on the chicory-leaf;
Yet within it

The sprung perch
Had time to absorb the shock,
Narrow its pitch and lurch,
Cease to rock.

A quiet spread
Over the neighbor ground;
No flower swayed its head
For yards around;

The wind shrank
Away with a swallowed hiss;
Caught in a widening, blank
Parenthesis,

Cry upon cry
Faltered and faded out;
Everything seemed to die.
Oh, without doubt

Peace like a plague
Had gone to the world's verge,
But that an aimless, vague
Grasshopper-urge

Leapt him aloft,
Giving the leaf a kick,
Starting the grasses' soft
Chafe and tick,

So that the sleeping
Crickets resumed their chimes,
And all things wakened, keeping
Their several times.

In gay release
The whole field did what it did,
Peaceful now that its peace
Lay busily hid.

SALVATORE QUASIMODO

THE AGRIGENTUM ROAD

That wind's still there that I remember afire
In the manes of the racing horses
Veering across the plains; a wind
That stains the sandstone and erodes the hearts
Of downed columnar statues in the grass.
Oh antique soul, bled white
By rancor, back you lean to that wind again,
Catching the delicate fetor of the moss
That clothes those giants tumbled down by heaven.
How lonely it will be, the time that is left you!
    Worse, worse, if you should hear
That sound again, borne toward the far-off sea
Which Hesperus already pinks with morning:
The jew's-harp quavering sadly in the mouth
Of the wagon-maker climbing
Slowly his moon-washed hill, amidst
The murmur of the Saracen olive trees.

THE ASPEN AND THE STREAM

THE ASPEN

Beholding element, in whose pure eye
My boughs upon a ground of heaven lie—
O deep surrendered mind, where cloud and stone
Compose their beings and efface your own,
Teach me, like you, to drink creation whole
And, casting out my self, become a soul.

THE STREAM

Why should the water drink,
Blithering little tree?
Think what you choose to think,
But lisp no more at me.

I seek an empty mind.
Reflection is my curse.
Oh, never have I been blind
To the damned universe,

Save when I rose in flood
And in my lathered flight
So fouled myself with mud
As to be purged of sight.

THE ASPEN

Your water livens me, but not your word,
If what you spoke was what I thought I heard.
But likely I mistook you. What with the claims
Of crow and cricket teaching me their names,
And all this flap and shifting in my head,
I must have lost the drift of what you said.

THE STREAM

There may be rocks ahead
Where, shivered into smoke

And brawling in my bed,
I'll shred this gaudy cloak;

Then, dodging down a trough
Into a rocky hole,
I'll shake the daylight off
And repossess my soul

In blackness and in fall,
Where self to self shall roar
Till, deaf and blind to all,
I shall be self no more.

THE ASPEN

Out of your sullen flux I shall distil
A gayer spirit and a clambering will,
And reach toward all about me, and ensnare
With roots the earth, with branches all the air—
Even if that blind groping but achieves
A darker head, a few more aspen-leaves.

A Fire-Truck

Right down the shocked street with a siren-blast
That sends all else skittering to the curb,
Redness, brass, ladders and hats hurl past,
    Blurring to sheer verb,

Shift at the corner into uproarious gear
And make it around the turn in a squall of traction,
The headlong bell maintaining sure and clear,
    Thought is degraded action!

Beautiful, heavy, unweary, loud, obvious thing!
I stand here purged of nuance, my mind a blank.
All I was brooding upon has taken wing,
    And I have you to thank.

As you howl beyond hearing I carry you into my mind,
Ladders and brass and all, there to admire
Your phoenix-red simplicity, enshrined
    In that not extinguished fire.

Someone Talking to Himself

Even when first her face,
Younger than any spring,
Older than Pharaoh's grain
And fresh as Phoenix-ashes,
Shadowed under its lashes
Every earthly thing,
There was another place
I saw in a flash of pain:
Off in the fathomless dark
Beyond the verge of love
I saw blind fishes move,
And under a stone shelf
Rode the recusant shark—
Cold, waiting, himself.

Oh, even when we fell,
Clean as a mountain source
And barely able to tell
Such ecstasy from grace,
Into the primal bed
And current of our race,
We knew yet must deny
To what we gathered head:
That music growing harsh,
Trees blotting the sky
Above the roaring course
That in the summer's drought
Slowly would peter out
Into a dry marsh.

Love is the greatest mercy,
A volley of the sun
That lashes all with shade,
That the first day be mended;
And yet, so soon undone,
It is the lover's curse

Till time be comprehended
And the flawed heart unmade.
What can I do but move
From folly to defeat,
And call that sorrow sweet
That teaches us to see
The final face of love
In what we cannot be?

IN THE SMOKING-CAR

The eyelids meet. He'll catch a little nap.
The grizzled, crew-cut head drops to his chest.
It shakes above the briefcase on his lap.
Close voices breathe, "Poor sweet, he did his best."

"Poor sweet, poor sweet," the bird-hushed glades repeat,
Through which in quiet pomp his litter goes,
Carried by native girls with naked feet.
A sighing stream concurs in his repose.

Could he but think, he might recall to mind
The righteous mutiny or sudden gale
That beached him here; the dear ones left behind...
So near the ending, he forgets the tale.

Were he to lift his eyelids now, he might
Behold his maiden porters, brown and bare.
But even here he has no appetite.
It is enough to know that they are there.

Enough that now a honeyed music swells,
The gentle, mossed declivities begin,
And the whole air is full of flower-smells.
Failure, the longed-for valley, takes him in.

BALLADE FOR THE DUKE OF ORLÉANS

who offered a prize at Blois, circa 1457, for the best ballade
employing the line "Je meurs de soif auprès de la fontaine."

Flailed from the heart of water in a bow,
He took the falling fly; my line went taut;
Foam was in uproar where he drove below;
In spangling air I fought him and was fought.
Then, wearied to the shallows, he was caught,
Gasped in the net, lay still and stony-eyed.
It was no fading iris I had sought.
I die of thirst, here at the fountain-side.

Down in the harbor's flow and counter-flow
I left my ships with hopes and heroes fraught.
Ten times more golden than the sun could show,
Calypso gave the darkness I besought.
Oh, but her fleecy touch was dearly bought:
All spent, I wakened by my only bride,
Beside whom every vision is but nought,
And die of thirst, here at the fountain-side.

Where does that Plenty dwell, I'd like to know,
Which fathered poor Desire, as Plato taught?
Out on the real and endless waters go
Conquistador and stubborn Argonaut.
Where Buddha bathed, the golden bowl he brought
Gilded the stream, but stalled its living tide.
The sunlight withers as the verse is wrought.
I die of thirst, here at the fountain-side.

   Envoi
Duke, keep your coin. All men are born distraught,
And will not for the world be satisfied.
Whether we live in fact, or but in thought,
We die of thirst, here at the fountain-side.

ANTÉROS

You ask me why I bear such rage in heart,
And on this pliant neck a rebel head;
Of great Antaeus' lineage was I bred;
I hurl to heaven again the Victor's dart.

Yea, I am one the Avenger God inspires;
He has marked my forehead with the breath of spite;
My face, like Abel's bloody—alas!—and white,
Burns red by turns with Cain's unsated fires!

The last, Jehovah! who by thy powers fell
And cried against thy tyranny from hell
Was Bel my grandsire, or my father Dagon.

By them thrice baptized in Cocytus' water,
I guard alone the Amalekite my mother,
And sow at her feet the teeth of the old dragon.

To Ishtar

Is it less than your brilliance, Ishtar,
How the snowfield smarts in the fresh sun,
And the bells of its melting ring, and we blink
    At the light flexing in trickles?

It is the Spring's disgrace
That already, before the prone arbutus
Will risk its whiteness, you have come down
    To the first gate and darkened.

Forgive us, who cannot conceive you
Elsewhere and maiden, but love you only
Fallen among us in rut and furrow,
    In the shade of amassing leaves,

Or scrawny in plucked harvest,
Your losses having fattened the world
Till crownless, starless, you stoop and enter
    The low door of Irkalla.

There too, in the year's dungeon
Where love takes you, even our itch
For defilement cannot find you out,
    Your death being so perfect.

It is all we can do to witness
The waste motions of empty trees,
The joyless tittering duff, the grass-mats
    Blanched and scurfy with ice,

And in the desert heat
Of vision force from rotten sticks
Those pure and inconceivable blooms
    Which, rising, you bear beyond us.

Pangloss's Song:

A COMIC-OPERA LYRIC

I

Dear boy, you will not hear me speak
    With sorrow or with rancor
Of what has paled my rosy cheek
    And blasted it with canker;
'Twas Love, great Love, that did the deed
    Through Nature's gentle laws,
And how should ill effects proceed
    From so divine a cause?

Sweet honey comes from bees that sting,
    As you are well aware;
To one adept in reasoning,
Whatever pains disease may bring
Are but the tangy seasoning
    To Love's delicious fare.

II

Columbus and his men, they say,
    Conveyed the virus hither
Whereby my features rot away
    And vital powers wither;
Yet had they not traversed the seas
    And come infected back,
Why, think of all the luxuries
    That modern life would lack!

All bitter things conduce to sweet,
    As this example shows;
Without the little spirochete
We'd have no chocolate to eat,
Nor would tobacco's fragrance greet
    The European nose.

III

Each nation guards its native land
    With cannon and with sentry,
Inspectors look for contraband
    At every port of entry,
Yet nothing can prevent the spread
    Of Love's divine disease:
It rounds the world from bed to bed
    As pretty as you please.

Men worship Venus everywhere,
    As plainly may be seen;
The decorations which I bear
Are nobler than the Croix de Guerre,
And gained in service of our fair
    And universal Queen.

Two Quatrains for First Frost

Hot summer has exhausted her intent
To the last rose and roundelay and seed.
No leaf has changed, and yet these leaves now read
Like a love-letter that's no longer meant.

Now on all things is the dull restive mood
Of some rich gambler who in quick disdain
Plumps all on zero, hoping so to gain
Fresh air, light pockets, and his solitude.

ANOTHER VOICE

The sword bites for peace,
Yet how should that be said
Now or in howling Greece
Above the sorry dead?
Corcyra! cry the crows,
And blacken all our sky.
The soul knows what it knows,
But may not make reply.

From a good face gone mad,
From false or hissing tongue,
What comfort's to be had,
What sweetness can be wrung?
It is the human thing
To reckon pain as pain.
If soul in quiet sing,
Better not to explain.

Great martyrs mocked their pain
And sang that wrong was right;
Great doctors proved them sane
By logic's drier light;
Yet in those I love the most
Some anger, love, or tact
Hushes the giddy ghost
Before atrocious fact.

Forgive me, patient voice
Whose word I little doubt,
Who stubbornly rejoice
When all but beaten out,
If I equivocate,
And will not yet unlearn
Anxiety and hate,
Sorrow and dear concern.

TARTUFFE

ACT I, SCENE 4

ORGON, CLÉANTE, DORINE

ORGON

Ah, Brother, good-day.

CLÉANTE

Well, welcome back. I'm sorry I can't stay.
How was the country? Blooming, I trust, and green?

ORGON

Excuse me, Brother; just one moment. (*to Dorine:*) Dorine...
      (to Cléante:)
To put my mind at rest, I always learn
The household news the moment I return.
      (to Dorine:)
Has all been well, these two days I've been gone?
How are the family? What's been going on?

DORINE

Your wife, two days ago, had a bad fever,
And a fierce headache that refused to leave her.

ORGON

Ah. And Tartuffe?

DORINE

      Tartuffe? Why, he's round and red,
Bursting with health, and excellently fed.

ORGON

Poor fellow!

DORINE

That night, the mistress was unable
To take a single bite at the dinner-table.
Her headache-pains, she said, were simply hellish.

ORGON

Ah. And Tartuffe?

DORINE

He ate his meal with relish,
And zealously devoured in her presence
A leg of mutton and a brace of pheasants.

ORGON

Poor fellow!

DORINE

Well, the pains continued strong,
And so she tossed and tossed the whole night long,—
Now icy-cold, now burning like a flame.
We sat beside her bed till morning came.

ORGON

Ah. And Tartuffe?

DORINE

Why, having eaten, he rose
And sought his room, already in a doze,
Got into his warm bed, and snored away
In perfect peace until the break of day.

ORGON

Poor fellow!

DORINE

After much ado, we talked her
Into dispatching someone for the doctor.
He bled her, and the fever quickly fell.

ORGON

Ah. And Tartuffe?

DORINE

He bore it very well.
To keep his cheerfulness at any cost,
And make up for the blood *Madame* had lost,
He drank, at lunch, four beakers full of port.

ORGON

Poor fellow!

DORINE

Both are much improved, in short.
I'll go and tell *Madame* that you've expressed
Keen sympathy and anxious interest.

FALL IN CORRALES

Winter will be feasts and fires in the shut houses,
Lovers with hot mouths in their blanched bed,
Prayers and poems made, and all recourses
Against the world huge and dead:

Charms, all charms, as in stillness of plumb summer
The shut head lies down in bottomless grasses,
Willing that its thought be all heat and hum,
That it not dream the time passes.

Now as these light buildings of summer begin
To crumble, the air husky with blown tile,
It is as when in bald April the wind
Unhoused the spirit for a while:

Then there was no need by tales or drowsing
To make the thing that we were mothered by;
It was ourselves who melted in the mountains,
And the sun dove into every eye.

Our desires dwelt in the weather as fine as bomb-dust;
It was our sex that made the fountains yield;
Our flesh fought in the roots, and at last rested
Whole among cows in the risen field.

Now in its empty bed the truant river
Leaves but the perfect rumples of its flow;
The cottonwoods are spending gold like water;
Weeds in their light detachments go;

In a dry world more huge than rhyme or dreaming
We hear the sentences of straws and stones,
Stand in the wind and, bowing to this time,
Practise the candor of our bones.

NEXT DOOR

The home for the aged opens its windows in May,
    And the stale voices of winter-long
Flap from their dusty curtains toward our wood,
    That now with robin-song

Rouses, and is regaled. Promptly the trees
    Break bud and startle into leaf,
Blotting the old from sight, while all the birds
    Repeal the winter's grief

Pitilessly, resolving every sigh
    Or quaver to a chipper trill,
And snaring the sick cough within the rapt
    Beat of the flicker's bill.

Must we not see or hear these worn and frail?
    They are such hearts, for all we know,
As will not cheat the world of their regard,
    Even as they let it go.

Seated, perhaps, along a shady porch
    In the calm, wicker stalls of age,
Old crones and played-out cronies, they project
    Upon a cloudy stage

Gossip of strong-man, dancer, priest, and all
    They knew who had the gift of life,
Artisan, lover, soldier, orator,
    Wild bitch and happy wife,

Lying the more as recollection fails,
    Until for their enchanted souls
The players are forgotten, and they see
    Only such naked rôles

As David was, or Helen, and invent
    Out of their fabulous memories
Alcestis climbing home again, with big
    Death-bullying Heracles.

Is it like this? We have no way to know.
    Our lawn is loud with girls and boys.
The leaves are full and busy with the sun.
    The birds make too much noise.

A CHRISTMAS HYMN

A stable-lamp is lighted
Whose glow shall wake the sky;
The stars shall bend their voices,
And every stone shall cry.
And every stone shall cry,
And straw like gold shall shine;
A barn shall harbor heaven,
A stall become a shrine.

This child through David's city
Shall ride in triumph by;
The palm shall strew its branches,
And every stone shall cry.
And every stone shall cry,
Though heavy, dull, and dumb,
And lie within the roadway
To pave his kingdom come.

Yet he shall be forsaken,
And yielded up to die;
The sky shall groan and darken,
And every stone shall cry.
And every stone shall cry
For stony hearts of men:
God's blood upon the spearhead,
God's love refused again.

But now, as at the ending,
The low is lifted high;
The stars shall bend their voices,
And every stone shall cry.
And every stone shall cry
In praises of the child
By whose descent among us
The worlds are reconciled.

Advice to a Prophet   Hephaestus, invoked by Achilles, scalded the river Xanthus (Scamander) in *Iliad*, xxi.

Junk   The epigraph, taken from a fragmentary Anglo-Saxon poem, concerns the legendary smith Wayland, and may roughly be translated: "Truly, Wayland's handiwork—the sword Mimming which he made—will never fail any man who knows how to use it bravely."

The Undead   The *Standard Dictionary of Folklore, Mythology, and Legend* defines the vampire as "One of the types of the undead; a living corpse or soulless body that comes from its burial place and drinks the blood of the living."

Eight Riddles from Symphosius   The answers to these riddles of Symphosius (A.D. fourth century?) are as follows: I, hobnail; II, mother of twins; III, onion; IV, stairs; V, chick in the egg; VI, river and fish; VII, saw; VIII, chain or fetter.

A Fire-Truck   Line 8 echoes a notion entertained by Henry Adams in his "Letter to American Teachers of History" (1910).

Things of This World

1956

———•———

*For
Ellen,
Christopher,
and
Nathan*

ALTITUDES

I

Look up into the dome:
It is a great salon, a brilliant place,
    Yet not too splendid for the race
Whom we imagine there, wholly at home

    With the gold-rosetted white
Wainscot, the oval windows, and the fault-
    Less figures of the painted vault.
Strolling, conversing in that precious light,

    They chat no doubt of love,
The pleasant burden of their courtesy
    Borne down at times to you and me
Where, in this dark, we stand and gaze above.

    For all they cannot share,
All that the world cannot in fact afford,
    Their lofty premises are floored
With the massed voices of continual prayer.

II

    How far it is from here
To Emily Dickinson's father's house in America;
    Think of her climbing a spiral stair
Up to the little cupola with its clear

    Small panes, its room for one.
Like the dark house below, so full of eyes
    In mirrors and of shut-in flies,
This chamber furnished only with the sun

    Is she and she alone,
A mood to which she rises, in which she sees
    Bird-choristers in all the trees
And a wild shining of the pure unknown

On Amherst. This is caught
In the dormers of a neighbor, who, no doubt,
Will before long be coming out
To pace about his garden, lost in thought.

LOVE CALLS US TO THE THINGS
OF THIS WORLD

The eyes open to a cry of pulleys,
And spirited from sleep, the astounded soul
Hangs for a moment bodiless and simple
As false dawn.
                    Outside the open window
The morning air is all awash with angels.

Some are in bed-sheets, some are in blouses,
Some are in smocks: but truly there they are.
Now they are rising together in calm swells
Of halcyon feeling, filling whatever they wear
With the deep joy of their impersonal breathing;

Now they are flying in place, conveying
The terrible speed of their omnipresence, moving
And staying like white water; and now of a sudden
They swoon down into so rapt a quiet
That nobody seems to be there.
                    The soul shrinks

From all that it is about to remember,
From the punctual rape of every blessèd day,
And cries,
          "Oh, let there be nothing on earth but laundry,
Nothing but rosy hands in the rising steam
And clear dances done in the sight of heaven."

Yet, as the sun acknowledges
With a warm look the world's hunks and colors,
The soul descends once more in bitter love
To accept the waking body, saying now
In a changed voice as the man yawns and rises,
          "Bring them down from their ruddy gallows;

Let there be clean linen for the backs of thieves;
Let lovers go fresh and sweet to be undone,
And the heaviest nuns walk in a pure floating
Of dark habits,
               keeping their difficult balance."

SONNET

The winter deepening, the hay all in,
The barn fat with cattle, the apple-crop
Conveyed to market or the fragrant bin,
He thinks the time has come to make a stop,

And sinks half-grudging in his firelit seat,
Though with his heavy body's full consent,
In what would be the posture of defeat,
But for that look of rigorous content.

Outside, the night dives down like one great crow
Against his cast-off clothing where it stands
Up to the knees in miles of hustled snow,

Flapping and jumping like a kind of fire,
And floating skyward its abandoned hands
In gestures of invincible desire.

PIAZZA DI SPAGNA, EARLY MORNING

I can't forget
How she stood at the top of that long marble stair
Amazed, and then with a sleepy pirouette
Went dancing slowly down to the fountain-quieted square;

Nothing upon her face
But some impersonal loneliness,—not then a girl,
But as it were a reverie of the place,
A called-for falling glide and whirl;

As when a leaf, petal, or thin chip
Is drawn to the falls of a pool and, circling a moment above it,
Rides on over the lip—
Perfectly beautiful, perfectly ignorant of it.

JOHN CHRYSOSTOM

He who had gone a beast
Down on his knees and hands
Remembering lust and murder
Felt now a gust of grace,
Lifted his burnished face
From the psalter of the sands
And found his thoughts in order
And cleared his throat at last.

What they heard was a voice
That spoke what they could learn
From any gelded priest,
Yet rang like a great choir,
He having taught hell's fire
A singing way to burn,
And borrowed of some dumb beast
The wildness to rejoice.

A BLACK NOVEMBER TURKEY

to A.M. and A.M.

Nine white chickens come
With haunchy walk and heads
Jabbing among the chips, the chaff, the stones
    And the cornhusk-shreds,

And bit by bit infringe
A pond of dusty light,
Spectral in shadow until they bobbingly one
    By one ignite.

Neither pale nor bright,
The turkey-cock parades
Through radiant squalors, darkly auspicious as
    The ace of spades,

Himself his own cortège
And puffed with the pomp of death,
Rehearsing over and over with strangled râle
    His latest breath.

The vast black body floats
Above the crossing knees
As a cloud over thrashed branches, a calm ship
    Over choppy seas,

Shuddering its fan and feathers
In fine soft clashes
With the cold sound that the wind makes, fondling
    Paper-ashes.

The pale-blue bony head
Set on its shepherd's-crook
Like a saint's death-mask, turns a vague, superb
    And timeless look

Upon these clocking hens
And the cocks that one by one,
Dawn after mortal dawn, with vulgar joy
Acclaim the sun.

MIND

Mind in its purest play is like some bat
That beats about in caverns all alone,
Contriving by a kind of senseless wit
Not to conclude against a wall of stone.

It has no need to falter or explore;
Darkly it knows what obstacles are there,
And so may weave and flitter, dip and soar
In perfect courses through the blackest air.

And has this simile a like perfection?
The mind is like a bat. Precisely. Save
That in the very happiest intellection
A graceful error may correct the cave.

After the Last Bulletins

After the last bulletins the windows darken
And the whole city founders readily and deep,
Sliding on all its pillows
To the thronged Atlantis of personal sleep,

And the wind rises. The wind rises and bowls
The day's litter of news in the alleys. Trash
Tears itself on the railings,
Soars and falls with a soft crash,

Tumbles and soars again. Unruly flights
Scamper the park, and taking a statue for dead
Strike at the positive eyes,
Batter and flap the stolid head

And scratch the noble name. In empty lots
Our journals spiral in a fierce noyade
Of all we thought to think,
Or caught in corners cramp and wad

And twist our words. And some from gutters flail
Their tatters at the tired patrolman's feet,
Like all that fisted snow
That cried beside his long retreat

Damn you! damn you! to the emperor's horse's heels.
Oh none too soon through the air white and dry
Will the clear announcer's voice
Beat like a dove, and you and I

From the heart's anarch and responsible town
Return by subway-mouth to life again,
Bearing the morning papers,
And cross the park where saintlike men,

White and absorbed, with stick and bag remove
The litter of the night, and footsteps rouse
With confident morning sound
The songbirds in the public boughs.

LAMARCK ELABORATED

"The environment creates the organ"

The Greeks were wrong who said our eyes have rays;
Not from these sockets or these sparkling poles
Comes the illumination of our days.
It was the sun that bored these two blue holes.

It was the song of doves begot the ear
And not the ear that first conceived of sound:
That organ bloomed in vibrant atmosphere,
As music conjured Ilium from the ground.

The yielding water, the repugnant stone,
The poisoned berry and the flaring rose
Attired in sense the tactless finger-bone
And set the taste-buds and inspired the nose.

Out of our vivid ambiance came unsought
All sense but that most formidably dim.
The shell of balance rolls in seas of thought.
It was the mind that taught the head to swim.

Newtonian numbers set to cosmic lyres
Whelmed us in whirling worlds we could not know,
And by the imagined floods of our desires
The voice of Sirens gave us vertigo.

A Plain Song for Comadre

Though the unseen may vanish, though insight fails
And doubter and downcast saint
Join in the same complaint,
What holy things were ever frightened off
By a fly's buzz, or itches, or a cough?
Harder than nails

They are, more warmly constant than the sun,
At whose continual sign
The dimly prompted vine
Upbraids itself to a green excellence.
What evening, when the slow and forced expense
Of sweat is done,

Does not the dark come flooding the straight furrow
Or filling the well-made bowl?
What night will not the whole
Sky with its clear studs and steady spheres
Turn on a sound chimney? It is seventeen years
Come tomorrow

That Bruna Sandoval has kept the church
Of San Ysidro, sweeping
And scrubbing the aisles, keeping
The candlesticks and the plaster faces bright,
And seen no visions but the thing done right
From the clay porch

To the white altar. For love and in all weathers
This is what she has done.
Sometimes the early sun
Shines as she flings the scrubwater out, with a crash
Of grimy rainbows, and the stained suds flash
Like angel-feathers.

MERLIN ENTHRALLED

In a while they rose and went out aimlessly riding,
Leaving their drained cups on the table round.
Merlin, Merlin, their hearts cried, where are you hiding?
In all the world was no unnatural sound.

Mystery watched them riding glade by glade;
They saw it darkle from under leafy brows;
But leaves were all its voice, and squirrels made
An alien fracas in the ancient boughs.

Once by a lake-edge something made them stop.
Yet what they found was the thumping of a frog,
Bugs skating on the shut water-top,
Some hairlike algae bleaching on a log.

Gawen thought for a moment that he heard
A whitethorn breathe *Niniane.* That Siren's daughter
Rose in a fort of dreams and spoke the word
Sleep, her voice like dark diving water;

And Merlin slept, who had imagined her
Of water-sounds and the deep unsoundable swell
A creature to bewitch a sorcerer,
And lay there now within her towering spell.

Slowly the shapes of searching men and horses
Escaped him as he dreamt on that high bed:
History died; he gathered in its forces;
The mists of time condensed in the still head

Until his mind, as clear as mountain water,
Went raveling toward the deep transparent dream
Who bade him sleep. And then the Siren's daughter
Received him as the sea receives a stream.

Fate would be fated; dreams desire to sleep.
This the forsaken will not understand.
Arthur upon the road began to weep
And said to Gawen *Remember when this hand*

Once haled a sword from stone; now no less strong
It cannot dream of such a thing to do.
Their mail grew quainter as they clopped along.
The sky became a still and woven blue.

A Voice from under the Table

to Robert and Jane Brooks

How shall the wine be drunk, or the woman known?
I take this world for better or for worse,
But seeing rose carafes conceive the sun
My thirst conceives a fierier universe:
And then I toast the birds in the burning trees
That chant their holy lucid drunkenness;
I swallowed all the phosphorus of the seas
Before I fell into this low distress.

You upright people all remember how
Love drove you first to the woods, and there you heard
The loose-mouthed wind complaining *Thou* and *Thou*;
My gawky limbs were shuddered by the word.
Most of it since was nothing but charades
To spell that hankering out and make an end,
But the softest hands against my shoulder-blades
Only increased the crying of the wind.

For this the goddess rose from the midland sea
And stood above the famous wine-dark wave,
To ease our drouth with clearer mystery
And be a South to all our flights of love.
And down by the selfsame water I have seen
A blazing girl with skin like polished stone
Splashing until a far-out breast of green
Arose and with a rose contagion shone.

"A myrtle-shoot in hand, she danced; her hair
Cast on her back and shoulders a moving shade."
Was it some hovering light that showed her fair?
Was it of chafing dark that light was made?
Perhaps it was Archilochus' fantasy,
Or that his saying sublimed the thing he said.

All true enough; and true as well that she
Was beautiful, and danced, and is now dead.

Helen was no such high discarnate thought
As men in dry symposia pursue,
But was as bitterly fugitive, not to be caught
By what men's arms in love or fight could do.
Groan in your cell; rape Troy with sword and flame;
The end of thirst exceeds experience.
A devil told me it was all the same
Whether to fail by spirit or by sense.

God keep me a damned fool, nor charitably
Receive me into his shapely resignations.
I am a sort of martyr, as you see,
A horizontal monument to patience.
The calves of waitresses parade about
My helpless head upon this sodden floor.
Well, I am down again, but not yet out.
O sweet frustrations, I shall be back for more.

THE BEACON

Founded on rock and facing the night-fouled sea
A beacon blinks at its own brilliance,
Over and over with cutlass gaze
Solving the Gordian waters,

Making the sea-roads out, and the lounge of the weedy
Meadows, finding the blown hair
As it always has, and the buxom, lavish
Romp of the ocean-daughters.

Then in the flashes of darkness it is all gone,
The flung arms and the hips, meads
And meridians, all; and the dark of the eye
Dives for the black pearl

Of the sea-in-itself. Watching the blinded waves
Compounding their eclipse, we hear their
Booms, rumors and guttural sucks
Warn of the pitchy whirl

At the mind's end. All of the sense of the sea
Is veiled as voices nearly heard
In morning sleep; nor shall we wake
At the sea's heart. Rail

At the deaf unbeatable sea, my soul, and weep
Your Alexandrine tears, but look:
The beacon-blaze unsheathing turns
The face of darkness pale

And now with one grand chop gives clearance to
Our human visions, which assume
The waves again, fresh and the same.
Let us suppose that we

See most of darkness by our plainest light.
It is the Nereid's kick endears
The tossing spray; a sighted ship
Assembles all the sea.

STATUES

These children playing at statues fill
The gardens with their shrillness; in a planned
And planted grove they fling from the swinger's hand
Across the giddy grass and then hold still

In gargoyle attitudes,—as if
All definition were outrageous. Then
They melt in giggles and begin again.
Above their heads the maples with a stiff

Compliance entertain the air
In abrupt gusts, losing the look of trees
In rushed and cloudy metamorphoses,
Their shadows all a brilliant disrepair,

A wash of dodging stars, through which
The children weave and then again undo
Their fickle zodiacs. It is a view
Lively as Ovid's Chaos, and its rich

Uncertainty compels the crowd:
Two nuns regard it with habitual love,
Moving along a path as mountains move
Or seem to move when traversed by a cloud;

The soldier breaks his iron pace;
Linked lovers pause to gaze; and every rôle
Relents,—until the feet begin to stroll
Or stride again. But settled in disgrace

Upon his bench, one aging bum,
Brought by his long evasion and distress
Into an adamantine shapelessness,
Stares at the image of his kingdom come.

LOOKING INTO HISTORY

I.

Five soldiers fixed by Mathew Brady's eye
Stand in a land subdued beyond belief.
Belief might lend them life again. I try
Like orphaned Hamlet working up his grief

To see my spellbound fathers in these men
Who, breathless in their amber atmosphere,
Show but the postures men affected then
And the hermit faces of a finished year.

The guns and gear and all are strange until
Beyond the tents I glimpse a file of trees
Verging a road that struggles up a hill.
They're sycamores.
                              The long-abated breeze

Flares in those boughs I know, and hauls the sound
Of guns and a great forest in distress.
Fathers, I know my cause, and we are bound
Beyond that hill to fight at Wilderness.

II.

But trick your eyes with Birnam Wood, or think
How fire-cast shadows of the bankside trees
Rode on the back of Simois to sink
In the wide waters. Reflect how history's

Changes are like the sea's, which mauls and mulls
Its salvage of the world in shifty waves,
Shrouding in evergreen the oldest hulls
And yielding views of its confounded graves

To the new moon, the sun, or any eye
That in its shallow shoreward version sees

The pebbles charging with a deathless cry
And carageen memorials of trees.

III.

Now, old man of the sea,
I start to understand:
The will will find no stillness
Back in a stilled land.

The dead give no command
And shall not find their voice
Till they be mustered by
Some present fatal choice.

Let me now rejoice
In all impostures, take
The shape of lion or leopard,
Boar, or watery snake,

Or like the comber break,
Yet in the end stand fast
And by some fervent fraud
Father the waiting past,

Resembling at the last
The self-established tree
That draws all waters toward
Its live formality.

CHARLES BAUDELAIRE

L'INVITATION AU VOYAGE

My child, my sister,
   dream
How sweet all things would seem
Were we in that kind land to live together,
  And there love slow and long,
  There love and die among
Those scenes that image you, that sumptuous weather.
  Drowned suns that glimmer there
  Through cloud-disheveled air
Move me with such a mystery as appears
  Within those other skies
  Of your treacherous eyes
When I behold them shining through their tears.

There, there is nothing else but grace and measure,
Richness, quietness, and pleasure.

  Furniture that wears
  The lustre of the years
Softly would glow within our glowing chamber,
  Flowers of rarest bloom
  Proffering their perfume
Mixed with the vague fragrances of amber;
  Gold ceilings would there be,
  Mirrors deep as the sea,
The walls all in an Eastern splendor hung—
  Nothing but should address
  The soul's loneliness,
Speaking her sweet and secret native tongue.

There, there is nothing else but grace and measure,
Richness, quietness, and pleasure.

See, sheltered from the swells
There in the still canals
Those drowsy ships that dream of sailing forth;
It is to satisfy
Your least desire, they ply
Hither through all the waters of the earth.
The sun at close of day
Clothes the fields of hay,
Then the canals, at last the town entire
In hyacinth and gold:
Slowly the land is rolled
Sleepward under a sea of gentle fire.

There, there is nothing else but grace and measure,
Richness, quietness, and pleasure.

DIGGING FOR CHINA

"Far enough down is China," somebody said.
"Dig deep enough and you might see the sky
As clear as at the bottom of a well.
Except it would be real—a different sky.
Then you could burrow down until you came
To China! Oh, it's nothing like New Jersey.
There's people, trees, and houses, and all that,
But much, much different. Nothing looks the same."

I went and got the trowel out of the shed
And sweated like a coolie all that morning,
Digging a hole beside the lilac-bush,
Down on my hands and knees. It was a sort
Of praying, I suspect. I watched my hand
Dig deep and darker, and I tried and tried
To dream a place where nothing was the same.
The trowel never did break through to blue.

Before the dream could weary of itself
My eyes were tired of looking into darkness,
My sunbaked head of hanging down a hole.
I stood up in a place I had forgotten,
Blinking and staggering while the earth went round
And showed me silver barns, the fields dozing
In palls of brightness, patens growing and gone
In the tides of leaves, and the whole sky china blue.
Until I got my balance back again
All that I saw was China, China, China.

A Prayer to Go to Paradise
with the Donkeys

to Máire and Jack

When I must come to you, O my God, I pray
It be some dusty-roaded holiday,
And even as in my travels here below,
I beg to choose by what road I shall go
To Paradise, where the clear stars shine by day.
I'll take my walking-stick and go my way,
And to my friends the donkeys I shall say,
"I am Francis Jammes, and I'm going to Paradise,
For there is no hell in the land of the loving God."
And I'll say to them: "Come, sweet friends of the blue skies,
Poor creatures who with a flap of the ears or a nod
Of the head shake off the buffets, the bees, the flies…"

Let me come with these donkeys, Lord, into your land,
These beasts who bow their heads so gently, and stand
With their small feet joined together in a fashion
Utterly gentle, asking your compassion.
I shall arrive, followed by their thousands of ears,
Followed by those with baskets at their flanks,
By those who lug the carts of mountebanks
Or loads of feather-dusters and kitchen-wares,
By those with humps of battered water-cans,
By bottle-shaped she-asses who halt and stumble,
By those tricked out in little pantaloons
To cover their wet, blue galls where flies assemble
In whirling swarms, making a drunken hum.
Dear God, let it be with these donkeys that I come,
And let it be that angels lead us in peace
To leafy streams where cherries tremble in air,
Sleek as the laughing flesh of girls; and there

In that haven of souls let it be that, leaning above
Your divine waters, I shall resemble these donkeys,
Whose humble and sweet poverty will appear
Clear in the clearness of your eternal love.

The Pelican

PELLICANUS is the word
  For a certain breed of bird
Who truly is a crane;
  Egypt is his domain.
There are two kinds thereof;
  Near to the Nile they live;
One of them dwells in the flood,
  The fishes are his food;
The other lives in the isles
  On lizards, crocodiles,
Serpents, and stinking creatures,
  And beasts of evil nature.
In Greek his title was
  Onocrotalos,
Which is *longum rostrum,* said
  In the Latin tongue instead,
Or *long-beak* in our own.
  Of this bird it is known
That when he comes to his young,
  They being grown and strong,
And does them kindly things,
  And covers them with his wings,
The little birds begin
  Fiercely to peck at him;
They tear at him and try
  To blind their father's eye.
He falls upon them then
  And slays them with great pain,
Then goes away for a spell,
  Leaving them where they fell.
On the third day he returns,
  And thereupon he mourns,
Feeling so strong a woe
  To see the small birds so

That he strikes his breast with his beak
    Until the blood shall leak.
And when the coursing blood
    Spatters his lifeless brood,
Such virtue does it have
    That once again they live.

KNOW that this pelican
    Signifies Mary's Son;
The little birds are men
    Restored to life again
From death, by that dear blood
    Shed for us by our God.
Now learn one meaning more,
    Revealed by holy lore:
Know why the small birds try
    To peck their father's eye,
Who turns on them in wrath
    And puts them all to death.
Men who deny the light
    Would blind God's blazing sight,
But on such people all
    His punishment will fall.
This is the meaning I find;
    Now bear it well in mind.

APOLOGY

A word sticks in the wind's throat;
A wind-launch drifts in the swells of rye;
Sometimes, in broad silence,
The hanging apples distil their darkness.

You, in a green dress, calling, and with brown hair,
Who come by the field-path now, whose name I say
Softly, forgive me love if also I call you
Wind's word, apple-heart, haven of grasses.

PAUL VALÉRY

HELEN

It is I, O Azure, come from the caves below
To hear the waves clamber the loudening shores,
And see those barks again in the dawn's glow
Borne out of darkness, swept by golden oars.

My solitary hands call back the lords
Whose salty beards beguiled my finger-tips;
I wept. They sang the prowess of their swords
And what great bays fled sternward of their ships.

I hear the martial trumpets and the deep-
Sea conches cry a cadence to the sweeps;
The oarsmen's chantey holds the storm in sway;

And high on the hero prows the Gods I see,
Their antique smiles insulted by the spray,
Reaching their carved, indulgent arms to me.

BEASTS

Beasts in their major freedom
Slumber in peace tonight. The gull on his ledge
Dreams in the guts of himself the moon-plucked waves below,
And the sunfish leans on a stone, slept
By the lyric water,

In which the spotless feet
Of deer make dulcet splashes, and to which
The ripped mouse, safe in the owl's talon, cries
Concordance. Here there is no such harm
And no such darkness

As the selfsame moon observes
Where, warped in window-glass, it sponsors now
The werewolf's painful change. Turning his head away
On the sweaty bolster, he tries to remember
The mood of manhood,

But lies at last, as always,
Letting it happen, the fierce fur soft to his face,
Hearing with sharper ears the wind's exciting minors,
The leaves' panic, and the degradation
Of the heavy streams.

Meantime, at high windows
Far from thicket and pad-fall, suitors of excellence
Sigh and turn from their work to construe again the painful
Beauty of heaven, the lucid moon
And the risen hunter,

Making such dreams for men
As told will break their hearts as always, bringing
Monsters into the city, crows on the public statues,
Navies fed to the fish in the dark
Unbridled waters.

EXEUNT

Piecemeal the summer dies;
At the field's edge a daisy lives alone;
A last shawl of burning lies
    On a gray field-stone.

All cries are thin and terse;
The field has droned the summer's final mass;
A cricket like a dwindled hearse
    Crawls from the dry grass.

MARGINALIA

Things concentrate at the edges; the pond-surface
Is bourne to fish and man and it is spread
In textile scum and damask light, on which
The lily-pads are set; and there are also
    Inlaid ruddy twigs, becalmed pine-leaves,
    Air-baubles, and the chain mail of froth.

Descending into sleep (as when the night-lift
Falls past a brilliant floor), we glimpse a sublime
Décor and hear, perhaps, a complete music,
But this evades us, as in the night meadows
    The crickets' million roundsong dies away
    From all advances, rising in every distance.

Our riches are centrifugal; men compose
Daily, unwittingly, their final dreams,
And those are our own voices whose remote
Consummate chorus rides on the whirlpool's rim,
    Past which we flog our sails, toward which we drift,
    Plying our trades, in hopes of a good drowning.

BOY AT THE WINDOW

Seeing the snowman standing all alone
In dusk and cold is more than he can bear.
The small boy weeps to hear the wind prepare
A night of gnashings and enormous moan.
His tearful sight can hardly reach to where
The pale-faced figure with bitumen eyes
Returns him such a god-forsaken stare
As outcast Adam gave to Paradise.

The man of snow is, nonetheless, content,
Having no wish to go inside and die.
Still, he is moved to see the youngster cry.
Though frozen water is his element,
He melts enough to drop from one soft eye
A trickle of the purest rain, a tear
For the child at the bright pane surrounded by
Such warmth, such light, such love, and so much fear.

SPEECH FOR THE REPEAL OF
THE MCCARRAN ACT

As Wulfstan said on another occasion,
The strong net bellies in the wind and the spider rides it out;
But history, that sure blunderer,
Ruins the unkempt web, however silver.

I am not speaking of rose windows
Shattered by bomb-shock; the leads touselled; the glass-grains
    broadcast;
If the rose be living at all
A gay gravel shall be pollen of churches.

Nor do I mean railway networks.
Torn-up tracks are no great trouble. As Wulfstan said,
It is oathbreach, faithbreach, lovebreach
Bring the invaders into the estuaries.

Shall one man drive before him ten
Unstrung from sea to sea? Let thought be free. I speak
Of the spirit's weaving, the neural
Web, the self-true mind, the trusty reflex.

ALL THESE BIRDS

Agreed that all these birds,
Hawk or heavenly lark or heard-of nightingale,
    Perform upon the kitestrings of our sight
    In a false distance, that the day and night
    Are full of wingèd words
                    gone rather stale,
       That nothing is so worn
       As Philomel's bosom-thorn,

       That it is, in fact, the male
Nightingale which sings, and that all these creatures wear
    Invisible armor such as Hébert beheld
    His water-ousel through, as, wrapped or shelled
    In a clear bellying veil
                 or bubble of air,
       It bucked the flood to feed
       At the stream-bottom. Agreed

       That the sky is a vast claire
In which the gull, despite appearances, is not
    Less claustral than the oyster in its beak
    And dives like nothing human; that we seek
    Vainly to know the heron
                 (but can plot
       What angle of the light
       Provokes its northern flight.)

       Let them be polyglot
And wordless then, those boughs that spoke with Solomon
    In Hebrew canticles, and made him wise;
    And let a clear and bitter wind arise
    To storm into the hotbeds
                 of the sun,
       And there, beyond a doubt,
       Batter the Phoenix out.

Let us, with glass or gun,
Watch (from our clever blinds) the monsters of the sky
Dwindle to habit, habitat, and song,
And tell the imagination it is wrong
Till, lest it be undone,
                                    it spin a lie
So fresh, so pure, so rare
As to possess the air.

Why should it be more shy
Than chimney-nesting storks, or sparrows on a wall?
Oh, let it climb wherever it can cling
Like some great trumpet-vine, a natural thing
To which all birds that fly
                                    come natural.
Come, stranger, sister, dove:
Put on the reins of love.

A BAROQUE WALL-FOUNTAIN
IN THE VILLA SCIARRA

for Dore and Adja

Under the bronze crown
Too big for the head of the stone cherub whose feet
    A serpent has begun to eat,
Sweet water brims a cockle and braids down

    Past spattered mosses, breaks
On the tipped edge of a second shell, and fills
    The massive third below. It spills
In threads then from the scalloped rim, and makes

    A scrim or summery tent
For a faun-ménage and their familiar goose.
    Happy in all that ragged, loose
Collapse of water, its effortless descent

    And flatteries of spray,
The stocky god upholds the shell with ease,
    Watching, about his shaggy knees,
The goatish innocence of his babes at play;

    His fauness all the while
Leans forward, slightly, into a clambering mesh
    Of water-lights, her sparkling flesh
In a saecular ecstasy, her blinded smile

    Bent on the sand floor
Of the trefoil pool, where ripple-shadows come
    And go in swift reticulum,
More addling to the eye than wine, and more

Interminable to thought
Than pleasure's calculus. Yet since this all
    Is pleasure, flash, and waterfall,
Must it not be too simple? Are we not

    More intricately expressed
In the plain fountains that Maderna set
    Before St. Peter's—the main jet
Struggling aloft until it seems at rest

    In the act of rising, until
The very wish of water is reversed,
    That heaviness borne up to burst
In a clear, high, cavorting head, to fill

    With blaze, and then in gauze
Delays, in a gnatlike shimmering, in a fine
    Illumined version of itself, decline,
And patter on the stones its own applause?

    If that is what men are
Or should be, if those water-saints display
    The pattern of our areté,
What of these showered fauns in their bizarre,

    Spangled, and plunging house?
They are at rest in fulness of desire
    For what is given, they do not tire
Of the smart of the sun, the pleasant water-douse

    And riddled pool below,
Reproving our disgust and our ennui
    With humble insatiety.
Francis, perhaps, who lay in sister snow

Before the wealthy gate
Freezing and praising, might have seen in this
    No trifle, but a shade of bliss—
That land of tolerable flowers, that state

    As near and far as grass
Where eyes become the sunlight, and the hand
    Is worthy of water: the dreamt land
Toward which all hungers leap, all pleasures pass.

AN EVENT

As if a cast of grain leapt back to the hand,
A landscapeful of small black birds, intent
On the far south, convene at some command
At once in the middle of the air, at once are gone
With headlong and unanimous consent
From the pale trees and fields they settled on.

What is an individual thing? They roll
Like a drunken fingerprint across the sky!
Or so I give their image to my soul
Until, as if refusing to be caught
In any singular vision of my eye
Or in the nets and cages of my thought,

They tower up, shatter, and madden space
With their divergences, are each alone
Swallowed from sight, and leave me in this place
Shaping these images to make them stay:
Meanwhile, in some formation of their own,
They fly me still, and steal my thoughts away.

Delighted with myself and with the birds,
I set them down and give them leave to be.
It is by words and the defeat of words,
Down sudden vistas of the vain attempt,
That for a flying moment one may see
By what cross-purposes the world is dreamt.

A CHRONIC CONDITION

Berkeley did not foresee such misty weather,
Nor centuries of light
Intend so dim a day. Swaddled together
In separateness, the trees
Persist or not beyond the gray-white
Palings of the air. Gone
Are whatever wings bothered the lighted leaves
When leaves there were. Are all
The sparrows fallen? I can hardly hear
My memory of those bees
Which only lately mesmerized the lawn.
Now, something, blaze! A fear
Swaddles me now that Hylas' tree will fall
Where no eye lights and grieves,
Will fall to nothing and without a sound.

I sway and lean above the vanished ground.

THE MILL

The spoiling daylight inched along the bar-top,
Orange and cloudy, slowly igniting lint,
And then that glow was gone, and still your voice,
Serene with failure and with the ease of dying,
Rose from the shades that more and more became you.
Turning among its images, your mind
Produced the names of streets, the exact look
Of lilacs, 1903, in Cincinnati,
—Random, as if your testament were made,
The round sums all bestowed, and now you spent
Your pocket change, so as to be rid of it.
Or was it that you half-hoped to surprise
Your dead life's sound and sovereign anecdote?
What I remember best is the wrecked mill
You stumbled on in Tennessee; or was it
Somewhere down in Brazil? It slips my mind
Already. But there it was in a still valley
Far from the towns. No road or path came near it.
If there had been a clearing now it was gone,
And all you found amidst the choke of green
Was three walls standing, hurdled by great vines
And thatched by height on height of hushing leaves.
But still the mill-wheel turned! its crazy buckets
Creaking and lumbering out of the clogged race
And sounding, as you said, as if you'd found
Time all alone and talking to himself
In his eternal rattle.
                            How should I guess
Where they are gone to, now that you are gone,
Those fading streets and those most fragile lilacs,
Those fragmentary views, those times of day?
All that I can be sure of is the mill-wheel.
It turns and turns in my mind, over and over.

For the New Railway Station in Rome

Those who said God is praised
By hurt pillars, who loved to see our brazen lust
    Lie down in rubble, and our vaunting arches
        Conduce to dust;

Those who with short shadows
Poked through the stubbled forum pondering on decline,
    And would not take the sun standing at noon
        For a good sign;

Those pilgrims of defeat
Who brought their injured wills as to a soldiers' home;
    Dig them all up now, tell them there's something new
        To see in Rome.

See, from the travertine
Face of the office block, the roof of the booking-hall
    Sails out into the air beside the ruined
        Servian Wall,

Echoing in its light
And cantilevered swoop of reinforced concrete
    The broken profile of these stones, defeating
        That defeat

And straying the strummed mind,
By such a sudden chord as raised the town of Troy,
    To where the least shard of the world sings out
        In stubborn joy,

"What city is eternal
But that which prints itself within the groping head
    Out of the blue unbroken reveries
        Of the building dead?

"What is our praise or pride
But to imagine excellence, and try to make it?
What does it say over the door of Heaven
But *homo fecit*?"

Ceremony and Other Poems

1950

———•———

To F.O.M.

THEN

Then when the ample season
Warmed us, waned and went,
We gave to the leaves no graves,
To the robin gone no name,
Nor thought at the birds' return
Of their sourceless dim descent,
And we read no loss in the leaf,
But a freshness ever the same.

The leaf first learned of years
One not forgotten fall;
Of lineage now, and loss
These latter singers tell,
Of a year when birds now still
Were all one choiring call
Till the unreturning leaves
Imperishably fell.

CONJURATION

Backtrack of sea, the baywater goes; flats
Bubble in sunlight, running with herringbone streams;
Sea-lettuce lies in oily mats
On sand mislaid; stranded
Are slug, stone, and shell, as dreams
Drain into morning shine, and the cheat is ended.

Oh, it was blue, the too amenable sea.
We heard of pearls in the dark and wished to dive.
But here in this snail-shell see, see
The crab-legs waggle; where,
If altered now, and yet alive,
Did softness get these bitter claws to wear?

As curtains from a fatal window blown
The sea's receding fingers terribly tell
Of strangest things together grown;
All join, and in the furl
Of waters, blind in muck and shell,
Pursue their slow paludal games. O pearl,

Rise, rise and brighten, wear clear air, and in
Your natal cloudiness receive the sun;
Hang among single stars, and twin
My double deep; O tides,
Return a truer blue, make one
The sky's blue speech, and what the sea confides.

"A World without Objects Is a Sensible Emptiness"

The tall camels of the spirit
Steer for their deserts, passing the last groves loud
With the sawmill shrill of the locust, to the whole honey of the arid
Sun. They are slow, proud,

And move with a stilted stride
To the land of sheer horizon, hunting Traherne's
Sensible emptiness, there where the brain's lantern-slide
Revels in vast returns.

O connoisseurs of thirst,
Beasts of my soul who long to learn to drink
Of pure mirage, those prosperous islands are accurst
That shimmer on the brink

Of absence; auras, lustres,
And all shinings need to be shaped and borne.
Think of those painted saints, capped by the early masters
With bright, jauntily worn

Aureate plates, or even
Merry-go-round rings. Turn, O turn
From the fine sleights of the sand, from the long empty oven
Where flames in flamings burn

Back to the trees arrayed
In bursts of glare, to the halo-dialing run
Of the country creeks, and the hills' bracken tiaras made
Gold in the sunken sun,

Wisely watch for the sight
Of the supernova burgeoning over the barn,
Lampshine blurred in the steam of beasts, the spirit's right
Oasis, light incarnate.

THE PARDON

My dog lay dead five days without a grave
In the thick of summer, hid in a clump of pine
And a jungle of grass and honeysuckle-vine.
I who had loved him while he kept alive

Went only close enough to where he was
To sniff the heavy honeysuckle-smell
Twined with another odor heavier still
And hear the flies' intolerable buzz.

Well, I was ten and very much afraid.
In my kind world the dead were out of range
And I could not forgive the sad or strange
In beast or man. My father took the spade

And buried him. Last night I saw the grass
Slowly divide (it was the same scene
But now it glowed a fierce and mortal green)
And saw the dog emerging. I confess

I felt afraid again, but still he came
In the carnal sun, clothed in a hymn of flies,
And death was breeding in his lively eyes.
I started in to cry and call his name,

Asking forgiveness of his tongueless head.
...I dreamt the past was never past redeeming:
But whether this was false or honest dreaming
I beg death's pardon now. And mourn the dead.

PART OF A LETTER

Easy as cove-water rustles its pebbles and shells
In the slosh, spread, seethe, and the backsliding
Wallop and tuck of the wave, and just that cheerful,
    Tables and earth were riding

Back and forth in the minting shades of the trees.
There were whiffs of anise, a clear clinking
Of coins and glasses, a still crepitant sound
    Of the earth in the garden drinking

The late rain. Rousing again, the wind
Was swashing the shadows in relay races
Of sun-spangles over the hands and clothes
    And the drinkers' dazzled faces,

So that when somebody spoke, and asked the question
Comment s'appelle cet arbre-là?
A girl had gold on her tongue, and gave this answer:
    Ça, c'est l'acacia.

La Rose des Vents

POET: The hardest headlands
       Gravel down,
       The seas abrade
       What coasts we know,
       And all our maps
       In azure drown,
       Forewarning us
       To rise and go.

       And we shall dwell
       On the rose of the winds,
       Which is the isle
       Of every sea,
       Surviving there
       The tinted lands
       Which could not last
       Our constancy.

LADY: That roving wave
       Where Venus rose
       Glints in the floods
       Of farthest thought;
       What beauty there
       In image goes
       Dissolves in other
       And is not.

       There are some shores
       Still left to find
       Whose broken rocks
       Will last the hour;
       Forsake those roses
       Of the mind
       And tend the true,
       The mortal flower.

EPISTEMOLOGY

I

Kick at the rock, Sam Johnson, break your bones:
But cloudy, cloudy is the stuff of stones.

II

We milk the cow of the world, and as we do
We whisper in her ear, "You are not true."

Castles and Distances

From blackhearted water colder
Than Cain's blood, and aching with ice, from a gunmetal bay
 No one would dream of drowning in, rises
 The walrus: head hunched from the oxen shoulder,
  The serious face made for surprises
  Looks with a thick dismay

At the camera lens which takes
Him in, and takes him back to cities, to volleys of laughter
 In film palaces, just as another, brought
 By Jonas Poole to England for the sakes
  Of James First and his court, was thought
  Most strange, and died soon after.

So strangeness gently steels
Us, and curiosity kills, keeping us cool to go
 Sail with the hunters unseen to the walrus rock
 And stand behind their slaughter: which of us feels
  The harpoon's hurt, and the huge shock
  When the blood jumps to flow?

Oh, it is hunters alone
Regret the beastly pain, it is they who love the foe
 That quarries out their force, and every arrow
 Is feathered soft with wishes to atone;
  Even the surest sword in sorrow
  Bleeds for its spoiling blow.

Sometimes, as one can see
Carved at Amboise in a high relief, on the lintel stone
 Of the castle chapel, hunters have strangely come
 To a mild close of the chase, bending the knee
  Instead of the bow, struck sweetly dumb
  To see from the brow bone

Of the hounded stag a cross
Grown, and the eyes clear with grace. Perfectly still
　　Are the cruising dogs as well, their paws aground
　　In a white hush of lichen. Beds of moss
　　　　Spread, and the clearing wreathes around
　　　　The dear suspense of will.

　　But looking higher now
To the chapel steeple, see among points and spines of the updrawn
　　Vanishing godbound stone, ringing its sped
　　Thrust as a target tatters, a round row
　　　　Of real antlers taken from dead
　　　　Deer. The hunt goes on.

II

　　They built well who made
Those palaces of hunting lords, the grounds planned
　　As ruled reaches, always with a view
　　Down tapered aisles of trees at last to fade
　　　　In the world's mass. The lords so knew
　　　　Of land beyond their land.

　　If, at Versailles, outdrawn
By the stairs or the still canals, by the gradual shrink of an urn
　　Or the thousand fountains, a king gave back his gaze
　　To the ample balanced windows vantaged on
　　　　The clearness near, and the far haze,
　　　　He learned he must return.

　　Seen from a palace stair
The wilderness was distance; difference; it spoke
　　In the strong king's mind for mercy, while to the weak,
　　To the weary of choice, it told of havens where
　　　　The Sabbath stayed, and all were meek,
　　　　And justice known a joke.

Some cast their crowns away
And went to live in the distance. There there was nothing seemed
Remotely strange to them, their innocence
Shone in the special features of the prey
They would not harm. The dread expense
Of golden times they dreamed

Was that their kingdoms fell
The deeper into tyranny, the more they stole
Through Ardens out to Eden isles apart,
Seeking a shore, or shelter of some spell
Where harmlessly the hidden heart
Might hold creation whole.

When to his solitude
The world became as island mists, then Prospero,
Pardoning all, and pardoned, yet aware
The full forgiveness cannot come, renewed
His reign, bidding the boat prepare
From mysteries to go

Toward masteries less sheer,
And Duke again, did rights and mercies, risking wrong,
Found advocates and enemies, and found
His bounded empire good, where he could hear
Below his walls the baying hound
And the loud hunting-song.

MUSEUM PIECE

The good gray guardians of art
Patrol the halls on spongy shoes,
Impartially protective, though
Perhaps suspicious of Toulouse.

Here dozes one against the wall,
Disposed upon a funeral chair.
A Degas dancer pirouettes
Upon the parting of his hair.

See how she spins! The grace is there,
But strain as well is plain to see.
Degas loved the two together:
Beauty joined to energy.

Edgar Degas purchased once
A fine El Greco, which he kept
Against the wall beside his bed
To hang his pants on while he slept.

ODE TO PLEASURE

from the French of La Fontaine

PLEASURE, whom had we lacked from earliest hour,
To live or die had come to seem as one,
Of all creatures the sole magnet-stone,
How surely are we drawn by thy great power!
    Here, thou art mover of all things.
    For thee, for thy soft blandishings
    We fly to troubles and to harms.
    No captain is, nor man-at-arms,
Nor subject, minister, nor royalty,
    Who does not singly aim at thee.
We other nurslings, did not our labors bear
The fruits of fame, delicious to the ear,
And were this sound not pleasurably heard,
    Then should we rhyme a single word?
That which the world calls glory, and acclaims,
Which served as guerdon in the Olympic games,
Truly is none but thee, O divine Pleasure.
And shall the joys of sense not fill thy measure?
    For whom are Flora's gifts outlaid,
    The Sunset and Aurora made,
    Pomona and her tasty fare,
    Bacchus, soul of banquets rare,
    Waters, and forest-lands, and leas,
    The nourishers of reveries?
Wherefore so many arts, thy children all?
Why all these Chlorises, whose charms enthrall,
    Unless to make thy commerce thrive?
My meaning's innocent: whatever limit
    Rigor may for desire contrive,
    Nevertheless there's pleasure in it.
O Pleasure, Pleasure, in the former age
    Mistress of Hellas' gayest sage,
Pray scorn me not, come thence and stop with me;
    Idle thou shalt never be:

For games I love, and love, and every art,
Country, and town, and all; there's nought my mood
    May not convert to sovereign good,
Even to the gloom of melancholy heart.
Then come; and wouldst thou know, O sweetest Pleasure,
What measure of these goods must me befall?
Enough to fill a hundred years of leisure;
    For thirty were no good at all.

In the Elegy Season

Haze, char, and the weather of All Souls':
A giant absence mopes upon the trees:
Leaves cast in casual potpourris
Whisper their scents from pits and cellar-holes.

Or brewed in gulleys, steeped in wells, they spend
In chilly steam their last aromas, yield
From shallow hells a revenance of field
And orchard air. And now the envious mind

Which could not hold the summer in my head
While bounded by that blazing circumstance
Parades these barrens in a golden trance,
Remembering the wealthy season dead,

And by an autumn inspiration makes
A summer all its own. Green boughs arise
Through all the boundless backward of the eyes,
And the soul bathes in warm conceptual lakes.

Less proud than this, my body leans an ear
Past cold and colder weather after wings'
Soft commotion, the sudden race of springs,
The goddess' tread heard on the dayward stair,

Longs for the brush of the freighted air, for smells
Of grass and cordial lilac, for the sight
Of green leaves building into the light
And azure water hoisting out of wells.

Marché aux Oiseaux

Hundreds of birds are singing in the square.
Their minor voices fountaining in air
And constant as a fountain, lightly loud,
Do not drown out the burden of the crowd.

Far from his gold Sudan, the travailleur
Lends to the noise an intermittent chirr
Which to his hearers seems more joy than rage.
He batters softly at his wooden cage.

Here are the silver-bill, the orange-cheek,
The perroquet, the dainty coral-beak
Stacked in their cages; and around them move
The buyers in their termless hunt for love.

Here are the old, the ill, the imperial child;
The lonely people, desperate and mild;
The ugly; past these faces one can read
The tyranny of one outrageous need.

We love the small, said Burke. And if the small
Be not yet small enough, why then by Hell
We'll cramp it till it knows but how to feed,
And we'll provide the water and the seed.

JUGGLER

A ball will bounce, but less and less. It's not
A light-hearted thing, resents its own resilience.
Falling is what it loves, and the earth falls
So in our hearts from brilliance,
Settles and is forgot.
It takes a sky-blue juggler with five red balls

To shake our gravity up. Whee, in the air
The balls roll round, wheel on his wheeling hands,
Learning the ways of lightness, alter to spheres
Grazing his finger ends,
Cling to their courses there,
Swinging a small heaven about his ears.

But a heaven is easier made of nothing at all
Than the earth regained, and still and sole within
The spin of worlds, with a gesture sure and noble
He reels that heaven in,
Landing it ball by ball,
And trades it all for a broom, a plate, a table.

Oh, on his toe the table is turning, the broom's
Balancing up on his nose, and the plate whirls
On the tip of the broom! Damn, what a show, we cry:
The boys stamp, and the girls
Shriek, and the drum booms
And all comes down, and he bows and says good-bye.

If the juggler is tired now, if the broom stands
In the dust again, if the table starts to drop
Through the daily dark again, and though the plate
Lies flat on the table top,
For him we batter our hands
Who has won for once over the world's weight.

PARABLE

I read how Quixote in his random ride
Came to a crossing once, and lest he lose
The purity of chance, would not decide

Whither to fare, but wished his horse to choose.
For glory lay wherever he might turn.
His head was light with pride, his horse's shoes

Were heavy, and he headed for the barn.

THE GOOD SERVANT

Its piers less black for sunny smiles above,
My roadstead hand takes all the world for sea,
Or lifts to wingèd love
Its limed and leafless tree,
Or creeps into a glove
To greet mine enemy.

Angers the noble face
Would suffer unexpressed
This lackey in his place
Must serve to manifest,
Be mailed without as any carapace,
But soft within, where self to self is pressed.

Nights, when the head to other glory sets,
The hand turns turtle, lying like a lake
Where men with broken nets
Seek, for their master's sake,
All that that lord forgets
Because he would not wake.

Above the ceded plains
Visored volition stands
And sees my lands in chains
And ponders the commands
Of what were not impossible campaigns
If I would take my life into my hands.

PITY

The following day was overcast, each street
A slow canal to float him to the place
Where he'd let fall the dear and staring face,
A funnel toward the thin reproachful tweet.

All day the starved canary called him back
In newsboy's whistle, crying of a tire,
Squeak of a squeegee, sirens finding fire,
Until the nightfall packed his head in black,

And he went back and climbed the stairs again,
Stepping across her body, freed the bird,
Which left its cage and out the window whirred
As a bad thought out of a cracked brain.

THE SIRENS

I never knew the road
From which the whole earth didn't call away,
With wild birds rounding the hill crowns,
Haling out of the heart an old dismay,
Or the shore somewhere pounding its slow code,
Or low-lighted towns
Seeming to tell me, stay.

Lands I have never seen
And shall not see, loves I will not forget,
All I have missed, or slighted, or foregone
Call to me now. And weaken me. And yet
I would not walk a road without a scene.
I listen going on,
The richer for regret.

Year's End

Now winter downs the dying of the year,
And night is all a settlement of snow;
From the soft street the rooms of houses show
A gathered light, a shapen atmosphere,
Like frozen-over lakes whose ice is thin
And still allows some stirring down within.

I've known the wind by water banks to shake
The late leaves down, which frozen where they fell
And held in ice as dancers in a spell
Fluttered all winter long into a lake;
Graved on the dark in gestures of descent,
They seemed their own most perfect monument.

There was perfection in the death of ferns
Which laid their fragile cheeks against the stone
A million years. Great mammoths overthrown
Composedly have made their long sojourns,
Like palaces of patience, in the gray
And changeless lands of ice. And at Pompeii

The little dog lay curled and did not rise
But slept the deeper as the ashes rose
And found the people incomplete, and froze
The random hands, the loose unready eyes
Of men expecting yet another sun
To do the shapely thing they had not done.

These sudden ends of time must give us pause.
We fray into the future, rarely wrought
Save in the tapestries of afterthought.
More time, more time. Barrages of applause
Come muffled from a buried radio.
The New-year bells are wrangling with the snow.

THE PURITANS

Sidling upon the river, the white boat
Has volleyed with its cannon all the morning,
Shaken the shore towns like a Judgment warning,
Telling the palsied water its demand
That the crime come to the top again, and float,
That the sunk murder rise to the light and land.

Blam. In the noon's perfected brilliance burn
Brief blooms of flame, which soil away in smoke;
And down below, where slowed concussion broke
The umber stroll of waters, water-dust
Dreamily powders up, and serves to turn
The river surface to a cloudy rust.

Down from his bridge the river captain cries
To fire again. They make the cannon sound;
But none of them would wish the murder found,
Nor wish in other manner to atone
Than booming at their midnight crime, which lies
Rotting the river, weighted with a stone.

GRASSE: THE OLIVE TREES

for Marcelle and Ferdinand Springer

Here luxury's the common lot. The light
Lies on the rain-pocked rocks like yellow wool
And around the rocks the soil is rusty bright
From too much wealth of water, so that the grass
Mashes under the foot, and all is full
Of heat and juice and a heavy jammed excess.

Whatever moves moves with the slow complete
Gestures of statuary. Flower smells
Are set in the golden day, and shelled in heat,
Pine and columnar cypress stand. The palm
Sinks its combs in the sky. The whole South swells
To a soft rigor, a rich and crowded calm.

Only the olive contradicts. My eye,
Traveling slopes of rust and green, arrests
And rests from plenitude where olives lie
Like clouds of doubt against the earth's array.
Their faint disheveled foliage divests
The sunlight of its color and its sway.

Not that the olive spurns the sun; its leaves
Scatter and point to every part of the sky,
Like famished fingers waving. Brilliance weaves
And sombers down among them, and among
The anxious silver branches, down to the dry
And twisted trunk, by rooted hunger wrung.

Even when seen from near, the olive shows
A hue of far away. Perhaps for this
The dove brought olive back, a tree which grows
Unearthly pale, which ever dims and dries,
And whose great thirst, exceeding all excess,
Teaches the South it is not paradise.

THE AVOWAL

from the French of Villiers de l'Isle Adam

I have lost the wood, the heath,
Fresh Aprils long gone by....
Give me your lips: their breath
Shall be the forest's sigh.

I have lost the sullen Sea,
Its glooms, its echoed caves;
Speak only: it shall be
The murmur of the waves.

By royal grief oppressed
I dream of a vanished light....
Hold me: in that pale breast
Shall be the calm of night.

THE GIFTS

from the French of Villiers de l'Isle Adam

If you speak to me, some night,
Of my sick heart's secret bale,
To ease you I'll recite
An ancient ballad-tale.

Or if you speak of pain
And hopes long fallen due,
I shall but gather then
The dew-filled rose for you.

If, like the flower which grows
In the exile soil of graves,
You beg to share my woes...
I'll bring you a gift of doves.

FIVE WOMEN BATHING IN MOONLIGHT

When night believes itself alone
It is most natural, conceals
No artifice. The open moon
With webs in sky and water wields

The slightest wave. This vision yields
To a cool accord of semblance, land
Leasing each wave the palest peals
Of bright apparent notes of sand.

The bathers whitely come and stand.
Water diffuses them, their hair
Like seaweed slurs the shoulders, and
Their voices in the moonstrung air

Go plucked of words. Now wading where
The moon's misprision salves them in-
To silver, they are unaware
How lost they are when they begin

To mix with water, making then
Gestures of blithe obedience,
As five Danilovas within
The soft compulsions of their dance.

The Terrace

De la vaporisation et de la centralisation du Moi. *Tout est là.*
—Baudelaire

We ate with steeps of sky about our shoulders,
High up a mountainside,
On a terrace like a raft roving
Seas of view.

The tablecloth was green, and blurred away
Toward verdure far and wide,
And all the country came to be
Our table too.

We drank in tilted glasses of rosé
From tinted peaks of snow,
Tasting the frothy mist, and freshest
Fathoms of air.

Women were washing linens in a stream
Deep down below,
The sound of water over their knuckles
A sauce rare.

Imminent towns whose weatherbeaten walls
Looked like the finest cheese
Bowled us enormous melons from their
Tolling towers.

Mixt into all the day we heard the spice
Of many tangy bees
Eddying through the miles-deep
Salad of flowers.

When we were done we had our hunger still;
We dipped our cups in light;

We caught the fine-spun shade of clouds
In spoon and plate;

Drunk with imagined breathing, we inhaled
The dancing smell of height;
We fished for the bark of a dog, the squeak
Of a pasture gate.

But for all our benedictions and our gay
Readily said graces,
The evening stole our provender and
Left us there,

And darkness filled the specious space, and fell
Betwixt our silent faces,
Pressing against our eyes its absent
Fathomless stare.

Out in the dark we felt the real mountains
Hulking in proper might,
And we felt the edge of the black wind's
Regardless cleave,

And we knew we had eaten not the manna of heaven
But our own reflected light,
And we were the only part of the night that we
Couldn't believe.

A Problem from Milton

In Eden palm and open-handed pine
Displayed to God and man their flat perfection.
Carefully coiled, the regulation vine
Submitted to our general sire's inspection.

And yet the streams in mazy error went;
Powdery flowers a potent odor gave;
The trees, on second thoughts, were lushly blent
And swashed forever like a piling wave.

The builded comber like a hurdling horse
Achieves the rocks. With wild informal roar
The spray upholds its freedom and its force,
But leaves the limpet and the whelk ashore.

In spirals of the whelk's eternal shell
The mind of Swedenborg to heaven flew,
But found it such a mathematic hell
That Emerson was damned if it would do.

Poor Adam, deviled by your energy,
What power egged you on to feed your brains?
Envy the gorgeous gallops of the sea,
Whose horses never know their lunar reins.

A Glance from the Bridge

Letting the eye descend from reeking stack
And black façade to where the river goes,
You see the freeze has started in to crack
(As if the city squeezed it in a vice),
And here and there the limbering water shows,
And gulls colonial on the sullied ice.

Some rise and braid their glidings, white and spare,
Or sweep the hemmed-in river up and down,
Making a litheness in the barriered air,
And through the town the freshening water swirls
As if an ancient whore undid her gown
And showed a body almost like a girl's.

CLEARNESS

There is a poignancy in all things clear,
In the stare of the deer, in the ring of a hammer in the morning.
Seeing a bucket of perfectly lucid water
We fall to imagining prodigious honesties.

And feel so when the snow for all its softness
Tumbles in adamant forms, turning and turning
Its perfect faces, littering on our sight
The heirs and types of timeless dynasties.

In pine-woods once that huge precision of leaves
Amazed my eyes and closed them down a dream.
I lost to mind the usual southern river,
Mud, mist, the plushy sound of the oar,

And pondering north through lifted veils of gulls,
Through sharpening calls, and blue clearings of steam,
I came and anchored by a fabulous town
Immaculate, high, and never found before.

This was the town of my mind's exacted vision
Where truths fell from the bells like a jackpot of dimes,
And the people's voices, carrying over the water,
Sang in the ear as clear and sweet as birds.

But this was Thulë of the mind's worst vanity;
Nor could I tell the burden of those clear chimes;
And the fog fell, and the stainless voices faded;
I had not understood their lovely words.

*

The asterisk
Says look below, as a star
We prize for its being far
And longing ask
For some release,
Joins to a dog or a bear,
A dipper, a tipping chair.
They give us peace
These downward looks
Of stars, the way they note
The birth of gods, and dote
On seaward brooks.
Some of the sea's
Stars are alive, I've seen
Them figure the white-green
Ocean frieze;
And I've known
The sea so rich and black
It gave the starlight back
Brighter. It shone
As if the high
Vault were its glass, and thus
It is. It's up to us
To gloss the sky.

GAMES TWO

:

From barren coldness birds
Go squadroned South;
So from the hollow mouth
The way of words
Is East. When written down
As here, they file
In broken bands awhile,
But never noun
Found what it named; for lame,
Lost, though they burn
For the East, all words must turn
Back where they came
From, back to their old
Capital. Still,
As pilgrims on a hill
Fallen, behold
With failing eyes from far
The desired city,
Silence will take pity
On words. There are
Pauses where words must wait,
Spaces in speech
Which stop and calm it, and each
Is like a gate:

Past which creation lies
In morning sun,
Where word with world is one
And nothing dies.

BEOWULF

The land was overmuch like scenery,
The flowers attentive, the grass too garrulous green;
In the lake like a dropped kerchief could be seen
The lark's reflection after the lark was gone;
The Roman road lay paved too shiningly
For a road so many men had traveled on.

Also the people were strange, were strangely warm.
The king recalled the father of his guest,
The queen brought mead in a studded cup, the rest
Were kind, but in all was a vagueness and a strain,
Because they lived in a land of daily harm.
And they said the same things again and again.

It was a childish country; and a child,
Grown monstrous, so besieged them in the night
That all their daytimes were a dream of fright
That it would come and own them to the bone.
The hero, to his battle reconciled,
Promised to meet that monster all alone.

So then the people wandered to their sleep
And left him standing in the echoed hall.
They heard the rafters rattle fit to fall,
The child departing with a broken groan,
And found their champion in a rest so deep
His head lay harder sealed than any stone.

The land was overmuch like scenery,
The lake gave up the lark, but now its song
Fell to no ear, the flowers too were wrong,
The day was fresh and pale and swiftly old,
The night put out no smiles upon the sea;
And the people were strange, the people strangely cold.

They gave him horse and harness, helmet and mail,
A jeweled shield, an ancient battle-sword,
Such gifts as are the hero's hard reward
And bid him do again what he has done.
These things he stowed beneath his parting sail,
And wept that he could share them with no son.

He died in his own country a kinless king,
A name heavy with deeds, and mourned as one
Will mourn for the frozen year when it is done.
They buried him next the sea on a thrust of land:
Twelve men rode round his barrow all in a ring,
Singing of him what they could understand.

STILL, CITIZEN SPARROW

Still, citizen sparrow, this vulture which you call
Unnatural, let him but lumber again to air
Over the rotten office, let him bear
The carrion ballast up, and at the tall

Tip of the sky lie cruising. Then you'll see
That no more beautiful bird is in heaven's height,
No wider more placid wings, no watchfuller flight;
He shoulders nature there, the frightfully free,

The naked-headed one. Pardon him, you
Who dart in the orchard aisles, for it is he
Devours death, mocks mutability,
Has heart to make an end, keeps nature new.

Thinking of Noah, childheart, try to forget
How for so many bedlam hours his saw
Soured the song of birds with its wheezy gnaw,
And the slam of his hammer all the day beset

The people's ears. Forget that he could bear
To see the towns like coral under the keel,
And the fields so dismal deep. Try rather to feel
How high and weary it was, on the waters where

He rocked his only world, and everyone's.
Forgive the hero, you who would have died
Gladly with all you knew; he rode that tide
To Ararat; all men are Noah's sons.

WELLFLEET: THE HOUSE

Roof overwoven by a soft tussle of leaves,
The walls awave with sumac shadow, lilac
Lofts and falls in the yard, and the house believes
It's guarded, garlanded in a former while.

Here one cannot intrude, the stillness being
Lichenlike grown, a coating of quietudes;
The portraits dream themselves, they are done with seeing;
Rocker and teacart balance in iron moods.

Yet for the transient here is no offense,
Because at certain hours a wallowed light
Floods at the seaside windows, vague, intense,
And lays on all within a mending blight,

Making the kitchen silver blindly gleam,
The yellow floorboards swim, the dazzled clock
Boom with a buoy sound, the chambers seem
Alluvial as that champed and glittering rock

The sea strokes up to fashion dune and beach
In strew by strew, and year by hundred years.
One is at home here. Nowhere in ocean's reach
Can time have any foreignness or fears.

THE DEATH OF A TOAD

A toad the power mower caught,
Chewed and clipped of a leg, with a hobbling hop has got
    To the garden verge, and sanctuaried him
    Under the cineraria leaves, in the shade
        Of the ashen heartshaped leaves, in a dim,
            Low, and a final glade.

The rare original heartsblood goes,
Spends on the earthen hide, in the folds and wizenings, flows
    In the gutters of the banked and staring eyes. He lies
    As still as if he would return to stone,
        And soundlessly attending, dies
            Toward some deep monotone,

Toward misted and ebullient seas
And cooling shores, toward lost Amphibia's emperies.
    Day dwindles, drowning, and at length is gone
    In the wide and antique eyes, which still appear
        To watch, across the castrate lawn,
            The haggard daylight steer.

DRIFTWOOD

In greenwoods once these relics must have known
A rapt, gradual growing,
That are cast here like slag of the old
Engine of grief;

Must have affirmed in annual increase
Their close selves, knowing
Their own nature only, and that
Bringing to leaf.

Say, for the seven cities or a war
Their solitude was taken,
They into masts shaven, or milled into
Oar and plank;

Afterward sailing long and to lost ends,
By groundless water shaken,
Well they availed their vessels till they
Smashed or sank.

Then on the great generality of waters
Floated their singleness,
And in all that deep subsumption they were
Never dissolved;

But shaped and flowingly fretted by the waves'
Ever surpassing stress,
With the gnarled swerve and tangle of tides
Finely involved.

Brought in the end where breakers dump and slew
On the glass verge of the land,
Silver they rang to the stones when the sea
Flung them and turned.

Curious crowns and scepters they look to me
Here on the gold sand,
Warped, wry, but having the beauty of
Excellence earned.

In a time of continual dry abdications
And of damp complicities,
They are fit to be taken for signs, these emblems
Royally sane,

Which have ridden to homeless wreck, and long revolved
In the lathe of all the seas,
But have saved in spite of it all their dense
Ingenerate grain.

A COURTYARD THAW

The sun was strong enough today
To climb the wall and loose the courtyard trees
(For two short hours, anyway)
From hardship of the January freeze.

Their icy cerements decayed
To silken moistures, which began to slip
In glints and spangles down, and made
On every twig a bauble at the tip.

No blossom, leaf or basking fruit
Showed ever such pure passion for the sun
As these cold drops that knew no root
Yet filled with light and swelled and one by one

(Or showered by a wingbeat, sown
From windbent branches in arpeggios)
Let go and took their shinings down
And brought their brittle season to a close.

O false gemmation! Flashy fall!
The eye is pleased when nature stoops to art,
Staging within a courtyard wall
Such twinkling scenes. But puzzling to the heart,

This spring was neither fierce nor gay;
This summer autumn fell without a tear:
No tinkling music-box can play
The slow, deep-grounded masses of the year.

LAMENT

Nashe's old queens who bartered young and fair
Their light tiaras for such ponderous stones:
Of them I'd think, how sunlit still their hair,
And fine as airship frames their balanced bones.

It is, I say, a most material loss.
Kept spirit is corporate; doubly the thought of you,
As air fills air, or waves together toss,
Out of my wishes and your being grew.

Water and air: such unclenched stuff can last,
But rarest things are visible and firm;
Grace falls the fastest from our failing past,
And I lament for grace's early term,

For casual dances that your body knows,
Whose spirit only sense can understand,
For times when spirit, doomed and single, flows
Into the speeches of your eye and hand.

FLUMEN TENEBRARUM

This night's colossal quiet, in heaven crowned
Immovable, at earth is slippered swift
With shore grasses' wind-ushering sound,
With the river's folding drift,

With our own vanishing voices as we go
By the stream side, watching our shadows dangled
Down the bank to the flood, trailed in the flow
And all in stars entangled.

There is the hunter hulking up the night
Who waded once the wildest of our seas,
With foiled eyes marking the still flight
Of the faint Pleiades.

And here are we, who hold each other now
So nearly, that our welded shadows seem,
There where they fall away, a ghostly prow
Steering into the stream.

As if to kiss were someway to embark;
As if to love were partly to be spent,
And send of us a hostage to the dark.
If so, I am content,

And would not have my lively longing freeze,
Nor your delays, in figures of the sky,
Since none outlasts the stream, and even these
Must come to life and die.

The hunter shall be tumbled in this tide,
Worse stricken than by Dian's steepest arrow,
And all his fire shall gutter out beside
This old embarcadero;

Those nymphs, so long preserved, at last be lost,
Be borne again along this blackening race,
And with their lover swept away, and tossed
In scintillant embrace.

FROM THE LOOKOUT ROCK

Oh wind I hear you faltering,
In long cessation dying down,
Failing the osprey's pillowed wing,
Franchising all the peaceful graves,
The lifted waters letting fall
And all the flags of every town,
Because your slackened voices crawl
To bass finales in their caves.

The parching stones along the shore
Hastily sip the listless waves,
In doubt the sea will pour them more
When lull has loitered into calm;
A tenantry of jays in swarm
Issues rebellious from the leaves
And rising makes a patch of storm
Above the quiet of their elm.

Good-bye the roving of the land:
The tumbling weed of all the West
Engraves its shadow on the sand.
Haphazard stand the weather-vanes,
Unrocked the cradles of the vales,
The ropes are loose of every mast,
Appalled are all the sagging sails
And overhushed the ocean-lanes.

The fishers for Atlantis see
A stillness on the ocean grow
Deeper than that of history.
Venturers to the pole turn round
And watch the southward cities fill
With space as barren as their snow.
The cities' voices fall and still
To hear the wide retreat of sound.

I from this rock espy a gull
Riding the raveled last of air
Who folds his wings, and tips to fall
Beside the pillar of the sun.
(The drumhead bay is like a lake,
A great and waiting skyward stare.)
The shoreline gives a timbrel shake:
Our last Icarian moment, done.

Gods of the wind, return again,
For this was not the peace we prayed;
Intone again your burdened strain,
And weave the world to harmony,
Voyage the seed along the breeze,
Reviving all your former trade,
Restore the lilting of the trees
And massive dances of the sea.

To an American Poet Just Dead

In the *Boston Sunday Herald* just three lines
Of no-point type for you who used to sing
The praises of imaginary wines,
And died, or so I'm told, of the real thing.

Also gone, but a lot less forgotten,
Are an eminent cut-rate druggist, a lover of Giving,
A lender, and various brokers: gone from this rotten
Taxable world to a higher standard of living.

It is out in the comfy suburbs I read you are dead,
And the soupy summer is settling, full of the yawns
Of Sunday fathers loitering late in bed,
And the ssshh of sprays on all the little lawns.

Will the sprays weep wide for you their chaplet tears?
For you will the deep-freeze units melt and mourn?
For you will Studebakers shred their gears
And sound from each garage a muted horn?

They won't. In summer sunk and stupefied
The suburbs deepen in their sleep of death.
And though they sleep the sounder since you died
It's just as well that now you save your breath.

GIACOMETTI

Rock insults us, hard and so boldly browed
Its scorn needs not to focus, and with fists
Which still unstirring strike:
Collected it resists
Until its buried glare begets a like
Anger in us, and finds our hardness. Proud,

Then, and armed, and with a patient rage
We carve cliff, shear stone to blocks,
And down to the image of man
Batter and shape the rock's
Fierce composure, closing its veins within
That outside man, itself its captive cage.

So we can baffle rock, and in our will
Can clothe and keep it. But if our will, though locked
In stone it clutches, change,
Then are we much worse mocked
Than cliffs can do: then we ourselves are strange
To what we were, which lowers on us still.

High in the air those habitants of stone
Look heavenward, lean to a thought, or stride
Toward some concluded war,
While we on every side,
Random as shells the sea drops down ashore,
Are walking, walking, many and alone.

What stony shape could hold us now, what hard
Bent can we bulk in air, where shall our feet
Come to a common stand?
Follow along this street
(Where rock recovers carven eye and hand),
Open the gate, and cross the narrow yard

And look where Giacometti in a room
Dim as a cave of the sea, has built the man
We are, and made him walk:
Towering like a thin
Coral, out of a reef of plaster chalk,
This is the single form we can assume.

We are this man unspeakably alone
Yet stripped of the singular utterly, shaved and scraped
Of all but being there,
Whose fullness is escaped
Like a burst balloon's: no nakedness so bare
As flesh gone in inquiring of the bone.

He is pruned of every gesture, saving only
The habit of coming and going. Every pace
Shuffles a million feet.
The faces in this face
Are all forgotten faces of the street
Gathered to one anonymous and lonely.

No prince and no Leviathan, he is made
Of infinite farewells. Oh never more
Diminished, nonetheless
Embodied here, we are
This starless walker, one who cannot guess
His will, his keel his nose's bony blade.

And volumes hover round like future shades
This least of man, in whom we join and take
A pilgrim's step behind,
And in whose guise we make
Our grim departures now, walking to find
What railleries of rock, what palisades?

HE WAS

a brown old man with a green thumb:
I can remember the screak on stones of his hoe,
The chug, choke, and high madrigal wheeze
Of the spray-cart bumping below
The sputtery leaves of the apple trees,
But he was all but dumb

Who filled some quarter of the day with sound
All of my childhood long. For all I heard
Of all his labors, I can now recall
Never a single word
Until he went in the dead of fall
To the drowsy underground,

Having planted a young orchard with so great care
In that last year that none was lost, and May
Aroused them all, the leaves saying the land's
Praise for the livening clay,
And the found voice of his buried hands
Rose in the sparrowy air.

A Simile for Her Smile

Your smiling, or the hope, the thought of it,
Makes in my mind such pause and abrupt ease
As when the highway bridgegates fall,
Balking the hasty traffic, which must sit
On each side massed and staring, while
Deliberately the drawbridge starts to rise:

Then horns are hushed, the oilsmoke rarefies,
Above the idling motors one can tell
The packet's smooth approach, the slip,
Slip of the silken river past the sides,
The ringing of clear bells, the dip
And slow cascading of the paddle wheel.

CEREMONY

A striped blouse in a clearing by Bazille
Is, you may say, a patroness of boughs
Too queenly kind toward nature to be kin.
But ceremony never did conceal,
Save to the silly eye, which all allows,
How much we are the woods we wander in.

Let her be some Sabrina fresh from stream,
Lucent as shallows slowed by wading sun,
Bedded on fern, the flowers' cynosure:
Then nymph and wood must nod and strive to dream
That she is airy earth, the trees, undone,
Must ape her languor natural and pure.

Ho-hum. I am for wit and wakefulness,
And love this feigning lady by Bazille.
What's lightly hid is deepest understood,
And when with social smile and formal dress
She teaches leaves to curtsey and quadrille,
I think there are most tigers in the wood.

The Beautiful Changes
and Other Poems

1947

For Charlee

CICADAS

You know those windless summer evenings, swollen to stasis
by too-substantial melodies, rich as a
running-down record, ground round
to full quiet. Even the leaves
have thick tongues.

And if the first crickets quicken then,
other inhabitants, at window or door
or rising from table, feel in the lungs
a slim false-freshness, by this
trick of the ear.

Chanters of miracles took for a simple sign
the Latin cicada, because of his long waiting
and sweet change in daylight, and his singing
all his life, pinched on the ash leaf,
heedless of ants.

Others made morals; all were puzzled and joyed
by this gratuitous song. Such a plain thing
morals could not surround, nor listening:
not "chirr" nor "cri-cri." There is no straight
way of approaching it.

This thin uncomprehended song it is
springs healing questions into binding air.
Fabre, by firing all the municipal cannon
under a piping tree, found out
cicadas cannot hear.

WATER WALKER

There was an infidel who
Walked past all churches crying,
Yet wouldn't have changed his tears,
Not for the smoothest-worn pew;
You've seen
Caddis flies walking on spring-surface, water walkers who breathe
Air and know water, with weakly wings
Drying to pelt and sheen;

There is something they mean

By breaking from water and flying
Lightly some hours in air,
Then to the water-top dropping,
Floating their heirs and dying:
It's like
Paulsaul the Jew born in Tarshish, who when at bay on the steps
With Hebrew intrigued those Jewsotted Jews
Crowding to stone and strike;

Always alike and unlike,

Walking the point where air
Mists into water, and knowing
Both, with his breath, to be real,
Roman he went everywhere:
I've been
Down in Virginia at night, I remember an evening door
A table lamp lit; light stretched on the lawn,
Seeming to ask me in;

I thought if I should begin

To enter entirely that door,
Saying, "I am a son of this house,

My birth and my love are here,"
I might never come forth any more:
Air mists
Into water, past odors of halls and the fade of familial voices,
Stair creaks, piano tones falling on rugs,
Wallpaper palimpsests:

Armored the larva rests

Dreaming the streambottom tides,
Writhing at times to respire, and
Sealing to him flat stones,
He closely abides, abides:
One night
I sat till dawn on a porch, rocked in a cane-bottom chair,
In Geneseo, in Illinois,
Rocking from light to light;

Silent and out of sight

I saw the houses sleep
And the autos beside them sleeping,
The neat plots, the like trustful houses,
Minute, armoreal, deep;
Wind went
Tamely and samely as puppies, tousling the Japanese maples,
Lawnsprays and tricycles waited for sun,
Shyly things said what they meant:

An old man stitching a tent

Could have been Saul in Tharsos,
Loved and revered; instead
He carried Jew visions to Greeks
For adoration or curses;
For he
Troubled them; whether they called him "babbler" or hailed him
        "Mercurios"

(Scarcely restrained from killing him oxen),
His wasn't light company:

Still pearled with water, to be

Ravished by air makes him grow
Stranger to both, and discover
Heaven and hell in the poise
Betwixt "inhabit" and "know";
I hold
Here in my head Maine's bit speech, lithe laughter of Mobile blacks,
Opinions of salesmen, ripe tones of priests,
Plaints of the bought and sold:

Can I rest and observe unfold

The imminent singletax state,
The Negro rebellion, the rise
Of the nudist cult, the return
Of the Habsburgs, watch and wait
And praise
The spirit and not the cause, and neatly precipitate
What is not doctrine, what is not bound
To enclosured ground; what stays?

Lives that the caddis fly lays

Twixt air and water, must lie
Long under water—how Saul
Cursed once the market babblers,
Righteous could watch them die!
Who learns
How hid the trick is of justice, cannot go home, nor can leave,
But the dilemma, cherished, tyrannical,
While he despairs and burns

Da capo da capo returns.

TYWATER

Death of Sir Nihil, book the *nth*,
Upon the charred and clotted sward,
Lacking the lily of our Lord,
Alases of the hyacinth.

Could flicker from behind his ear
A whistling silver throwing knife
And with a holler punch the life
Out of a swallow in the air.

Behind the lariat's butterfly
Shuttled his white and gritted grin,
And cuts of sky would roll within
The noose-hole, when he spun it high.

The violent, neat and practiced skill
Was all he loved and all he learned;
When he was hit, his body turned
To clumsy dirt before it fell.

And what to say of him, God knows.
Such violence. And such repose.

MINED COUNTRY

They have gone into the gray hills quilled with birches,
Drag now their cannon up the chill mountains;
But it's going to be long before
Their war's gone for good.

I tell you it hits at childhood more than churches
Full up with sky or buried town fountains,
Rooms laid open or anything
Cut stone or cut wood,

Seeing the boys come swinging slow over the grass
(Like playing pendulum) their silver plates,
Stepping with care and listening
Hard for hid metal's cry.

It's rightly-called-chaste Belphoebe some would miss,
Some, calendar colts at Kentucky gates;
But the remotest would guess that
Some scheme's gone awry.

Danger is sunk in the pastures, the woods are sly,
Ingenuity's covered with flowers!
We thought woods were wise but never
Implicated, never involved.

Cows in mid-munch go splattered over the sky;
Roses like brush-whores smile from bowers;
Shepherds must learn a new language; this
Isn't going to be quickly solved.

Sunshiny field grass, the woods floor, are so mixed up
With earliest trusts, you have to pick back
Far past all you have learned, to go
Disinherit the dumb child,

Tell him to trust things alike and never to stop
Emptying things, but not let them lack
Love in some manner restored; to be
Sure the whole world's wild.

POTATO

for André du Bouchet

An underground grower, blind and a common brown;
Got a misshapen look, it's nudged where it could;
Simple as soil yet crowded as earth with all.

Cut open raw, it looses a cool clean stench,
Mineral acid seeping from pores of prest meal;
It is like breaching a strangely refreshing tomb:

Therein the taste of first stones, the hands of dead slaves,
Waters men drank in the earliest frightful woods,
Flint chips, and peat, and the cinders of buried camps.

Scrubbed under faucet water the planet skin
Polishes yellow, but tears to the plain insides;
Parching, the white's blue-hearted like hungry hands.

All of the cold dark kitchens, and war-frozen gray
Evening at window; I remember so many
Peeling potatoes quietly into chipt pails.

"It was potatoes saved us, they kept us alive."
Then they had something to say akin to praise
For the mean earth-apples, too common to cherish or steal.

Times being hard, the Sikh and the Senegalese,
Hobo and Okie, the body of Jesus the Jew,
Vestigial virtues, are eaten; we shall survive.

What has not lost its savor shall hold us up,
And we are praising what saves us, what fills the need.
(Soon there'll be packets again, with Algerian fruits.)

Oh, it will not bear polish, the ancient potato,
Needn't be nourished by Caesars, will blow anywhere
Hidden by nature, counted-on, stubborn and blind.

You may have noticed the bush that it pushes to air,
Comical-delicate, sometimes with second-rate flowers
Awkward and milky and beautiful only to hunger.

First Snow in Alsace

The snow came down last night like moths
Burned on the moon; it fell till dawn,
Covered the town with simple cloths.

Absolute snow lies rumpled on
What shellbursts scattered and deranged,
Entangled railings, crevassed lawn.

As if it did not know they'd changed,
Snow smoothly clasps the roofs of homes
Fear-gutted, trustless and estranged.

The ration stacks are milky domes;
Across the ammunition pile
The snow has climbed in sparkling combs.

You think: beyond the town a mile
Or two, this snowfall fills the eyes
Of soldiers dead a little while.

Persons and persons in disguise,
Walking the new air white and fine,
Trade glances quick with shared surprise.

At children's windows, heaped, benign,
As always, winter shines the most,
And frost makes marvelous designs.

The night guard coming from his post,
Ten first-snows back in thought, walks slow
And warms him with a boyish boast:

He was the first to see the snow.

On the Eyes of an SS Officer

I think of Amundsen, enormously bit
By arch-dark flurries on the ice plateaus,
An amorist of violent virgin snows
At the cold end of the world's spit.

Or a Bombay saint asquat in the market place,
Eyes gone from staring the sun over the sky,
Who still dead-reckons that acetylene eye,
An eclipsed mind in a blind face.

But this one's iced or ashen eyes devise,
Foul purities, in flesh their wilderness,
Their fire; I ask my makeshift God of this
My opulent bric-a-brac earth to damn his eyes.

Place Pigalle

Now homing tradesmen scatter through the streets
Toward suppers, thinking on improved conditions,
While evening, with a million simple fissions,
Takes up its warehouse watches, storefront beats,
By nursery windows its assigned positions.

Now at the corners of the Place Pigalle
Bright bars explode against the dark's embraces;
The soldiers come, the boys with ancient faces,
Seeking their ancient friends, who stroll and loll
Amid the glares and glass: electric graces.

The puppies are asleep, and snore the hounds;
But here wry hares, the soldier and the whore,
Mark off their refuge with a gaudy door,
Brazen at bay, and boldly out of bounds:
The puppies dream, the hounds superbly snore.

Ionized innocence: this pair reclines,
She on the table, he in a tilting chair,
With Arden ease; her eyes as pale as air
Travel his priestgoat face; his hand's thick tines
Touch the gold whorls of her Corinthian hair.

"Girl, if I love thee not, then let me die;
Do I not scorn to change my state with kings?
Your muchtouched flesh, incalculable, which wrings
Me so, now shall I gently seize in my
Desperate soldier's hands which kill all things."

VIOLET AND JASPER

Outside, the heirs of purity pick by,
Pecked by petite damnations, sweatless still
Along the burning marle of Cambridge; here
The light that spanks the windows takes a spill
Over the lint-bright curtain to the floor
Or frays through glasses, curly as a vine.

Broad Violet, her lettuce head all full
Of bawdry and novenas, yanks the tap,
Carries a beer to Jasper where he dreams
Of lucky numbers, falls upon his lap:
Her wandy fingers paddling on his dome
Trouble the face of El Dorado's pool.

Rumors of plenty flutter these around,
Riot, mercy and treasure haven here,
In silly brains monastically kept,
In Cambridge, where I homing saw appear
In a pharmacy window-globe ruddily rapt
Suddenly streaming with blood this turnip town.

THE PEACE OF CITIES

Terrible streets, the manichee hell of twilight
Glides like a giant bass between your windows,

Dark deploying in minnows into your alleys
Stirs and hushes the reefs of scudding trash.

Withinwalls voices, past the ports and locks,
Murmur below the shifting of crockery

I know not what; the barriered day expires
In scattered sounds of dread inconsequence.

Ah, this is no andante, there will come
No primavera, there was a louder and deeper

Peace in those other cities, when silver fear
Drove the people to fields, and there they heard

The Luftwaffe waft what let the sunshine in
And blew the bolt from everybody's door.

THE GIAOUR AND THE PACHA

(EUGÈNE DELACROIX, 1856)

The Pacha sank at last upon his knee
And saw his ancient enemy reared high
In mica dust upon a horse of bronze,
The sun carousing in his either eye,

Which of a sudden clouds, and lifts away
The light of day, of triumph; and the scene
Takes tenderly the one already dead
With secret hands of strong and bitter green.

As secretly, the cloak becomes aware
Of floating, mane and tail turn tracery;
Imbedded in the air, the Giaour stares
And feels the pistol fall beside his knee.

"Is this my anger, and is this the end
Of gaudy sword and jeweled harness, joy
In strength and heat and swiftness, that I must
Now bend, and with a slaughtering shot destroy

The counterpoise of all my force and pride?
These falling hills and piteous mists; O sky,
Come loose the light of fury on this height,
That I may end the chase, and ask not why."

Up, Jack

Prince Harry turns from Percy's pouring sides,
Full of the kind of death that honor makes
By pouring all the man into an act;
So simplified by battle, he mistakes

A hibernating Jack for dead Sir John.
"Poor pumpkin, I am cold since you are done,
For if you proved but yellow pulp within,
You were this nature's kindest earthly sun."

Exit the Prince; now Jack will rise again,
No larger now, nor spun of stuff more fine,
And only to his feet, and yet a god
To our short summer days and the world's wine.

Up, Jack! For Percy sinks in darker red,
And those who walk away are dying men.
Great Falstaff (*rising*) clears his thirsty throat,
And I'm content, and Hal is hale again.

IN A BIRD SANCTUARY

Because they could not give it too much ground
they closely planted it with fir and shrub.
A plan of pathways, voted by the Club,
contrived to lead the respiter around
a mildly wandring wood, still at no cost
to get him lost.

Now over dear Miss Drury's favored trees
they flutter (birds) and either stop or not,
as if they were unconscious that the spot
is planned for them, and meant to buy release
for one restrained department of the soul,
to "make men whole."

It's hard to tell the purpose of a bird;
for relevance it does not seem to try.
No line can trace no flute exemplify
its traveling; it darts without the word.
Who wills devoutly to absorb, contain,
birds give him pain.

Commissioners of Public Parks have won
a partial wisdom, know that birds exist.
And seeing people equally insist
on birds and statues, they go hire a man
to swab sans rancor dung from granite stare
and marble hair.

BIRDS HAVE BEEN SEEN IN TOWERS AND ON ISLES;
ALSO ON PRIVY TOPS, IN FANEUIL HALL;
BIRDS HAVE SOME OF THEM NOT BEEN SEEN AT ALL;
BIRDS, IF THEY CARE TO, WALK ALONG IN FILE.
BIRDS DO NOT FEEL ESPECIALLY GOOD IN FLIGHT:
LET'S TREAT THEM RIGHT!

The liberty of any things becomes
the liberty of all. It also brings
their abolition into anythings.
In order's name let's not turn down our thumbs
on routine visions; we must figure out
what all's about.

JUNE LIGHT

Your voice, with clear location of June days,
Called me—outside the window. You were there,
Light yet composed, as in the just soft stare
Of uncontested summer all things raise
Plainly their seeming into seamless air.

Then your love looked as simple and entire
As that picked pear you tossed me, and your face
As legible as pearskin's fleck and trace,
Which promise always wine, by mottled fire
More fatal fleshed than ever human grace.

And your gay gift—Oh when I saw it fall
Into my hands, through all that naïve light,
It seemed as blessed with truth and new delight
As must have been the first great gift of all.

A Song

As at the bottom of a seething well
A phosphorus girl is singing,
Up whispering galleries trellised notes
Climb and cling.

It is a summer-song an old man wrote
Out of the winter's wringing,
He hunched in a cold room, back to frost's
Sledge and sting.

Desperate, gentle, every phrase declines
As fruit to groundward weighs,
As all things seek their shadows, yearn,
Yearn and fall.

She may be singing Iowa afternoons,
Lightshifting corn ballets,
Scattering stutter of windmills, each throat's
Very clear call;

Nevertheless, the balconies are in tune
And all but a single child
Are hushed in sweet relinquishing, in
Praise of time.

But the white child is puzzled, cannot hear,
To loss not reconciled
Has heartroom still for sorrows, needs no
Song or rhyme.

The Walgh-Vogel

More pleasurable to look than feed upon,
Hence unconserved in dodo-runs, the round,
Unfeathered, melancholy, more than fifty pound
Dodo is gone,

Who when incarnate wore two token wings
And dined on rocks, to mock at mockeries.
Empowered now by absence, blessed with tireless ease,
It soars and sings

Elated in our skies, wherever seen.
Absolute retractility allows
Its wings be wavy wide as heaven; silence endows
Its hoots serene

With airy spleenlessness all may unhear.
Alive the dodo strove for lack of point,
Extinct won superfluity, and can disjoint
To joy our fear.

Dive, dodo, on the earth you left forlorn,
Sit vastly on the branches of our trees,
And chant us grandly all improbabilities.

THE MELONGÈNE

Our uncrowned kings have no such regal rind
As this; their purple stain
Is in the mind.
God was more kind to this wronged kingly fruit
And pedigreed it plain.
It makes no suit

For rule in gardens, yields to the Brussels sprout,
Knows that the scornful sun
Will seek it out
In exile, and so blazon in its sheen
That it may cow and stun
Turnip and bean.

Natural pomp! Excessive Nightshades' Prince!
Polished potato, you wear
An Egyptian rinse
Of Belladonna's hues, a crown that's green,
And do not have the care
Of storing spleen,

Because your purple presence is reproof!
Before God gave him rue
And raised the roof,
Unoriginal Adam, bloat with cant
Celestial, christened you
The *Egg*-plant.

Objects

Meridians are a net
Which catches nothing; that sea-scampering bird
The gull, though shores lapse every side from sight, can yet
Sense him to land, but Hanno had not heard

Hesperidean song,
Had he not gone by watchful periploi:
Chalk rocks, and isles like beasts, and mountain stains along
The water-hem, calmed him at last near-by

The clear high hidden chant
Blown from the spellbound coast, where under drifts
Of sunlight, under plated leaves, they guard the plant
By praising it. Among the wedding gifts

Of Herë, were a set
Of golden McIntoshes, from the Greek
Imagination. Guard and gild what's common, and forget
Uses and prices and names; have objects speak.

There's classic and there's quaint,
And then there is that devout intransitive eye
Of Pieter de Hooch: see feinting from his plot of paint
The trench of light on boards, the much-mended dry

Courtyard wall of brick,
And sun submerged in beer, and streaming in glasses,
The weave of a sleeve, the careful and undulant tile. A quick
Change of the eye and all this calmly passes

Into a day, into magic.
For is there any end to true textures, to true
Integuments; do they ever desist from tacit, tragic
Fading away? Oh maculate, cracked, askew,

Gay-pocked and potsherd world
I voyage, where in every tangible tree
I see afloat among the leaves, all calm and curled,
The Cheshire smile which sets me fearfully free.

A Dutch Courtyard

What wholly blameless fun
To stand and look at pictures. Ah, they are
Immune to us. This courtyard may appear
To be consumed with sun,

Most mortally to burn,
Yet it is quite beyond the reach of eyes
Or thoughts, this place and moment oxidize;
This girl will never turn,

Cry what you dare, but smiles
Tirelessly toward the seated cavalier,
Who will not proffer you his pot of beer;
And your most lavish wiles

Can never turn this chair
To proper uses, nor your guile evict
These tenants. What surprising strict
Propriety! In despair,

Consumed with greedy ire,
Old Andrew Mellon glowered at this Dutch
Courtyard, until it bothered him so much
He bought the thing entire.

My Father Paints the Summer

A smoky rain riddles the ocean plains,
Rings on the beaches' stones, stomps in the swales,
Batters the panes
Of the shore hotel, and the hoped-for summer chills and fails.
The summer people sigh,
"Is this July?"

They talk by the lobby fire but no one hears
For the thrum of the rain. In the dim and sounding halls,
Din at the ears,
Dark at the eyes well in the head, and the ping-pong balls
Scatter their hollow knocks
Like crazy clocks.

But up in his room by artificial light
My father paints the summer, and his brush
Tricks into sight
The prosperous sleep, the girdling stir and clear steep hush
Of a summer never seen,
A granted green.

Summer, luxuriant Sahara, the orchard spray
Gales in the Eden trees, the knight again
Can cast away
His burning mail, Rome is at Anzio: but the rain
For the ping-pong's optative bop
Will never stop.

Caught Summer is always an imagined time.
Time gave it, yes, but time out of any mind.
There must be prime
In the heart to beget that season, to reach past rain and find
Riding the palest days
Its perfect blaze.

FOLK TUNE

When Bunyan swung his whopping axe
The forests strummed as one loud lute,
The timber crashed beside his foot
And sprung up stretching in his tracks.

He had an ox, but his was blue.
The flower in his buttonhole
Was brighter than a parasol.
He's gone. Tom Swift has vanished too,

Who worked at none but wit's expense,
Putting dirigibles together
Out in the yard, in the quiet weather,
Whistling behind Tom Sawyer's fence.

Now when the darkness in my street
Nibbles the last and crusty crumbs
Of sound, and all the city numbs
And goes to sleep upon its feet,

I listen hard to hear its dreams:
John Henry is our nightmare friend,
Whose shoulders roll without an end,
Whose veins pump, pump and burst their seams,

Whose sledge is smashing at the rock
And makes the sickly city toss
And half awake in sighs of loss
Until the screaming of the clock.

John Henry's hammer and his will
Are here and ringing out our wrong,
I hear him driving all night long
To beat the leisured snarling drill.

SUN AND AIR

The air staggers under the sun, and heat-morasses
Flutter the birds down; wind barely climbs the hills,
Saws thin and splinters among the roots of the grasses;

All stir sickens, and falls into barn shadows, spills
Into hot hay and heat-hammered road dust, makes no sound,
Waiting the sun's siege out to collect its wills.

As a hound stretched sleeping will all on a sudden bound,
Air will arise all sinews, crack-crying, tear tether,
Plow sheets of powder high, heave sky from milling ground.

So sun and air, when these two goods war together,
Who else can tune day's face to a softest laugh,
Being sweet beat the world with a most wild weather,

Trample with light or blow all heaven blind with chaff.

Two Songs in a Stanza of Beddoes'

I

That lavished sunlight, where
And lilac-mottled air,
And where the fair-skinned winds
    That touched the plum
To fall? All gone; my mind's
Lost all the summer, binds
    No beauty home.

How have such seas of sun
Cast me so dry here? Run,
Mindseye, and find a field
    Embered with clover...
Why is my heart congealed,
All the sweet season sealed
    Off from her lover?

Stretch, tamarack, and strain;
Lash, poplar; and complain,
Guttering grasses; seek
    For summer, swallow:
And mind, fill full of creak
And hustling scraps, be bleak
    And howling-hollow.

Come tender winter, weep
This raving earth to sleep;
Your deadly tears disguise
    In lightest white.
Frost these forgetful eyes
From day's sheet-metal skies
    And viselike night.

II

Through tossing views, the gull,
All-balancing, can scull
The sky, and strew its calls
    On the breeze;
Its shivered shadow crawls
The leisured azure brawls
    Of the seas.

When then from day's blue brink
Its rapt reflections sink,
A bird made dark, unclear,
    To sea-deep flies,
And monstrous flutters there,
And slow and loud with fear
    Cries and cries.

THE WATERS

From powdery Palmyre, the tireless wind,
Braided by waves but cradling to this shore,
Where folding water leaves Atlantis' gold,
Dust of Aurelian's sack, scrawls in the sand,
Streams in the salty grass the stainless cries
Of fighters at the gate, and strews the trees
With, milled by many days, Zenobia's priceless robe.

And the sunned wind, as the wave thins and slips
Into rock-pools, lies in the shallows of the spine.
And the mind, as the sand rises and rolls in the pull
Of the wave, yields to the cry of the buried child.

The sea so sings us back to histories
On every perilous beach. At Juan-les-Pins
Or Coney Isle, the bathers lie between
Yellow and blue, in the handling of such soft air
That real caresses leaf the thinnest hair,
Maternal murmurs sweep the dozing head;
And gazing out from underneath our arms,
We see the spring of feet from brightened sand;
We feel the world lie warm beneath the hand;
And hear the cry of voices over water,
Or horns of vessels very far from land.

And only the dull are safe, only the dead
Are safe from the limitless swell and the bitter seethe,
The sea's lumbering sigh that says it carries
So many stars and suns, and yet will wreathe
A rock with webs of foam and maidenhair.
Von Aschenbach, when he perceived the fair
Aureate child before the endless sea,
Shingled his painted face in agony.

For the damnedest lovers of water dread the waves:
The inland painters in whose canvases
We read some vaporized and fierce devotion
To "the smiling of women, and the motion
Of great waters"; the pauper poet who dreamed
Of sunken rivers, yet who scorned to seek
Their sources in the caves of the world; and he
Who mad and weak, became a sailingcraft
On heilignüchterne lakes of memory.

SUPERIORITIES

Malachy stamped the diving decks
And shouted to the frigging wind
"Frig on!," and hove an empty quart
Into the stomach of a wave.

Phipps at the bucking rail was still
And keenly modest as a star,
Attentive to each blast and surge,
And so becalmed the storm in him.

How far superior to those
Huddled below with wives and buddies
Comforting, caring, sharing pills,
Prayers and other proper studies.

A SIMPLIFICATION

Those great rough ranters, Branns
And catarrhal Colonels, who hurled
Terrible taunts at the vault, ripped down Jesus' banns
And widowed the world

With Inquisitorial thunder, dammed-
Up Biblical damnations, were
The last with tongues to topple heaven; they hammed
Jahweh away and here

We are. The decorous god
Simply withdrew. If you hear
A good round rhetoric anywhere tip me the nod.
I'd like to hear

Bryan lying and quoting sic
Transit nux vomica. These foetal-
Voiced people lack eloquence to blow a sick
Maggot off a dead beetle.

A Dubious Night

A bell diphthonging in an atmosphere
Of shying night air summons some to prayer
Down in the town, two deep lone miles from here,

Yet wallows faint or sudden everywhere,
In every ear, as if the twist wind wrung
Some ten years' tangled echoes from the air.

What kyries it says are mauled among
The queer elisions of the mist and murk,
Of lights and shapes; the senses were unstrung,

Except that one star's synecdochic smirk
Burns steadily to me, that nothing's odd
And firm as ever is the masterwork.

I weary of the confidence of God.

L'Etoile

(DEGAS, 1876)

A rushing music, seizing on her dance,
Now lifts it from her, blind into the light;
And blind the dancer, tiptoe on the boards
Reaches a moment toward her dance's flight.

Even as she aspires in loudening shine
The music pales and sweetens, sinks away;
And past her arabesque in shadow show
The fixt feet of the maître de ballet.

So she will turn and walk through metal halls
To where some ancient woman will unmesh
Her small strict shape, and yawns will turn her face
Into a little wilderness of flesh.

SUNLIGHT IS IMAGINATION

Each shift you make in the sunlight somewhere
Cleaves you away into dark. Now
You are clarion hair, bright brow,
Lightcaped shoulder and armside here, and there
Gone into meadow shadow. Where
Are my eyes to run?
Shall I say you are fair
In the sun,
Or mermaid you in the grass waving away?

Shall I say
    The whole green day builds hither to lift
    This flare of your hair?, I wielding such sight
    As did Juan Ponce, climbing to light
    On a morning of the Feast of the Resurrection. Aloft
    On the ocean shelf he saw the soft
    Signals of trees
    And gulls, and the sift
    Of the sea's
    Long landward airs offering trails to him.

And dim
    Each flower of Florida, but all
    Was shining; parrots prophesied;
    Vines ciphered; to each waterside
    Paths pitched in hopes to the fair and noble well
    Of sweetest savor and reflaire
    Whose ghostly taste
    And cleanse repair
    All waste,
    And where was ageless power from the first.

Yet thirst
    Makes deserts, barrens to a sign
    Deckled and delicate arbors, bleeds
    The rose, parches the prodigal seeds

That spring toward time in air, and breaks the spine
Of the rock. No; I shall resign
That power, and crave
Kindly to pine
And to save
The sprout and the ponderation of the land.

My hand
    Can touch but mysteries, and each
    Of a special shadow. I shall spare
    The larch its shattering ghost, the pear
    Its dark awaiter too, for shades beseech
    Originals: they running reach
    On windy days
    To touch, to teach
    What stays
    Is changed, and shadows die into dying things.

Now swings
    The sky to noon, and mysteries run
    To cover; let our love not blight
    The various world, but trust the flight
    Of love that falls again where it begun.
    All creatures are, and are undone.
    Then lose them, lose
    With love each one,
    And choose
    To welcome love in the lively wasting sun.

&

A slopeshouldered shape from scurrying burdens
Backward and forth, or perhaps a lyre
Or a clef wrung wry in tuning untunable tones,
Or a knot for tugging an out-of-hand

Vine to the trellis in clerical gardens:
Sweetness & light, ice & fire,
Nature & art have dissocketed all your bones,
Porter, poor pander ampersand.

O

The idle dayseye, the laborious wheel,
The osprey's tours, the pointblank matin sun
Sanctified first the circle; thence for fun
Doctors deduced a shape, which some called real
(So all games spoil), a shape of spare appeal,
Cryptic and clean, and endlessly spinning unspun.
Now I go backward, filling by one and one
Circles with hickory spokes and rich soft shields
Of petalled dayseyes, with herehastening steel
Volleys of daylight, writhing white looks of sun;
And I toss circles skyward to be undone
By actual wings, for wanting this repeal
I should go whirling a thin Euclidean reel,
No hawk or hickory to true my run.

THE REGATTA

A rowdy wind pushed out the sky,
Now swoops the lake and booms in sails;
Sunlight can plummet, when it fails,
Brighten on boats which pitch and fly.

Out on the dock-end, Mrs. Vane,
Seated with friends, lifts lenses to
Delighted eyes, and sweeps the view
Of "galleons" on the "raging main."

A heeling boat invades the glass
To turn a buoy; figures duck
The crossing sail—"There's Midge and Buck!
I know his scarf!"—the sailors pass.

The hotel guests make joking bets,
And Mrs. Vane has turned, inquired
If Mr. Vane is feeling "tired."
He means to answer, but forgets.

She offers him binoculars:
A swift, light thing is slipping on
The bitter waters, always gone
Before the wave can make it hers;

So simply it evades, evades,
So weightless and immune may go,
The free thing does not need to know
How deep the waters are with shades.

It's but a trick; and still one feels
Franchised a little—God knows I
Would be the last alive to cry
To Whatzisname, "I love thy wheels!"

Freedom's a pattern. I am cold.
I don't know what I'm doing here.
And Mrs. Vane says, "Home now, dear."
He rises, does as he is told;
Hugging her arm, he climbs the pier.
Behind him breaks the triumph cheer.

BELL SPEECH

The selfsame toothless voice for death or bridal:
It has been long since men would give the time
To tell each someone's-change with a special chime,
And a toll for every year the dead walked through.
And mostly now, above this urgent idle
Town, the bells mark time, as they can do.

This bavardage of early and of late
Is what is wanted, and yet the bells beseech
By some excess that's in their stricken speech
Less meanly to be heard. Were this not so,
Why should Great Paul shake every window plate
To warn me that my pocket watch is slow?

Whether or not attended, bells will chant
With a clear dumb sound, and wide of any word
Expound our hours, clear as the waves are heard
Crashing at Mount Desert, from far at sea,
And dumbly joining, as the night's descent
Makes deltas into dark of every tree.

Great Paul, great pail of sound, still dip and draw
Dark speech from the deep and quiet steeple well,
Bring dark for doctrine, do but dim and quell
All voice in yours, while earth will give you breath.
Still gather to a language without flaw
Our loves, and all the hours of our death.

POPLAR, SYCAMORE

Poplar, absolute danseuse,
Wind-wed and faithless to wind, troweling air
Tinily everywhere faster than air can fill,
Here whitely rising, there
Winding, there
Feinting to earth with a greener spill,
Never be still, whose pure mobility
Can hold up crowding heaven with a tree.

Sycamore, trawled by the tilt sun,
Still scrawl your trunk with tattered lights, and keep
The spotted toad upon your patchy bark,
Baffle the sight to sleep,
Be such a deep
Rapids of lacing light and dark,
My eye will never know the dry disease
Of thinking things no more than what he sees.

Winter Spring

A script of trees before the hill
Spells cold, with laden serifs; all the walls
Are battlemented still;
But winter spring is winnowing the air
Of chill, and crawls
Wet-sparkling on the gutters;
Everywhere
Walls wince, and there's the steal of waters.

Now all this proud royaume
Is Veniced. Through the drift's mined dome
One sees the rowdy rusted grass,
And we're amazed as windows stricken bright.
This too-soon spring will pass
Perhaps tonight,
And doubtless it is dangerous to love
This somersault of seasons;
But I am weary of
The winter way of loving things for reasons.

ATTENTION MAKES INFINITY

The kingdom of air, of lightly looming air
That crowns us all king spinners, let it swing
Wide of the earth and any foundering
In the sea's reflection, the forest's manifold snare.

Air is refreshment's treasury; earth seems
Our history's faulted sink, and spring of love;
And we between these dreamt-of empires move
To coop infinity away from dreams.

See, every yard, alive with laundry white,
Billowing wives and leaves, gives way to air:
A blown pedestrian upon the square
Tosses a clanging trolley out of sight.

Then air relents to skyward with a sigh,
Earth's adamant variety is remade;
The hanging dust above the streets is staid
And solid as the walls of Central High.

Contagious of the solid make this day
An infiniteness any eye may prove.
Let asphalt bear us up to walk in love,
Electric towers shore the clouds away.

GRACE

"'The young lambs bound As to the tabor's sound.' They toss and toss; it is as if it were the earth that flung them, not themselves. It is the pitch of graceful agility when we think that."

—G. M. Hopkins, NOTEBOOKS

So active they seem passive, little sheep
Please, and Nijinsky's out-the-window leap
And marvelous midair pause please too
A taste for blithe brute reflex; flesh made word
Is grace's revenue.

One is tickled, again, by the dining-car waiter's absurd
Acrobacy—tipfingered tray like a wind-besting bird
Plumblines his swinging shoes, the sole things sure
In the shaken train; but this is all done for food,
Is habitude, if not pure

Hebetude. It is a graph of a theme that flings
The dancer kneeling on nothing into the wings,
And Nijinsky hadn't the words to make the laws
For learning to loiter in air; he "merely" said,
"I merely leap and pause."

Lambs are constrained to bound. Consider instead
The intricate neural grace in Hamlet's head;
A grace not barbarous implies a choice
Of courses, not in a lingo of leaps-in-air
But in such a waiting voice

As one would expect to hear in the talk of Flaubert.
Piety makes for awkwardness, and where
Balance is not urgent, what one utters
May be puzzled and perfect, and we respect
Some scholars' stutters.

Even fraction-of-a-second action is not wrecked
By a graceful still reserve. To be unchecked
Is needful then: choose, challenge, jump, poise, run...
Nevertheless, the praiseful, graceful soldier
Shouldn't be fired by his gun.

A birdsnest built on the palm of the high-
Most bough of an elm, this morning as I came by
A brute gust lifted-and-left in the midst of the air;
    Whereat the leaves went quiet, and there
    Was a moment of silence in honor of
The sweetness of danger. The chalice now bobbing above,
Of interlaid daintiest timber, began the chute
    Down forty fell feet toward stone and root
    With a drift and a sampan spin, and gripped
Loosely its fineshelled life; now viciously tipped
By a ripple of air, with an acrobat's quick not-quite-
    Lost, dipped lower to whirl upright;
    Then, with a straight-down settling, it
Descended into sunshine, and, with a hushed touch, lit
On a mesa of strenuous grass. Oh risk-hallowed eggs, oh
    Triumph of lightness! Legerity begs no
    Quarter: my Aunt Virginia, when
She'd relapsed and recovered, would sit in the garden again
Waiting, all lapped in an indigo-flowered shawl,
    In white for her "regular customers'" call;
    Whose pity she parried with very-blue-eyed
Attention, and giggled and patted their hands when they tried
To do-something-for-her; she sat in the heart of her days
    And watched with a look of peculiar praise;
    Her slight voice could catch a pleasure complete
As a gull takes a fish at the flash of his side. Her great
Heavy husband adored her, would treat with a sudden blind sally
    Of softness his "visitor from the valley";
    He called her "Birdie," which was good, for him.
And he and the others, the strong, the involved, in-the-swim,
Seeing her there in the garden, in her gray shroud
    As vague and as self-possessed as a cloud,
    Requiring nothing of them any more,
And one hand lightly laid on a fatal door,
Thought of the health of the sick, and, what mocked their sighing,
    Of the strange intactness of the gladly dying.

FOR ELLEN

On eyes embarked for sleep the only light
Goes off, and there is nothing that you know
So well, it may not monster in this sea.
The vine leaves pat the screen. Viciously free,
The wind vaults over the roof with Mister Crow
To drop his crooked laughter in your night.

And morning's cannonades of brightness come
To a little utter blueness in your eyes.
You stagger goldenly, bestowing blue;
Blue heal-all breaks the pavingstone where you
Expect it, and you laugh in pure surprise
At the comic cripple hurdling to his slum.

But sometime you will look at the lazy sun
Hammocked in clouds, dead-slumbering in the sky.
That casual fire will blister blue, and night
Will strand its fears; then with a starker sight
And newer darker love, you will supply
The world of joy which never was begun.

CASERTA GARDEN

Their garden has a silent tall stone-wall
So overburst with drowsing trees and vines,
None but a stranger would remark at all
The barrier within the fractured lines.

I doubt they know it's there, or what it's for—
To keep the sun-impasted road apart,
The beggar, soldier, renegade and whore,
The dust, the sweating ox, the screeching cart.

They'd say, "But this is how a garden's made":
To fall through days in silence dark and cool,
And hear the fountain falling in the shade
Tell changeless time upon the garden pool.

See from the tiptoe boy—the dolphin throats—
The fine spray bending; jets collapse in rings
Into the round pool, and each circle floats
Wide to the verge, and fails in shimmerings.

A childhood by this fountain wondering
Would leave impress of circle-mysteries:
One would have faith that the unjustest thing
Had geometric grace past what one sees.

How beauties will grow richer walled about!
This tortile trunk, old paradigm of pain,
These cherished flowers—they dream and look not out,
And seem to have no need of earth or rain.

In heavy peace, walled out necessity,
How devious the lavish grapevine crawls,
And trails its shade, irrelevant and free,
In delicate cedillas on the walls.

And still without, the dusty shouting way,
Hills lazar-skinned, with hungry-rooted trees,
And towns of men, below a staring day,
Go scattered to the turning mountain frieze.

The garden of the world, which no one sees,
Never had walls, is fugitive with lives;
Its shapes escape our simpler symmetries;
There is no resting where it rots and thrives.

Praise in Summer

Obscurely yet most surely called to praise,
As sometimes summer calls us all, I said
The hills are heavens full of branching ways
Where star-nosed moles fly overhead the dead;
I said the trees are mines in air, I said
See how the sparrow burrows in the sky!
And then I wondered why this mad *instead*
Perverts our praise to uncreation, why
Such savor's in this wrenching things awry.
Does sense so stale that it must needs derange
The world to know it? To a praiseful eye
Should it not be enough of fresh and strange
That trees grow green, and moles can course in clay,
And sparrows sweep the ceiling of our day?

THE BEAUTIFUL CHANGES

One wading a Fall meadow finds on all sides
The Queen Anne's Lace lying like lilies
On water; it glides
So from the walker, it turns
Dry grass to a lake, as the slightest shade of you
Valleys my mind in fabulous blue Lucernes.

The beautiful changes as a forest is changed
By a chameleon's tuning his skin to it;
As a mantis, arranged
On a green leaf, grows
Into it, makes the leaf leafier, and proves
Any greenness is deeper than anyone knows.

Your hands hold roses always in a way that says
They are not only yours; the beautiful changes
In such kind ways,
Wishing ever to sunder
Things and things' selves for a second finding, to lose
For a moment all that it touches back to wonder.

Mined Country   Silver plates: mine detectors.

Up, Jack   *King Henry IV, Part I,* Act V, Scene 4.

The Walgh-Vogel   Title and first stanza derived from Sir Thomas Herbert's *Travels,* quoted in Phipson's *Animal-Lore of Shakespeare's Time.*

Objects   *A Dutch Courtyard,* by Pieter de Hooch, is in the National Gallery in Washington, D.C.

The Waters   The last section refers to Leonardo via Walter Pater, Villiers de l'Isle Adam, and Holderlin. These artists, particularly the two last, seem to me to have suffered similar emotional tragedies.

A Simplification   Brann the iconoclast was shot dead on the streets of Waco in 1898. Not an important figure, but his name has the irascible sound I was seeking.

Show Lyrics

OH, HAPPY WE!

This lyric was written for Candide *(1956), on which I collaborated with Lillian Hellman and Leonard Bernstein. In it, Candide and Cunegonde are anticipating the joys of marriage.*

CANDIDE *sings*

Soon, when we feel we can afford it,
We'll build a modest little farm.

CUNEGONDE *sings*

We'll buy a yacht and live aboard it,
Rolling in luxury and stylish charm.

CANDIDE

Cows and chickens.

CUNEGONDE

Social whirls.

CANDIDE

Peas and cabbage.

CUNEGONDE

Ropes of pearls.

CANDIDE

Soon there'll be little ones beside us;
We'll have a sweet Westphalian home.

CUNEGONDE

Somehow we'll grow rich as Midas;
We'll live in Paris when we're not in Rome.

CANDIDE

Smiling babies.

CUNEGONDE

Marble halls.

CANDIDE

Sunday picnics.

CUNEGONDE

Costume balls.

CUNEGONDE

Oh, won't my robes of silk and satin
Be chic! I'll have all that I desire.

CANDIDE

Pangloss will tutor us in Latin
And Greek, while we sit before the fire.

CUNEGONDE

Glowing rubies.

CANDIDE

Glowing logs.

CUNEGONDE

Faithful servants.

CANDIDE

Faithful dogs.

CUNEGONDE

We'll round the world enjoying high life;
All will be pink champagne and gold.

CANDIDE

We'll lead a rustic and a shy life,
Feeding the pigs and sweetly growing old.

CUNEGONDE

Breast of peacock.

CANDIDE

Apple pie.

CUNEGONDE

I love marriage.

CANDIDE

So do I.

CUNEGONDE

Oh, happy pair!
Oh, happy we!
It's very rare
How we agree.

BOTH

Oh, happy pair!
Oh, happy we!
It's very rare
How we agree.

GLITTER AND BE GAY

A second lyric from Candide.

CUNEGONDE *sings*

Glitter and be gay,
That's the part I play.
Here am I in Paris, France,
Forced to bend my soul
To a sordid role,
Victimized by bitter, bitter circumstance.

Alas for me, had I remained
Beside my lady mother,
My virtue had remained unstained
Until my maiden hand was gained
By some Grand Duke or other.

Ah, 'twas not to be;
Harsh necessity
Brought me to this gilded cage.
Born to higher things,
Here I droop my wings,
Singing of a sorrow nothing can assuage.

(*Suddenly brighter*)

And yet, of course, I rather like to revel, ha, ha!
I have no strong objection to champagne, ha, ha!
My wardrobe is expensive as the devil, ha, ha!
Perhaps it is ignoble to complain...

Enough, enough
Of being basely tearful!
I'll show my noble stuff
By being bright and cheerful!

Ha, ha ha ha... (*Sings "ha" at some length*)

(Reciting, to music)

Pearls and ruby rings...
Ah, how can worldly things
Take the place of honor lost?
Can they compensate
For my fallen state,
Purchased as they were at such an awful cost?

Bracelets...lavalieres...
Can they dry my tears?
Can they blind my eyes to shame?
Can the brightest brooch
Shield me from reproach?
Can the purest diamond purify my name?

(Suddenly bright again; singing as she puts on enormous bracelets)

And yet, of course, these trinkets are endearing, ha ha!
I'm oh, so glad my sapphire is a star, ha ha!
I rather like a twenty-carat earring, ha ha!
If I'm not pure, at least my jewels are!

(Puts on three more bracelets)

Enough, enough!
I'll *take* their diamond necklace,
And show my noble stuff
By being gay and reckless!

Ha ha ha ha ha...

Observe how bravely I conceal
The dreadful, dreadful shame I feel.
Ha ha ha ha ha, ha...

(Puts on a giant diamond necklace)

Ha!

THE RAGPICKER'S SONG

This number was written in 1966 for a musical version—almost completed but never produced—of Giraudoux' La Folle de Chaillot. My collaborators were Michel Legrand (music) and Maurice Valency (book).

RAGPICKER

There was a time when the ragpicker's life was akin to
The pearl-diver's life, or the life of a hunter for treasure.
There was a time when the trash-cans were worth looking into:
Now it's no pleasure.

Once you could hope to find hats that had come from a hatter's,
And not from the shelves of a general merchandise monger.
Once there were clothes that were beautiful even in tatters:
Not any longer.

CHORUS OF VAGABONDS

Then there were wonderful rags,
Gay and exciting as flags!
Then there were chokers and muffs!
Shirts with magnificent cuffs!
Those were the days when a vest
Argued a soldierly chest!
Days when a feminine glove
Seemed to be pulsing with love!
Then people knew how to live!
Then people knew how to give
Life to whatever they wore:
Not any more!

RAGPICKER

There was a time when the garbage was wholesome and fragrant,
And scavengers lived on a diet both varied and pleasant.
No one ate better, back then, than a tramp or a vagrant:
Not at the present.

Then one could dine upon scraps of delectable dishes
That came not from freezer and tin but from pantry or larder.
Once there was never an end to the loaves and the fishes:
Now life is harder.

CHORUS OF VAGABONDS

Then one was properly fed!
Then there was wheat in the bread!
Then there was savory salt!
Beer that was hopping with malt!
People were different then!
People were women and men!
Even their garbage expressed
Gusto and passion and zest!
Then there was gold in the eggs!
Wine tasted good to the dregs!
Apples were sweet to the core!
Not any more!

*(after an interval of dialogue, there is a reprise by the Madwoman
herself.)*

THE COUNTESS

There was a time when a calling-card brought by one's servant
Gave some expectation of meeting a man or a woman.
People were formerly charming and lively and fervent:
Now they're not human.

Now we're surrounded by robots with cigarette cases,
Whose lighters ignite with a sound that's as fearful as thunder.
Once there were people with some sort of life in their faces:
Now they've gone under.

CHORUS OF VAGABONDS

Then there were feet that could dance!
Hearts that were wild with romance!
Hair that could stand up on end!

Hands that could help out a friend!
Those were the days when an eye
Knew how to sparkle or cry!
Men were a different breed!
Women had not gone to seed!
Then there were hats that could tip!
Men with a stiff upper lip!
Ladies that men could adore!
Not any more!

Poems for Children and Others

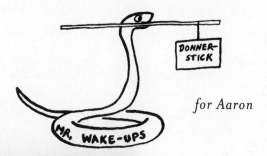

for Aaron

OPPOSITES

1

What is the opposite of *nuts*?
It's *soup*! Let's have no ifs or buts.
In any suitable repast
The soup comes first, the nuts come last.
Or that is what *sane* folk advise;
You're nuts if you think otherwise.

2

What is the opposite of *flying*?
For birds, it would be *just not trying*.

Perhaps the opposite for us
Would be *to take a train or bus*.

3

The opposite of *foot* is what?
A *mountain top*'s one answer, but
If you are thinking of a bed,
The opposite of foot is *head.*
To ancient generals, of course,
The opposite of foot was *horse.*

4

What is the opposite of *cheese*?
For mice, it's *anything you please*.
So fond are they of cheese, that mice
Think nothing else is very nice.

I too like cheese, I must admit.
I'm certainly not opposed to it.

The opposite of *junk* is *stuff*
Which someone thinks is good enough,

Or *any vessel on the seas*
That isn't in the least Chinese.

6

What is the opposite of *string*?
It's *gnirts*, which doesn't mean a thing.

7

The opposite of *standing still*
Is *walking up or down a hill,*
Running backwards, creeping, crawling,
Leaping off a cliff and falling,

Turning somersaults in gravel,
Or any other mode of travel.

What is the opposite of *riot*?
It's *lots of people keeping quiet*.

9

The opposite of a *hole's* a *heap*
Just as high as the hole is deep.
How deep's the hole? Go on and measure,
If it will give you any pleasure.

10

What is the opposite of *fox*?
Foxes are clever, while the *ox*,
So we are told, could not be duller:
But is it opposite in color?

The fox is reddish-brown in hue;
Perhaps *a greenish ox* would do.

11

The opposite of *making faces*
Is *not indulging in grimaces,*
Wrinkling your nose, with tongue stuck out,
And rolling both your eyes about,
But letting eyes, and mouth, and nose
Remain entirely in repose.
It's true, however, that a *very*
Fixed expression can be scary.

12

What is the opposite of *two*?
A lonely me, a lonely you.

13

What is the opposite of *doe*?
The answer's *buck*, as you should know.
A buck *is* dough, you say? Well, well,
Clearly you don't know how to spell.
Moreover, get this through your head:
The current slang for dough is *bread*.

14

What is the opposite of *penny*?
I'm sorry, but there isn't any—
Unless you count the change, I guess,
Of someone who is *penniless*.

When people flip a penny, its
Two *sides*, of course, are opposites.

I'll flip one now. Go on and choose:
Which is it, heads or tails? You lose.

15

The opposite of *squash*? Offhand,
I'd say that it might be *expand*,
Enlarge, uncrumple, or *inflate.*

However, on a dinner plate
With yellow vegetables and green,
The opposite of squash is *bean.*

16

What is the opposite of *actor*?
The answer's very simple: *tractor.*
I said that just because it rhymes,
As lazy poets do at times.

However, to be more exact,
An actor's one who likes to act
King Lear in some unlikely plot,
Pretending to be what he's not.

The opposite of *actor,* friend,
Is *someone who does not pretend,*
But is *himself,* like you and me.
I'm Romeo. Who might you be?

17

There's more than one way to be right
About the opposite of *white*,
And those who merely answer *black*
Are very, very single-track.
They make one want to scream, "I beg
Your pardon, but within an egg
(A fact known to the simplest folk)
The opposite of white is *yolk*!"

18

The opposite of *doughnut*? Wait
A minute while I meditate.

This isn't easy. Ah, I've found it!
A cookie with a hole around it.

19

Because what's *present* doesn't last,
The opposite of it is *past*.
Or if you choose to look ahead,
Future's the opposite instead.
Or look around to see what's here,
And *absent* things will not appear.
There's one more opposite of *present*
That's really almost too unpleasant:
It is *when someone takes away*
Something with which you like to play.

20

What is the opposite of *hat*?
It isn't hard to answer that.
It's *shoes,* for shoes and hat together
Protect our two extremes from weather.

Between these two extremes there lies
A middle, which you would be wise
To clothe as well, or you'll be chilly
And run the risk of looking silly.

21

The opposites of *earth* are two,
And which to choose is up to you.
One opposite is called *the sky,*
And that's where larks and swallows fly;
But angels, there, are few if any,
Whereas in *heaven* there are many.
Well, which word are you voting for?
Do birds or angels please you more?
It's very plain that you are loath
To choose. All right, we'll keep them both.

22

The opposite of a *cloud* could be
A white reflection in the sea,

Or *a huge blueness in the air,*
Caused by a cloud's not being there.

23

Not to have any *hair* is called
Hairlessness, or being *bald.*
It is a fine thing to be hairy,
Yet it's not always necessary.
Bald heads on men are very fine,
Particularly if they shine,
And who conceivably could wish
To see a hairy frog or fish?

Some creatures, though, do well to wear
A normal covering of hair.
I don't think I should care to know
Those hairless dogs of Mexico
Who ramble naked out of doors
And must be patted on their pores.

24

What is the opposite of *Cupid*?
If you don't know, you're pretty stupid.
It's *someone with a crossbow who*
Delights in shooting darts at you.
Not with the kind intention of
Persuading you to fall in love,
But to be mean, and make you shout,
"I hate you," "Ouch," and "Cut it out."

25

What is the opposite of a *shoe*?
Either the *right* or *left* will do,
Depending on which one you've got.
The question's foolish, is it not?

26

What is the opposite of *fleet*?
Someone who's *slow* and drags his feet.

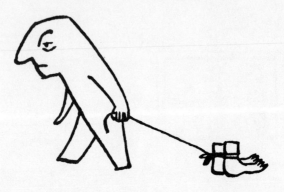

Another's an *armada* that'll
Engage the first fleet in a battle.

What is the opposite of *July*?
That's hard to answer, but I'll try.
In San Francisco and Quebec,
Duluth, Big Forks, Mamaroneck,
And every other city here
In the upper Western Hemisphere,
July can be extremely hot;
But far to southward it is not.
The month can be extremely chill
In Paraguay or in Brazil,
And furthermore, July can mean a
Blizzard or so in Argentina.
These unexpected facts are why
The opposite of July's *July*.

28

What is the opposite of *bat*?
It's easy enough to answer that.
A bat sleeps upside down in trees,
Whereas a *horse,* with equal ease,
Can sleep while upright in his stall.

Another answer might be *ball.*

29

The opposite of *well* is *sick*.

Another answer's to be quick
And tell what you have got to tell,
Without a lot of "Well…well…well…"

30

The opposite of *tiller*? Well,
It's *when some farmer in the dell*
Has grown so lazy that by now
He lacks the energy to plow.

A *bowsprit* also comes to mind,
Since, like a tiller, it's a kind
Of stick, and since on sailing craft
The bowsprit's fore, the tiller aft.

I also think of *butter, brads,*
Shoe polish, cannon, shoulder pads,
Daisies, and *stock exchange,* and *goat,*
Since none of these can steer a boat.

31

The opposite of *fast* is *loose*,
And if you doubt it you're a goose,
"Nonsense!" you cry. "As you should know,
The opposite of fast is *slow.*"
Well, let's not quarrel: have a chair
And see what's on the bill of fare.

We should agree on this at least:
The opposite of fast is *feast.*

What is the opposite of a *prince*?
A *frog* must be the answer, since,
As all good fairy stories tell,
When some witch says a magic spell,
Causing the prince to be disguised
So that he won't be recognized,
He always ends up green and sad
And sitting on a lily pad.

33

The opposite of a *king*, I'm sure,
Is someone humble and obscure—
A *peasant,* or some *wretched soul*
Who begs through life with staff and bowl.

Another opposite's the *queen,*
If she is quarrelsome and mean.

34

The opposite of *spit*, I'd say,
Would be *a narrow cove or bay*.

(There is another sense of *spit*,
But I refuse to think of it.
It stands opposed to *all refined*
And decent instincts of mankind!)

35

What is the opposite of *ball*?
It's *meteor*. Though meteors fall
As balls do, and like balls are round,
And though they sometimes hit the ground,
They don't know how to bounce or roll
And merely make a dreadful hole.

The opposite of *trunk* could be
The taproot of a cedar tree.
In terms of elephants, however,
The answer *tail* is rather clever.

Another answer is *when all*
Your things are tied up in a ball
And carried on your head, for lack
Of anything in which to pack.

37

The opposite of *post,* were you
On horseback, would be *black and blue;*

Another answer is *to fail*
To put your letters in the mail.

38

What is the opposite of *mirror*?
The answer hardly could be clearer:
It's *anything which, on inspection,*
Is not all full of your reflection.

For instance, it would be no use
To brush your hair before a moose,
Or try a raincoat on for size
While looking at a swarm of flies.

39

The opposite of *opposite*?
That's much too difficult. I quit.

MORE
OPPOSITES

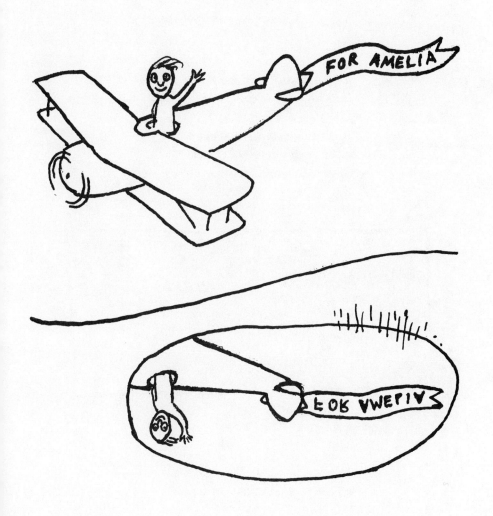

1

The opposite of *duck* is *drake*.
Remember that, for heaven's sake!
One's female, and the other's male.
In writing to a *drake*, don't fail
To start your letter off, "Dear Sir."
"Dear Madam" is what *ducks* prefer.

Mrs. Millard K, Mallard
The Pond
Cummington

In snowball fights, the opposite
Of *duck*, of course, is *getting hit*.

2

The opposite of *doctor*? Well,
That's not so very hard to tell.
A *doctor's* nice, and when you're ill
He makes you better with a pill.
Then what's his opposite? Don't be thick!
It's *anyone who makes you sick.*

3

What is the opposite of *baby*?
The answer is a *grown-up*, maybe.

4

What is the opposite of *pillow*?
The answer, child, is *armadillo*.
"Oh, don't talk nonsense!" you protest.
However, if you tried to rest
Your head upon the creature, you
Would find that what I say is true.
It isn't soft. From head to tail
It wears a scratchy coat of mail.
And furthermore, it won't hold still
Upon a bed, as pillows will,
But squirms, and jumps at every chance
To run away and eat some ants.

So there! Admit that I was right,
Or else we'll have a *pillow fight*.

5

The opposite of *tar* is *rat*.
If you don't see the sense of that,
Just spell *tar* backwards, and you will.
And there's another reason still:
Though *rats* desert a sinking ship,
A *tar*, with stiffened upper lip,
Will man the bilge-pumps like a sport
And bring the vessel into port.

6

The opposite of *sheep*, I think,
Is when you cannot sleep a wink
And find that you're not counting rams
And ewes and little jumping lambs
But countless *vultures* flocking by
With bony head and searching eye,
Each giving you a sidewise glare
To let you know it knows you're there.

7

How often travelers who mean
To tell us of some cave they've seen
Fall mute, forgetting how to use
Two dreadful words which they confuse!
The word *stalactite* is the first;
Stalagmite means the same, reversed.
Though both these things are formed in time
By dripping carbonate of lime,
Stalactites *hang,* while from beneath,
Stalagmites *rise* like lower teeth.

Can you remember that? You'll find
That you can fix those facts in mind
If you will frequently repeat,
While strolling down the village street
Or waiting for a bus to town,
"Stalagmites up! Stalactites down!"

Take care, though, not to be too loud,
Or you may draw a curious crowd.

8

An *omen* is a sign of some
Occurrence that is *yet to come,*
As when a star, by tumbling down,
Warns that a king will lose his crown.

A *clue,* by contrast, is a sign
By means of which we can divine
What has already taken place—
As when, to cite a common case,
A fish is missing from a platter,
And the cat looks a little fatter.

9

What is the opposite of *road*?
I'd say the answer is *abode*.
"What's an abode?" you ask. I'd say
It's ground that doesn't lead away—
Some patch of earth where you *abide*
Because it makes you satisfied.

Abodes don't take you anywhere,
Because you are already there.

10

The opposite of *"Gee!"* is some
Reaction that is bored and glum,
Like *saying "Big deal" with a shrug,*
Or *staring mutely at the rug.*

When *"Gee!"* is spoken to a horse,
It bids him take a right-hand course.
Conversely, *"Haw!"* is how to say
"Turn left" and make a horse obey.

"But will a SEA-horse," you inquire,
"Turn *gee* or *haw* as you desire,
Or must you speak of *starboard* and
Of *port* to make him understand?"

How foolish such a question is!
Don't interrupt me, please. *Gee whiz!*

11

The opposite of *kite*, I'd say,
Is *yo-yo*. On a breezy day
You take your *kite* and let it *rise*
Upon its string into the skies,
And then you pull it *down* with ease
(Unless it crashes in the trees).
A *yo-yo*, though, drops *down*, and then
You quickly bring it *up* again
By pulling deftly on its string
(If you can work the blasted thing).

12

When ships send out an *S.O.S.*
It means that they are in distress.
Is there an opposite sort of call
Which means "There's nothing wrong at all"?
Of course not. Ships would think it sappy
To send us word that they are happy.
If you hear *nothing* from a liner,
It means that things could not be finer.

13

When some poor thirsty nomad sees
A far-off fountain fringed with trees
And, making for the spot in haste
Across the blazing desert waste,
Finds that his vision had no basis,
That is the opposite of *oasis*.
What do we call such sad confusion?
Mirage, or *optical illusion*.

Another opposite might be
A *sandy islet in the sea*.

14

The opposite of *robber*? Come,
You know the answer. Don't be dumb!
While robbers *take things* for a living,
Philanthropists are fond of *giving*.
"And yet," you say, "that's not quite true;
Philanthropists are takers, too,
And often have been very greedy
Before they thought to help the needy."

Well, let's be obvious, then: the op-
Posite of *robber* is a *cop*.

15

The opposite of *less* is *more*.
What's better? Which one are you for?
My question may seem simple, but
The catch is—more or less of *what*?

"Let's have more everything!" you cry.
Well, after we have had more pie,
More pickles, and more layer cake,
I think we'll want *less stomach-ache.*

The best thing's to avoid excess.
Try to be temperate, more or less.

16

An *echo*'s opposite is the *cry*
To which the echo makes reply.
Of course I do not mean to claim
That what they say is not the same.
If one of them calls out "Good day"
Or "Who are you?" or "Hip, hooray"
Or "Robert has an ugly hat,"
The other says exactly that.
But still they're opposites. Know why?
A cry is *bold*; an echo's *shy,*
And though it loves to shout yoo-hoo,
It won't until it hears from you.

17

What is the opposite of *root*?
It's *stem and branch and leaf and fruit*—
All of a plant that we can see.
Another answer, possibly,
Is *when a truffle-hunter's pig
Has grown too proud to sniff and dig,
And stands there with his snout in air.*
(Such happenings are very rare.)

18

A *dragon* is a wingèd snake
Who's always fierce and wide awake
And squats in front of caves which hold
Enormous bags and chests of gold.
If you approach, he bares his nails
And roars at you, and then exhales
Fire, smoke, and sulphur—all of which
Dissuade you from becoming rich.

A dragon's opposite is a *goose*,
A bird who likes to be of use
And who (if of a special breed)
Will give you all you really need
By laying for you every day
A golden egg (or so they say).

19

The opposite of *stunt*? You're right!
It's *making someone grow in height*
By feeding him nutritious bran
Till he's a large and smiling man.
Another answer is *when you*
Do something not too hard to do,
Some act that doesn't call for nerve
And isn't thrilling to observe,
Like sipping from a water glass
Or merely lying on the grass.

20

The opposite of *so-and-so*
Is *anyone whose name you know,*

Or *someone good* who would not take
Your skateboard or your piece of cake,
Making you tell him, with a thwack,
"You so-and-so! I want that back!"

The opposite of *punch*, I think,
Might be some sort of *fruitless drink*,
Unless we say that *punch* means *hit*,
In which event the opposite
Is *counter-punch* or *shadowbox*.
Or if we think of *punching clocks*,
I guess the opposite of *punch*
Is *always to be out to lunch*.

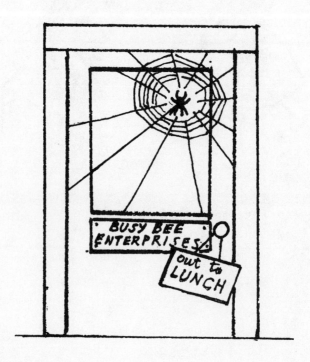

What if we capitalize the P?
Judy's the answer then, since she
And *Punch,* although they chose to marry,
Are each the other's adversary—
Each having, ever since they wed,
Pounded the other on the head.

How many things we've thought of! Whew!
I'm getting punchy. That will do.

A *spell* is something you are under
When put to sleep, or filled with wonder.
The opposite of *spell*, I guess,
Is *normal waking consciousness,*
In which you're not enthralled or sleepy,
And things are only *fairly* creepy.

Another answer could be *writing*
"Recieve," "Occassional," and *"fiteing,"*
"Emporer," "mackeral," and *"snaiks,"*
And other *horribel mistaiks.*

23

The opposite of *hot*, we know,
Is *icy cold* or *ten below.*
Some other answers to the question
Are *leaky buckets, indigestion,*
E-minus, or a *granny knot,*
Since all those things are *not so hot.*

24

The opposite of *moth*? It's *moth*!
One kind is fond of chewing cloth
And biting holes in woolen hats
And coats and dresses and cravats.

However, it's another story
With a nice moth called *Bombyx Mori,*
Who, when it is of tender age
And passing through the larval stage,
Sits munching in a mulberry tree
And spinning silk for you and me—
Of which we make, of course, cravats
As well as dresses, coats, and hats.

25

The opposite of *top*, in case
You haven't heard, is *bottom, base,*
Foundation, underside, or *foot.*
I also think of *chimney soot*
And *mattresses* and *margarine,*
Since none of those is fun to spin.

When you are playing on a harp,
The opposite of *flat* is *sharp*,
And both sound very good if they
Are what the music says to play.
But when you think it's time to stop
And drink a bit of soda pop,
How bad the thought of flatness is!
A soda should be *full of fizz*.

27

Gray is the opposite of *blue*,
Or was in 1862.

At present, *blue* means *sad and tearful*,
And so its opposite is *cheerful*.

28

What is the opposite of *chew*?
It's *wolf*, which you must never do.
A wolf is said to *wolf* his food,
Because he gulps it down unchewed.
If you must imitate a beast,
Then let it be the cow, at least,
Who eats in such a placid way
And never hurries through her hay.

The cow, however, has a trait
Which there's no need to imitate.
Don't go too far! Don't overdo it!
Chew what you eat, but don't *re*-chew it.
I fear you'd be a social dud
If you were seen to have a *cud*.

29

What is the opposite of a *U*?
An *arch* to knock croquet balls through,
Using a mallet which could be
Described as an inverted *T*.

But how can you invert an *O*?
It's round on top and round below.
It looks as though a croquet ball
May have no opposite at all.

30

I wonder if you've ever seen a
Willow sheltering a *hyena*?
Nowhere in nature can be found
An opposition more profound:
A sad tree weeping inconsolably!
A wild beast laughing uncontrollably!

31

The opposite of *pluck*, my dear,
Is *being overcome by fear*.
(I've thought of one more opposite,
But I don't think I'll mention it,
Since, frankly, I have never heard
Of *adding feathers to a bird*.)

32

The opposite of *sound*? Well, that's
When someone's *ill,* or *wrong,* or *bats,*
Or when some firm is *deep in debt.*
Another answer's *what you get*
By strumming cobwebs with a feather
Or banging powder puffs together.

33

What is the opposite of *Missouri*?
The answer's *California*, surely.
Missouri folk are *doubters* who
Won't take your word for two plus two
Until they add them up, by heck,
And then they like to double-check.

But people on our Western Coast
Believe in everything, almost.
The Californians think, I'm told,
That every river's full of gold,

That stars give good advice to men
On what they ought to do, and when,
And that we all had former lives
As Pharaohs or as Pharaohs' wives.

That's how those states are opposite.
I may exaggerate a bit,
But I have told you what we say
In *Massachusetts,* anyway.

34

The opposite of *stop* is *go*,
But sometimes one does both, you know.
We've come at last, by pleasant stages,
To where there are no further pages,
And since our book is at an end,
I'll *stop*. And *go*. Farewell, my friend.

A FEW
DIFFERENCES

1

Dawn is a thing that poets write
Verses about till late at night.
At *daybreak,* when the poets' eyes
Are closed in sleep, their neighbors rise
And put the coffee on to perk
And drink it, and go off to work.

2

An *owl* is like a *cat* because
Both pounce on rodents with their claws,
And look about the same in size,
And pierce the dark with round, bright eyes.
But cats are *beasts,* whereas an owl
Has wings, of course, and is a *fowl.*
An *owl* can fly up into trees
And then swoop down again with ease;
But when a *cat* is on a limb
A sudden dread can madden him
And make him howl, and grow still madder,
Until some person brings a ladder.

You don't confuse a *cake of soap*
With *other sorts of cake,* I hope.
Were you to eat a helping of
Camay, or *Ivory,* or *Dove,*
I think you'd have digestive troubles
Caused by a stomach full of bubbles.

How horrible! But the reverse
Confusion might be even worse.
Be careful, if you please: I'd rather
Not see you bathe in *mocha* lather,
Or watch as you shampoo your head
With *angel food* or *gingerbread.*

4

How is a *room* unlike a *moor*?
They're not the same, you may be sure.
A *room* has walls, a *moor* does not.
Inquire of any honest Scot
And he will say, I have no doubt,
That one's indoors and one is out.
A *room*, then, fits inside a dwelling;
A *moor* is its reverse in spelling,
And has such wild outdoorish weather,
Such rocks, such miles and miles of heather
All full of flocks of drumming grouse,
You wouldn't have one in the house.

In what way do your two lips differ?
The *upper one* is somewhat stiffer,
And useful for expressing pluck
When faced with danger or ill-luck.

The *lower one's* for sticking out
When there's a need to sulk and pout.

6

The kindly barber trims your *nape*,
Then gives your hair a pleasing shape,
And lastly, with his busy shears,
Snips carefully around your ears.
How nice he is! But what if you
Refused to pay when he was through?
I think he'd take you by the *scruff*
And shake you, and be pretty rough.

7

A *jester* differs from a *dunce*
In ways that one can state at once:
Each of them is a kind of fool,
One at the court, and one at school,
And both are given funny caps:
But one of them is bright, perhaps.

THE DISAPPEARING ALPHABET

If the alphabet began to disappear,
Some words would soon look raggedy and queer
(Like QUIRREL, HIMPANZEE, and CHOOCHOO-TRAI),
While others would entirely fade away;
And since it is by words that we construe
The world, the world would start to vanish, too!
Good heavens! It would be an awful mess
If everything dissolved to nothingness!
Be careful, then, my friends, and do not let
Anything happen to the alphabet.

*

What if there were no letter A?
Cows would eat HY instead of HAY.
What's HY? It's an unheard-of diet,
And cows are happy not to try it.

*

In the word DUMB, the letter B is mute,
But elsewhere its importance is acute.
If it were absent, say, from BAT and BALL,
There'd be no big or little leagues AT ALL.

*

If there were no such thing as C,
Whole symphonies would be off key,
And under every nut-tree, you'd
See HIPMUNKS gathering winter food.

*

If D did not exist, some creatures might
Wish, like the Dodo bird, to fade from sight.
For instance, any self-respecting DUCK
Would rather be extinct than be an UCK.

*

The lordly ELEPHANT is one whom we
Would have no word for if there were no E,
And how it would offend him, were we to
Greet him as "Bud," or "Mac," or "Biggy-poo!"
The ELEPHANT is thick-skinned, but I'll bet
That that's a thing he never would forget.

*

Hail, letter F! If it were not for you,
Our raincoats would be merely "WATERPROO,"
And that is such a stupid word, I doubt
That it would help to keep the water out.

*

If G did not exist, the color GREEN
Would have to vanish from the rural scene.
Would oak trees, then, be blue, and pastures pink?
We would turn green at such a sight, I think.

*

An H can be too scared to speak, almost.
In *gloomy* words like GHASTLY, GHOUL, and GHOST,
The sound of H can simply not be heard.
But how it loves to say a *cheerful* word
Like HEALTH, or HAPPINESS, or HOLIDAY!
Or HALLELUJAH! Or HIP, HIP, HURRAY!

*

Without the letter I, there'd be
No word for your IDENTITY,
And so you'd find it very tough
To tell yourself from other stuff.
Sometimes, perhaps, you'd think yourself
A jam-jar on the pantry shelf.
Sometimes you'd make a ticking sound
And slowly move your hands around.
Sometimes you'd lie down like a rug,
Expecting to be vacuumed. Ugh!

Surely, my friends, you now see why
We need to keep the letter I.

*

If, all at once, there were no letter J,
A cloud of big blue birds might fly away,
And though they'd been an angry, raucous crew,
I think that I would miss them, wouldn't you?

*

Is K unnecessary? "Heavens, no!
It's in my name!" exclaims the ESKIMO,
"And if there were no K, my little craft
The KAYAK, would be scuttled fore and aft."

*

It would be bitter, if there were no L,
To bid the LEMON or the LOON farewell,
And if the LLAMA, with its two-L name,
Should leave us, it would be a *double* shame;
But certainly it would be *triply* sad
If LOLLIPOPS no longer could be had.

*

M is a letter, but it alternates
As a *Roman numeral* often found in dates.
If M should vanish, we would lose, my dears,
MINCE PIE, MARSHMALLOWS, and a thousand years.

*

No N? In such a state of things,
Birds would have WIGS instead of WINGS,
And though a wig might suit the *Owl*,
Who is a staid and judgelike fowl,
Most birds would rather fly than wear
A mat of artificial hair.
What would our proud *Bald Eagle* say
If he were offered a toupee?

569

I think it would be better, then,
For us to keep the letter N.

*

What if there were no letter O?
You couldn't COME, you couldn't GO,
You couldn't ROVE, you couldn't ROAM,
And yet you couldn't stay at HOME!
Where would you be, had heaven not sent you
The letter O to orient you?

*

How strange that the banana's slippery PEEL,
Without its P, would be a slippery EEL!
It makes you think! However, it is not
Profound enough to think about *a lot.*

*

What if the letter Q should be destroyed?
Millions of U's would then be unemployed,
For Q and U belong like *tick* and *tock,*
Except, of course, in places like Iraq.

*

What if there were no R? Your boat, I fear,
Would have no RUDDER, and so you couldn't steer.
How helplessly you'd drift, then, seeing more
Of the Seven Seas than you had bargained for!
But happily you couldn't come to grief
On ROCKS, or run aground upon a REEF.

*

What if the letter S were missing?
COBRAS would have no way of hissing,
And all their kin would have to take
The name of ERPENT or of NAKE.

*

At breakfast time, the useful letter T
Preserves us all from eating SHREDDED WHEA.

*

Without the letter U, you couldn't say,
"I think I'd like to visit URUGUAY,"
And so you'd stay forever in *North Platte,*
New Paltz, or *Scranton,* or some place like that.

*

Were there no V, would geese still fly
In V-formation in the sky,
Calling it something else instead,
Like "angle," "wedge," or "arrowhead"?
Perhaps. Or they might take the shape
Of *smoke-rings* or of *ticker-tape*
Or spell out words like HERE WE GO
Or NUTS TO YOU. You never know.

*

What if there were no letter W?
The WEREWOLF would no longer trouble you,
And you'd be free of many evils
Like WARTS, and WEARINESS, and WEEVILS.
But then there'd be (*alas!*) no sweet
WATERMELONS for you to eat.
(What's more, I guess there'd have to be a
Different shape in CASSIOPEIA.)

*

The letter X will never disappear.
The more you cross it out, the more it's here.
But if it vanished, treasure maps would not
Have anything with which to *mark the spot,*
And treasure isles would ring with the despair
Of puzzled pirates digging everywhere.

*

Lacking the letter Y, I guess
We'd have no way of saying YES,
Or even saying MAYBE, and so
There'd be no answer left but *No*.
How horrible! Who wants to live
A life so very negative,
Refusing presents, raspberry ice,
Fudge cake, and everything that's nice?

*

Because they're always BUZZING, honey bees
Could not be with us if there were no Z's,
And many Z's are needed, furthermore,
When people feel the need to SNOOZE and snore.
Long live the Z, then! Not for any money,
Would I give up such things as *sleep* and *honey*.

THE PIG IN THE SPIGOT

Because he swings so neatly through the trees,
An *ape* feels natural in the word *trapeze*.

*

It's seldom that you see a hen or cock
Come strolling down a busy city block
They much prefer the country, for their part,
Because a *chicken* is a *hick* at heart.

*

Because some moths can think of nothing better
Than chewing wool, there is an *eat* in *sweater*.

*

When in your *neighborhood* you hear a *neigh*,
It means that there's a horse not far away.

*

The *Devil* is at home, as you can see,
In *Mandeville, Louisiana,* but he
Is often on the road, and in the line
Of work he visits both your town and mine.

*

Some tiny insects make a seething sound,
And swarm and jitter furiously around,
Which seems to me sufficient explanation
Of why there is a *gnat* in *indignation*.

*

I don't see why a *belfry* should contain
An *elf*. The notion strikes me as insane.
A bell-tower, or a church's lofty steeple,
Is not the place for so-called "little people."
Belfries should be inhabited by bats,
Not small, fictitious men in pointed hats.

There's an *ant,* you say, in *pantry*? I don't doubt it.
There's something quite inevitable about it.
Like you, the ant knows where the sweet things are,
And on what shelf to find the cookie jar.

It's hard to think in crowded places where
Loud music, squeals, and clatter fill the air,
And brainless persons holler "Yo!" and "Hey!"
That's why *idea* is found in *hideaway.*

Emphatic has a *hat* inside it. Why?
Because some people, if you doubt them, cry
"By golly, if I'm wrong I'll eat my hat!"
What could be more emphatic, friends, than that?

An *obol* is an old Greek coin. To think
That one should be inside a *bobolink*!
We know that birds have bills, but it is strange
That one of them should have a taste for change.

When battling airplanes chase each other 'round
Till one is hit and crashes to the ground,
It's called a "dog-fight." Is that, do you suppose,
Why there's an *arf* in *warfare*? Heaven knows.

Look! There's a *bug* in *bugle*! We must warn
The bugler not to breathe *in* when his horn
Is playing "taps" or "call to quarters," lest
He find a beetle awkward to digest.

Sea is in *nausea,* which seems strange to me,
Since *nausea* comes of tossing in the *sea.*

*

The mother kangaroo makes long, long jumps
And comes to earth with very heavy bumps.
That is the reason why, inside her *pouch,*
Her child is constantly exclaiming *"Ouch!"*

*

When there's a *pig* inside your *spigot,* you
Must not cry out, "There's nothing I can do!"
Be sensible, and take the obvious course,
Which is to turn the spigot on full force.
Sufficient water pressure will, I think,
Oblige the pig to flow into the sink.

*

If you'd been on *Mount Ararat,* would you
Have smelled a *rat?* Of course. Not one, but two.
For Noah's ark, we're told, contained a pair
Of every creature when it landed there.

*

If you're fond of road-blocks, this one can't be beat:
A big *tree* in the middle of the *street.*

*

Moms weep when children don't do as they say.
That's why there is a *sob* in *disobey.*

*

Look closely, and you'll see that there's a *cat*
In *Pocatello.* Don't be surprised by that.
Cats are all over. Don't tell me there's not a
Cat in *Decatur, Muscat,* or *Licata,*
Or in a million other places still,
Like *Acatlán, Catania, Catonsville,*

And that enormous country far away
Which old map-makers used to call *Cathay.*
In fact, in all the pages of the atlas,
There's no lo*cat*ion that's completely catless.

*

Proprietors of china shops are full
Of dread when they're invaded by a bull,
And so are gardeners, when a trampling *ox*
Makes its appearance in a bed of *phlox.*

*

If you can't find a daisy with which to settle
Your fate by asking, petal after petal,
Whether "she loves you" or "she loves you not,"
Than ask a *clover* to foretell your lot.
Clovers are full of *love,* as you will find.
I'm sure you'll pick the lucky four-leaf kind.

*

You've heard about that old moon-jumping cow,
But no one, I suspect, has told you how
On her last jump, she leveled off too soon.
That's why we hear a *moo*-sound from the *moon.*

*

Inside a *taxi,* why do we find an *ax?*
It's because cabs are also known as "hacks."
And "hacking" is the taxi-driver's trade.
(No doubt the explanation I have made
Strikes you as forced, and of no use whatever.
Make up your own, then, if you're so darn clever.)

*

Mustn't includes the letters *TNT.*
Does that mean something? What can the message be?
Children, you know exactly what it means:
You're not to blow things into smithereens.

*

The *emu* is a bird of noble size,
But out of modesty she never flies.
Her nature's gentle, and that is why, I'm sure,
She fits so well inside the word *demure*.

*

The reason why there is a *one* in *throne*
Is that a monarch has to reign alone.
There isn't room upon a throne for two,
And three or four would clearly never do.
If five kings tried to fit in one gold chair,
Think how they'd fight, and pull each other's hair,
And do the sort of thing that isn't done!
A *throne*, friends, is a seat reserved for *one*.

*

Now that you've read this *book*, I hope you'll say
That what you found inside it was *OK*.
(The other word inside of *book* is *boo*,
But don't say that! I'll hate it if you do.)

PERMISSIONS ACKNOWLEDGMENTS

April," "The Eye," "In Limbo," "A Sketch," "The Fourth of July," "To His Skeleton," "John Chapman," "Children of Darkness," "Rillons, Rillettes," "On the Marginal Way," "Complaint," "In a Churchyard," "Seed Leaves," "In the Field," "A Wood," "Running," "Thyme Flowering Among Rocks," "A Late Aubade," "Walking to Sleep," "Two Voices in a Meadow," "Advice to a Prophet," "Loves of the Puppets," "A Summer Morning," "A Hole in the Floor," "The Undead," "October Maples, Portland," "A Grasshopper," "The Aspen and the Stream," "A Fire-Truck," "Someone Talking to Himself," "In the Smoking-Car," "Ballade for the Duke of Orléans," "Two Quatrains for First Frost," "Next Door," "A Black November Turkey," "After the Last Bulletins," "Merlin Enthralled," "The Beacon," "Exeunt," "Boy at the Window," "All These Birds," "A Baroque Wall-Fountain in the Villa Sciarra," "In the Elegy Season," "Juggler," "The Sirens," "Year's End," "Grasse: The Olive Trees," and "Clearness."

Other poems appeared originally in *21st*, *Accent*, *American Letters*, the *American Poetry Review*, the *American Scholar*, the *Antioch Review*, the *Atlantic Monthly*, *Audience*, *Beloit Poetry Journal*, *Between Worlds*, the *Boston University Journal*, *Botteghe Oscure*, the *Carolina Review*, *Chicago Choice*, *Daedalus*, *Encounter*, the *Epigrammatist*, *Foreground*, *A Festschrift for Marianne Moore's Seventy-seventh Birthday*, the *Formalist*, *Furioso*, *Gallery Press*, the *Georgia Review*, *Harvard Advocate*, *Hispanic Arts*, the *Hollins Critic*, *Hopkins Review*, the *Hudson Review*, *Image*, *Imagi*, *Inventario*, the *Iowa Review*, *Junior Bazaar*, *Kansas Quarterly*, *Kayak*, *Kenyon Review*, *Mandrake*, *Michigan Quarterly Review*, *Mill Mountain Review*, the *Nation*, *New Directions No. 10*, the *New Republic*, the *New York Review of Books*, *Nimbus*, *Origin*, the *Oxford American*, *Palaemon Press*, the *Paris Review*, *Partisan Review*, *Penny Poems from Midwestern University*, *Ploughshares*, *Poetry*, *Poetry New York*, *Poetry Northwest*, *Poetry on the Buses*, *Poetry Quarterly* (London), *Quagga*, *Quarterly Review of Literature*, *Trinity College Review*, the *Sewanee Review*, *Sheepmeadow Press*, *Spectrum*, *Strike News*, *Tiger's Eye*, the *Tin Drum*, *Transatlantic Review*, *Tri-Quarterly*, the *Vassar Review*, *Virginia Quarterly*, *Wake*, and the *Yale Review*.

TITLE INDEX

&, 447

Advice from the Muse, 104
Advice to a Prophet, 258
After the Last Bulletins, 315
Agent, The, 225
Agrigentum Road, The (SALVATORE
  QUASIMODO), 280
Alatus, 81
Albatross, The (CHARLES BAUDELAIRE), 55
All That Is, 112
All These Birds, 342
Altitudes, 305
An Arrow in the Wall (ANDREI
  VOZNESENSKY), 177
Another Voice, 293
Antéros (GÉRARD DE NERVAL), 288
Antiworlds (ANDREI VOZNESENSKY), 247
Apology, 335
April 5, 1974, 153
Asides, 10
Aspen and the Stream, The, 281
At Moorditch, 32
Attention Makes Infinity, 454
Avowal, The, 378

Ballad of the Jack of Diamonds (NINA
  CASSIAN), 45
Ballade for the Duke of Orléans, 287
Ballade in Old French (FRANÇOIS
  VILLON), 252
Ballade of Forgiveness (FRANÇOIS
  VILLON), 159
Ballade of the Ladies of Time Past
  (FRANÇOIS VILLON), 251

Ballade to End With, A (FRANÇOIS
  VILLON), 253
Baroque Wall-Fountain in the Villa
  Sciarra, A, 344
Barred Owl, A, 29
Beacon, The, 323
Beasts, 337
Beautiful Changes, The, 462
Bell Speech, 451
Beowulf, 388
Blackberries for Amelia, 16
Black Birch in Winter, A, 147
Black November Turkey, A, 312
Bonds, 33
Bone Key, 47
Boy at the Window, 340

Canto xxv of the Inferno (DANTE
  ALIGHIERI), 66
Caserta Garden, 459
Castles and Distances, 362
Catch, The, 91
Ceremony, 406
Children of Darkness, 155
Christmas Hymn, A, 300
Chronic Condition, A, 348
Cicadas, 409
Clearness, 385
C Minor, 149
Compass (JORGE LUIS BORGES), 241
Complaint, 200
Conjuration, 356
Correspondences (CHARLES
  BAUDELAIRE), 56
Cottage Street, 1953, 143

Courtyard Thaw, A, 395

Crow's Nests, 43

Cry from Childhood, A (VALERI PETROV), 49

Dead Still (ANDREI VOZNESENSKY), 249

Death, from a Distance (JORGE GUILLÉN), 268

Death of a Toad, The, 392

Digging for China, 330

Digression, A, 51

Disappearing Alphabet, The, 567

Driftwood, 393

Dubious Night, A, 443

Dutch Courtyard, A, 433

Eightieth-Birthday Ballade for Anthony Hecht, An, 22

Eight Riddles from Symphosius, 275

Elsewhere, 54

Epistemology, 361

Event, An, 347

Everness (JORGE LUIS BORGES), 242

Ewigkeit (JORGE LUIS BORGES), 243

Exeunt, 338

Eye, The, 131

Fable, A, 107

Fabrications, 38

Fall in Corrales, 297

Fern-Beds in Hampshire County, 202

Few Differences, A, 559

Finished Man, A, 114

Fire-Truck, A, 283

First Snow in Alsace, 418

Five Women Bathing in Moonlight, 380

Flippancies, 167

Flumen Tenebrarum, 397

Foggy Street (ANDREI VOZNESENSKY), 245

Folk Tune, 435

For C., 30

For Dudley, 211

For Ellen, 458

For K. R. on Her Sixtieth Birthday, 231

For the New Railway Station in Rome, 350

For the Student Strikers, 148

For W. H. Auden, 100

Fourth of July, The, 144

From the Lookout Rock, 399

Funeral of Bobò, The (JOSEPH BRODSKY), 173

Gambler, The, 34

Games One, 386

Games Two, 387

Gemini, 271

Giacometti, 402

Giaour and the Pacha, The, 423

Gifts, The, 379

Glance from the Bridge, A, 384

Glitter and Be Gay, 468

Gnomons, 80

Good Servant, The, 372

Grace, 455

Grasse: The Olive Trees, 377

Grasshopper, A, 278

Grasshopper and the Ant, The (JEAN DE LA FONTAINE), 160

Green, 15

Hamlen Brook, 115

Happy the Man (JOACHIM DU BELLAY), 161

Helen (PAUL VALÉRY), 336

He Was, 404

Hole in the Floor, A, 265

Horses, The (JORGE GUILLÉN), 267

Icarium Mare, 94

Icons, 41

In a Bird Sanctuary, 425

In a Churchyard, 203

In Limbo, 138

In the Elegy Season, 368

In the Field, 207

In the Smoking-Car, 286
In Trackless Woods, 12

John Chapman, 152
John Chrysostom, 311
Juggler, 370
June Light, 427
Junk, 261

Lamarck Elaborated, 317
Lament, 396
La Rose des Vents, 360
Late Aubade, A, 229
Leaving, 89
L'Etoile, 444
Lightness, 457
Lilacs, The, 195
L'Invitation au Voyage (CHARLES
    BAUDELAIRE), 328
Looking into History, 326
Lot's Wife (ANNA AKHMATOVA), 244
Love Calls Us to the Things of This
    World, 307
Loves of the Puppets, 263
Lying, 83

Man Running, 8
March, 137
Marché aux Oiseaux, 369
Marginalia, 339
Matthew VIII, 28 ff., 230
Mayflies, 36
Mechanist, The, 224
Melongène, The, 430
Merlin Enthralled, 319
Mill, The, 349
Miltonic Sonnet for Mr. Johnson, A,
    221
Mind, 314
Mind-Reader, The, 183
Mined Country, 414
Mirabeau Bridge (GUILLAUME
    APOLLINAIRE), 102

More Opposites, 515
Museum Piece, 365
My Father Paints the Summer, 434

Next Door, 298

O, 448
Objects, 431
October Maples, Portland, 274
Ode to Pleasure, 366
Oh, Happy We!, 465
Once, 46
On Freedom's Ground, 119
On Having Mis-identified a Wild Flower,
    86
On the Eyes of an SS Officer, 419
On the Marginal Way, 197
Opposites, 473
Orchard Trees, January, 101

Pangloss's Song: A Comic-Opera Lyric,
    290
Parable, 371
Pardon, The, 358
Part of a Letter, 359
Peace of Cities, The, 422
Pelican, The (PHILIPPE DE THAUN), 333
Personae, 48
Peter, 142
Phone Booth (ANDREI VOZNESENSKY),
    175
Photos from the Archives (VALERI
    PETROV), 50
Piazza di Spagna, Early Morning, 310
Piccola Commedia, 134
Pig in the Spigot, The, 573
Pity, 373
Place Pigalle, 420
Plain Song for Comadre, A, 318
Playboy, 223
Poplar, Sycamore, 452
Potato, 416
Praise in Summer, 461

Prayer to Go to Paradise with the
    Donkeys, A (FRANCIS JAMMES), 331
Prisoner of Zenda, The, 170
Problem from Milton, A, 383
Prologue to Molière's *Amphitryon,* The, 61
Proof, The, 228
Puritans, The, 376

Ragpicker's Song, The, 470
Reader, The, 5
Regatta, The, 449
Riddle, A, 222
Ride, The, 79
Rillons, Rillettes, 169
Rondeau (CHARLES D'ORLÉANS), 250
Rule, The, 106
Running, 213

Sea Breeze, (STÉPHANE MALLARMÉ), 44
Security Lights, Key West, 7
Seed Leaves, 205
Shad-Time, 109
Shallot, A, 146
Shame, 277
She, 269
Short History, A, 37
Signatures, 40
Simile for Her Smile, A, 405
Simplification, A, 442
Sir David Brewster's Toy, 6
Sirens, The, 374
Six Years Later (JOSEPH BRODSKY), 87
Sketch, A, 140
Sleepless at Crown Point, 133
Sleepwalker, The, 13
Someone Talking to Himself, 284
Some Riddles from Symphosius, 96
Song, A, 428
Song (VINICIUS DE MORAES), 93
Sonnet, 309
Speech for the Repeal of the McCarran
    Act, 341
Statues, 325

Still, Citizen Sparrow, 390
Stop, 260
Storm in April, A, 127
Summer Morning, A, 264
Sun and Air, 436
Sunlight Is Imagination, 445
Superiorities, 441

Tanka, 11
Tartuffe, Act I, Scene 4 (MOLIÈRE), 294
Teresa, 154
Terrace, The, 381
Then, 355
This Pleasing Anxious Being, 57
Three Tankas, 35
Thyme Flowering among Rocks, 219
To a Comedian, 21
To an American Poet Just Dead, 401
To His Skeleton, 151
To Ishtar, 289
To Madame du Châtelet (VOLTAIRE), 162
To the Etruscan Poets, 130
Transit, 108
Trolling for Blues, 103
Twelve Riddles from Symphosius, 19
Two Poems (NIKOLAI MORSHEN), 179
Two Quatrains for First Frost, 292
Two Riddles from Aldhelm, 168
Two Songs in a Stanza of Beddoes', 437
Two Voices in a Meadow, 257
Tywater, 413

Undead, The, 272
Under a Tree, 98
Under Cygnus, 216
Up, Jack, 424

Violet and Jasper, 421
Voice from under the Table, A, 321

Walgh-Vogel, The, 429
Walking to Sleep, 235
Wall in the Woods, A: Cummington, 52

Waters, The, 439
Water Walker, 410
Wedding Toast, A, 136
Wellfleet: The House, 391
Winter Spring, 453
Wood, A, 210
Worlds, 111
"World without Objects Is a Sensible
      Emptiness, A", 357

Writer, The, 128
Wyeth's Milk Cans, 99

Year's End, 375

Zea, 31